Does Parliament Matter?

CONTEMPORARY POLITICAL STUDIES

Series Editor: John Benyon, *Director, Centre for the Study of Public Order, University of Leicester*

A series which provides authoritative, yet concise introductory accounts of key topics in contemporary political studies.

CONTEMPORARY POLITICAL STUDIES

Does Parliament Matter?

PHILIP NORTON
University of Hull

HARVESTER
WHEATSHEAF

New York   London   Toronto   Sydney   Tokyo   Singapore

First published 1993 by
Harvester Wheatsheaf
Campus 400, Maylands Avenue,
Hemel Hempstead,
Hertfordshire, HP2 7EZ
A division of
Simon & Schuster International Group

Typeset in 10pt Times by
Inforum, Rowlands Castle, Hants

Printed and bound in Great Britain by
Biddles Ltd, Guildford and King's Lynn

British Library Cataloguing in Publication Data

A catalogue record for this book is available from the
British Library

ISBN 0–7450–1207–8
ISBN 0–7450–1208–6 (pbk)

3 4 5   97 96 95

Contents

* Accountability + Investigation.

Scrutiny Accountability. — Actions
Information   "   — Info
Pecunary   "   — Malfesance.
Administrative   "   — Dept. + C.S.
Agenda   "   — Policy + Proposals

Preface

This book has a dual purpose. One is to provide a contemporary introduction to Parliament in the United Kingdom. The institution is ever changing and there is a need for texts to keep abreast of those changes. The reader is therefore introduced to the Parliament of the 1990s. The other purpose is to provide a broader perspective of Parliament than is offered by most existing works. Those who have studied Parliament have tended to focus on the relationship between Parliament and government. That relationship is clearly important but so too is the relationship between Parliament and the citizen. This work considers the relationship of Parliament to both government and the citizen.

In taking this broader context, the book addresses one particular question: does Parliament matter? That question provides the basis for a structured analysis. The question runs through each chapter. At the same time, I have tried to ensure that each chapter is as self-contained as possible, thus allowing chapters to be utilized as appropriate for class assignments. Where there is an overlap of subject matter, I have identified the chapter where the principal material appears and, if necessary to maintain internal coherence, briefly mentioned the essential point of the earlier material.

In writing the book, I have incurred a number of debts. My thanks are owing to Clare Grist, of Simon & Schuster, for her customary skill and enthusiasm in seeing it through to publication. I am especially grateful to Dr Nicholas Baldwin, Cliff Grantham, Thomas Saalfeld and Paul Willis for reading and commenting on all or parts of the manuscript. Their comments have helped strengthen the text considerably. Responsibility for any errors and omissions remains entirely mine.

Philip Norton
University of Hull

1

Parliament in Perspective

It is common for a country to have a legislature – a body created to approve measures that will form the law of the land. Legislatures exist under a variety of names, of which Congress is the most popular. In the United Kingdom, and in Commonwealth countries influenced by British experience, Parliament is preferred. Some, such as the French, use the term National Assembly.

Two assumptions inform contemporary perceptions of legislatures. One is longstanding: that is, that legislatures exist to make law. The second, a notable feature of twentieth-century perceptions, is that legislatures are in decline.

The first perception derives from the very name *legislature*. *Legis* is the genitive of *lex*, meaning law; *lator* means carrier or proposer. A *legislator* was therefore someone who carried law. Legislatures, have thus, by definition, been treated as bodies for carrying, or making, law. 'The legislative' declared John Locke in his *Second Treatise on Government* in 1689, 'is no otherwise legislative of the society but by the right it has to make laws for all parts and for every member of society, prescribing rules for their actions, and giving power of execution where they are transgressed.' Baron de Montesquieu, in *The Spirit of Laws* published in 1748, a work that was to have a powerful influence in America, similarly defined legislative power as that of enacting temporary or perpetual laws and the amending or abrogating of those already made. Law was thus created by legislatures. It was the very task that gave them their name and justified their existence.

The second assumption has existed for more than a century. Various nineteenth century scholars, such as the English journalist

Walter Bagehot (1867) and the American academic A. Lawrence Lowell (1896), identified the likely consequences for legislatures of the growth of party. However, it was to be a twentieth-century work by the scholar–statesman Lord Bryce that popularised the perception of decline. In *Modern Democracies*, published in 1921, Bryce titled Chapter 58 'The decline of legislatures'. In the following chapter, he identified five 'chronic ailments' that had undermined representative assemblies, with party as the principal ailment. Though Bryce qualified his assertion, the notion of decline became associated with his work. It is one that has found a resonance in the subsequent study of legislatures.

The decline of legislatures

That there should be a perception of decline is not surprising. In the nineteenth century, legislatures grew in number and political significance. This growth in significance was not uniform. Some countries, such as Germany, witnessed no 'golden age' of parliament. However, such countries were exceptional. Parliamentarianism was a feature of the century (Sontheimer 1984). Yet no sooner had this condition been reached than it began to deteriorate. Legislatures were unable to withstand the various pressures favouring executive dominance in the formulation and determination of public policy.

Industrialization generated an increasingly urban population with no political voice. Pressure for such a voice was to result in the widening of the franchise and the growth of political parties. In Britain, for example, the 1867 Reform Act – which increased the size of the electorate by almost ninety per cent – spurred the creation of mass-membership parties. Parties served to aggregate the demands of an electorate that lacked the willingness and the sophistication to consider the merits of individual candidates. Parties were beholden to electors for their success and successful candidates owed their position to the party label. Continued party success came to depend on parties being able to implement promises made to the electorate. Implementation of such promises depended on party loyalty in the legislature. Scope for independent action by the elected members was squeezed out.

Party thus came to dominate the electoral and parliamentary processes. The party chose the candidates and set the agenda.

Party leaders occupied the central positions of government and decided what measures were to be laid before the legislature for approval. The locus of policy making shifted from the legislature to the government.

Industrialization had a further effect. Not only did it generate a mass franchise, it also resulted in a more specialized society. Interests became more differentiated – and more organized. In Britain, trade associations grew in number in the first half of the nineteenth century and various professional and employers' organizations were established. These organizations began to compete to protect their own interests. What was notable in the first half of the century became more pronounced in the latter half. Organized groups became more extensive in number and more national in structure. Trade unions, legalized in the 1870s, began to organize. The greater and more specialized the demands made of government by these groups, the greater the specificity of government policy (Richardson and Jordan 1979: 44–45). The more specialized government policy became, the more government relied on groups for advice, information and for co-operation in implementing policy.

The support of the party could usually be taken for granted by government: that of interest groups could not. Groups were increasingly drawn into the policy-making process. In Britain, a number of groups were effectively co-opted into that process and given statutory representation on advisory bodies. The National Health Insurance Act of 1924, for example, gave the medical profession representation on bodies set up to administer the system of social insurance. Co-option was extended in succeeding decades and groups continued to grow in number. Government itself became more specialized and dependent on a growing bureaucracy. Contact with government departments became frequent and institutionalized (Norton 1990a: Chapter 7). By the 1970s, the links were extensive.

Hence, in the process of making law, legislatures came to be seen as increasingly marginalized. Party – or parties – dominate in the legislature. The thrust of public policy is determined by party and confirmed by the electorate at periodic elections. The specific measures of public policy are formulated by government departments following consultation with affected interests. Those measures are presented to the legislature for approval. The legislature will usually lack the political will to challenge them: a partisan majority will exist to pass them. It may also lack the resources to challenge them: if presented with a measure that has the support of the different groups affected by it, it may have no alternative source of information or advice to challenge the agreed package. Consequently, the measures are passed.

The paradox of legislatures

The position of legislatures, on the basis of this analysis, thus appears straightforward. They are marginal bodies in policy making. Yet legislatures present us with a seeming paradox.

On the one hand, legislatures are in decline. On the other, they are ubiquitous. They span the globe. Almost nine out of every ten countries listed in *The Statesman's Year Book* have one (see Norton 1990b: 1). Of countries that have existed for more than twenty years, the number that have never had a legislature can be counted on one's fingers (see Blondel 1973: 7). Furthermore, they show no signs of diminishing in number. As military regimes have been toppled or have handed over power, so legislatures have been established. Following periods of military rule, countries such as Brazil and Greece have reverted to elected legislatures. As the Iron Curtain has rusted and disappeared, the legislatures of the old regimes of central and eastern Europe have given way to new legislatures. The creation of legislatures is seen clearly as important.

If they are so marginal, why bother? Why give so much attention to their creation and operation? One explanation for their continued existence in western Europe is the importance ascribed to them by the population. A survey of six countries in 1983 found that in every one an absolute majority of respondents regarded their legislature as very important or important 'in the life of our country nowadays' (*Euro-Barometre* survey, reported in Norton 1990a: 37). In the United Kingdom, an absolute majority – fifty-six per cent – said Parliament was very important. Only in Italy did the number saying it was not very or not at all important exceed one in four, and then only just: twenty-eight per cent, compared with seventy-two per cent saying it was very important or important. Levels of confidence in legislatures vary, with the Japanese and Italian legislatures, for example, attracting less confidence among electors than the German, Spanish and Swedish parliaments (Merkl 1988: 61; Arter 1990: 137); in the latter cases, an absolute majority of respondents when questioned expressed confidence. In most countries, though, confidence in the legislature normally exceeds that in a number of other national institutions. But confidence to do what?

Why are legislatures still seen as important? Are electors deluding themselves? Are the new regimes of Europe unnecessarily creating bodies that will have little consequence for the new political systems? This seeming paradox is simply resolved.

The generic name of legislatures masks rather than illuminates what they actually do. Parliaments are not simply law-making bodies. Indeed, most are not even predominantly law-making bodies. Their core defining role, as suggested by our opening sentence, is not to *make* law but rather to *give assent* to it. For some that has not only been their core but their only function. The parliament of the former German Democratic Republic (East Germany), for example, sometimes met on only three days a year to approve measures put before it, an example of what Michael Mezey (1979) has defined as a 'minimal legislature'. With the collapse of the Soviet-dominated regimes of central and eastern Europe, the number of such legislatures has declined significantly. Furthermore, such legislatures have been exceptional. Most legislatures engage in other activities and have wider consequences for their political systems. Their significance lies not so much in law making but rather in a range of other functions they fulfil. Those functions will vary in extent and significance over time and from legislature to legislature. Indeed, even in central and eastern Europe during the era of Soviet domination, there was some variation in activity and consequences. The Polish parliament (the Sejm), for example, exhibited a capacity for some independent action that set it apart from its German neighbour.

That, then, is an essential starting point for our study. There is more to legislatures, much more, than formulating – making – law. That is apparent from a cursory observation of the demands made in Britain of the House of Commons and its members. The House of Commons spends as much time dealing with other items of business as it does with legislation. Question time and debates on declaratory motions are not part of the law making process. Some of the most significant occasions in the House in recent years which have had a major political impact, such as Sir Geoffrey Howe's resignation speech in November 1990, have had nothing to do directly with legislation. The most extensive media coverage is of the partisan clash between the Prime Minister and the Leader of the Opposition during the Prime Minister's twice-weekly appearance at the despatch box to answer questions. Constituents will write to Members of Parliament seeking their intervention in cases where benefits have not been paid or where some government department has apparently mishandled a request or complaint. No change in the law is being sought, yet members of the legislature – in their capacity as members – are expected to act, and do act, in pursuit of particular demands. In surveys of what constituents expect of their MP, law making comes way down the list (Jeger 1978: 12; Cain *et al.*, 1979: 16). 'Constituents clearly want their MP to protect the constituency, to put local interests first, and most definitely to be available for help at all times' (Marsh 1985: 77; see also Crewe 1975: 320–21). Those expectations have increased rather than diminished in recent years.

Britain may enjoy a legislature that is distinctive for its longevity, but observation of other legislatures suggests that it is not unusual in the range of its activities and the demands made of it. Constituency pressures are notable, to take two fairly random examples, in the United States (Cain *et al.*, 1987) and in Ireland (Arkins 1990). Most parliamentary assemblies have a facility for asking oral questions on the floor of the House (Bruyneel 1978). A fixed period for asking such questions – question time – is a feature of many European parliaments. In some countries, such as Austria and Finland, the procedure for asking questions is enshrined in the constitution.

Formally, then, as well as in practice, expectations of legislatures extend beyond involvement in the formal process of law making. Hence the apparent paradox falls. Legislatures cannot be assessed solely in terms of their capacity to make law. Given this, a prerequisite is to identify the functions that they variously fulfil.

The functions of legislatures

In a seminal study, Robert Packenham (1970) identified a total of eleven functions of legislatures. He defined functions in terms of consequences for the political system. In other words, they were not necessarily planned or formally delineated tasks undertaken

Table 1.1 Packenham's legislative functions

Legitimation
    Latent (through meeting regularly and uninterruptedly)
    Manifest (the formal stamp of approval)
    'Safety valve' or 'tension release' (outlet for tensions)

Recruitment, socialization and training
    Recruitment
    Socialization
    Training

Decisional or influence functions
    Law making
    'Exit' function (resolving an impasse in the system)
    Interest articulation
    Conflict resolution
    Administrative oversight and patronage (including 'errand running' for
    constituents)

Source: derived from Packenham (1970).

by the legislature. The functions are listed in Table 1.1. Packenham drew on a study of the Brazilian congress in the 1960s in order to identify them. His study of that legislature allowed him to determine a rank ordering – those at the top of the list had the greatest consequences for the political system, those at the bottom the least. The decisional functions such as law making, on which most observers concentrate, came at the bottom of the ranking. Those functions would clearly rank higher in any analysis of the United States Congress but, as Packenham observed, 'what knowledge we have suggests that the Brazilian case is much closer to the mode than the U.S. Congress.' For Packenham, it is the other functions that merit particular scrutiny. 'In fact, even if it [the Brazilian congress] had no decision-making power whatsoever, the other functions which it performs would be significant.'

Packenham's delineation of a number of functions is neither original nor exhaustive. Walter Bagehot in *The English Constitution* (1867) provided a list of functions of the House of Commons more than a century before Packenham's work appeared. They were five in number: the elective (choosing the government), expressive ('to express the mind of the ... people on all matters which come before it'), teaching ('to teach the nation what it does not know' and so alter society), informing (to raise grievances and

make people hear 'what otherwise we should not'), and, finally, the
⑤legislative function,'of which of course it would be preposterous to
deny the great importance'. Parliament's responsibility in the
sphere of finance he subsumed under the last heading. A year
short of a century after Bagehot's work appeared, Samuel Beer
identified another function – that of support mobilization, that is,
helping raise popular support for a particular measure of public
policy. It was, he contended, a function that was significant in the
United States but not in the United Kingdom (Beer 1966). It is a
function that, to some extent, marries Bagehot's informing and
teaching functions.

Packenham's work, however, marked a major advance. It is
significant for its breadth, sophistication and empirical support. It
still provides the most extensive delineation of functions available
in the field of comparative legislative studies. In an adapted form,
it will provide the basic structure for this study. It will be adapted
in two ways. First, it will be reworked to provide slightly greater
breadth and sophistication. The category of seeking a redress of
grievance will be employed, thus separating out – and going
beyond – the errand running activity identified by Packenham; the
law making category will be broken up into separate categories of
the early stages of policy making (initiation and formulation) and
legislation; and the study will be complemented by a consideration
of Parliament's capacity to educate and to mobilize support for
particular policies. Second, it will not be utilised in the rank order
provided by Packenham. Instead, the functions will be grouped
under two basic heads: government and the citizen.

Parliament, like other legislatures, serves as a buckle between
the citizen and the executive. The buckle may not always be a
strong one. However, what is important for our immediate purposes is that Parliament has two sets of relationships, one with the
executive and one with the citizen. The relationships are not mutually exclusive but they are analytically separable. The focus of
scholarly attention has been on the link with the executive and, in
particular, on the capacity of Parliament to influence government
in the initiation and formulation – the making – of public policy.

The relationship with the citizen has rarely been explored to the
same extent as Parliament's relationship with the executive. The
literature is growing but is still relatively sparse. Yet the link is a
vital one, underpinning the health of a political system. Political

authority rests on the twin pillars of effectiveness and consent. 'An organization that cannot effectively influence the society around it is not', according to Richard Rose (1979: 353), 'a government. A government that acts without the consent of the governed is not a government as we like to think of it in the western world.' The legislature serves as a central, indeed *the* central, agent of support. The consequences that Parliament has for the citizen thus need to be teased out and assessed in order to determine the extent to which it serves to underpin the stability of the political system.

Does Parliament matter?

The relationship of Parliament with government, and the consequences of that relationship, will form the basis of Part 1 (Chapters 3 to 7) of our study, the relationship of Parliament with the citizen the basis of Part 2 (Chapters 8 to 12). As a prerequisite to this analysis, the second part of our introductory section (Chapter 2) offers a brief descriptive history of Parliament and an overview of recent changes.

In Part 1, drawing on Packenham's taxonomy, we will consider the consequences of Parliament for the recruitment and training of ministers, for the initiation and formulation of public policy, for legislation, for the administration of government, and, focusing on a new dimension to Parliament's activities, for the European Community. The order is chosen not to reflect the relative significance of each but rather the succeeding stages of the policy-making process. Ministers have to be in place. Then, in terms of specific measures of public policy, the policy has to be initiated and drawn up before entering the legislative process.

Not all policies require parliamentary approval. Some may be generated under prerogative powers (the powers that traditionally have inhered in the crown and have not been superseded by statutory powers) and some may be formulated under powers already granted by Act of Parliament. Since the UK became a member of the European Community on 1 January 1973, some policies may be drawn up for determination at the supra-national level. Hence the particular importance of the distinction drawn in this section between the categories of policy formulation and legislation.

After formulation and (where necessary) approval, comes the implementation. Our consideration of Parliament's consequences for administration will encompass not only the implementation of public policy but also the general administration of government. The European Community is considered last not only by virtue of its newness but also by virtue of its uniqueness. The institutions of the EC are *sui generis* and Parliament's relationship with them are consequently distinct.

In Part 2, we look at the relationship of Parliament to citizen. Chapter 8 – 'The seal of approval' – considers the importance of Parliament as a body for approving, or legitimizing, measures on behalf of the citizenry. Chapter 9 – 'The voice of the constituents' – focuses on MPs as the principal link between the individual and government, serving as 'grievance chasers' (in traditional terminology, seeking a redress of grievance) and as a safety valve for constituents wanting to give vent to particular problems and concerns. Chapter 10 looks at Parliament's role as a means of expressing particular interests and demands channelled through party and, at a more particular level, through pressure groups. Chapter 11 – 'Other voices, other interests' – goes beyond organized interests to consider the extent to which Parliament fulfils a similar role for sectors of society that are not organized, a category that on occasion includes majority opinion. The final chapter in this section considers the extent to which Parliament plays a role in raising popular knowledge about, and changing attitudes toward, particular policies.

A number of these functions have a close affinity with one another and, in some cases, overlap considerably. They are not mutually exclusive. Neither are they necessarily exhaustive. However, they take us beyond existing narrow studies and identify the principal consequences of Parliament for the British political system. They are sufficiently extensive for the purpose of our enquiry, which is to answer a basic but fundamental question: does Parliament matter? The question is a simple one, reflecting a commonly asked question about a range of phenomena. 'Matter' is taken quite simply as meaning 'to be of importance'. This question forms the title of the book. It could equally have been titled – but to avoid confusion has not been – 'Does Parliament Make a Difference?'

In a major work first published in 1980, Richard Rose addressed the question embodied in his book's title: *Do Parties Make a*

Difference? The prevailing view in the literature at the time was that they did. This view formed the basis of much of the writing on adversary politics. This argued that British politics were characterised by the partisan clash between the two major parties, each competing for the all-or-nothing gains of electoral victory, with negative consequences for economic continuity and stability. One party succeeding another in office, it was contended, reversed much if not most of the policy of its predecessor, thus generating discontinuity in public policy (see Finer 1975). Rose's careful study suggested that the received wisdom was misplaced. He found that parties made some difference to public policy but that their impact on economic indicators and performances was very limited indeed. Economic trends did not mirror changes in government.

This study addresses a similar question about Parliament in the United Kingdom. As we have seen, the prevailing view in the literature is that Parliament is marginal in the political system. However, that view derives from a fairly narrow view of Parliament: it focuses on Parliament's capacity to influence the outcome of particular issues on the agenda of political debate. As we have seen, there is a wider context in which Parliament operates. That context is more diffuse than that of Rose's enquiry. Our focus is not a particular consequence but a range of consequences. Our starting point is that there is more to Parliament than law making. However, it is no more than a starting point. The purpose of this study is to explore the different consequences of Parliament and assess their significance. Given popular perceptions of Parliament as an important body in the life of the nation, and our cursory observations about parliamentary activity, there is a working assumption that Parliament matters to some extent. But just how important *is* Parliament in the British polity?

2

The Development of
Parliament

In legal terms, Parliament is not just the House of Commons and House of Lords: it is the Queen-in-Parliament. The assent of the monarch is necessary for a measure to be recognised by the courts as constituting an Act of Parliament. However, the Queen, as sovereign, occupies a position distinct from the two Houses, forming what Bagehot referred to as a 'dignified' element of the constitution. Her actions as sovereign are determined almost exclusively by convention. As such, her actions are predictable, involving little if any real scope for independent, and hence partisan, judgement. The role of the monarch will not form part of our enquiry. That will accord with popular perceptions of what constitutes Parliament: few electors would include the monarch if asked to define the term.

Many electors, though, would tend to define Parliament in terms of the House of Commons. It is not uncommon for writers on British politics to use 'Parliament' as a synonym for the House of Commons. In this study, though, the focus is on both Houses occupying the Palace of Westminster. The House of Lords may be a poor relation, but it is part of the family.

However, though both Houses may be part of the same family, they are certainly not twins. They have different origins, different characteristics, different roles and – formally since 1911 – different powers. Today, as an elected Lower House, the House of Commons is not dissimilar in character to many other lower chambers. There are some differences. It is a relatively large chamber (651 members, second only – as a Lower House – to the newly-enlarged German Bundestag).[1] It also tends to sit for more hours than other legislatures (Blondel 1973; Select Committee on Sittings of the House 1992). However, it is the House of Lords that has the claim to be atypical. Not only is it extraordinarily large (1,194 members at the beginning of 1992), but the basis of selection sets it apart. It is not unique in that it is an unelected upper chamber. A number of upper chambers, such as the Canadian, share that characteristic. However, it is the only major legislative chamber in the world based predominantly on the hereditary principle.

The House of Commons

The House of Commons is the younger, but now the more active and politically significant, chamber. However, it is only in the past century that it has established itself as the politically superior chamber.

Origins

The House has its origins in the thirteenth century. In 1254 two knights from each shire were summoned to the King's Great Council, the *Curia*, 'to consider what aid they will be willing to grant us in our great need' (McKenzie 1968: 15). Ten years later, Simon de Montfort – then the most powerful baron and effectively ruling the country – issued writs in the King's name for the return of four knights from each shire to discuss the state of the realm. The following year – 1265 – he issued writs for the return not only of two knights from each shire but also of two leading figures (burgesses) from each borough. This, as McKenzie noted, is often seen as the beginning of the House of Commons: 'the Commons had arrived' (McKenzie 1968: 15).

In 1275, Edward I held his 'first general Parliament', to which knights, burgesses and citizens were summoned in addition to the barons and leading churchmen (McKenzie 1968: 17). He held some thirty Parliaments during the first twenty-five years of his reign. However, those summoned from the local communities, or *communes* (Commons), played no part in the deliberations on high policy. Nor were they always summoned. There is no evidence, for example, of them having been summoned to more than four of Edward's Parliaments. Their attendance became more regular under Edward II and they were summoned regularly after 1325.

The Commons grew in importance in the fourteenth and fifteenth centuries. At various times in the fourteenth century, the knights and burgesses met separately from the barons and churchmen and so there developed the separation of the two chambers. It was also during this time that the Commons acquired functions that are still associated with it today.

Early functions

original function The knights and burgesses had initially been summoned to confirm the assent of local communities to the raising of additional taxation. There was no suggestion that they had the power to refuse that assent. Nor was such assent sought for all forms of taxation. However, in 1341 the King agreed that the people should not be 'charged nor grieved to make common aid or to sustain charge' without the assent of Parliament (White 1908: 364). Granting supply thus became an important parliamentary function.

Even before the measure of 1341, Parliament had begun to use its power of the purse to ensure that public petitions were accepted by the King. Citizens had the right to petition the monarch for a redress of grievances. Parliament presented such petitions and began to make the voting of supply conditional on a redress being granted. The first known instance of this was as early as 1309 (White 1908: 369). From such petitions developed what came to be called statutes, which required the assent of the Commons, the Lords and the King, and were thus distinguishable from ordinances, which were the product solely of the King. Statute law soon displaced ordinances as the most extensive form of written law and in the fifteenth century the task of writing statutes was taken from the King's scribes and undertaken instead by the Commons.

Those returned to Parliament also began to take an interest in how money was actually collected as well as how it was spent. As early as 1340, commissioners were appointed to audit the accounts of the collectors of subsidies. Where public officials were found wanting, Parliament employed the power of impeachment, the Commons voting impeachment, the Lords trying the case. Though impeachment has since fallen into disuse, it provided the basis for the development of Parliament's scrutiny of administrative actions.

Sixteenth to eighteenth century

Parliament's position was strengthened under the Tudors, when monarchs needed supply and the support of Parliament in their various political and religious battles. Henry VIII had little difficulty achieving the support he wanted in his battles with Rome, but in so doing he accorded Parliament a significant status in helping determine the high policy of the realm. During the Tudor era, a seat in the House of Commons actually became something that was sought after, rather than service in the House simply being treated as an expensive chore. It was also during this era that there were the first signs of embryonic specialization by the Commons. In 1571 there is the first official reference to a bill being sent to a committee of the House. Committees to undertake particular enquiries – select committees – were often employed in both Tudor and Stuart Parliaments.

The seventeenth century witnessed the clash between an assertive Parliament and a monarch believing in the divine right of kings. James I and, more especially his son, Charles I, variously denied the privileges of Parliament and the clash between Charles and Parliament resulted in the Civil War. The defeat of the royalist forces brought in its wake not only the abolition of the monarchy but also of the House of Lords. The country was ruled by a council of state, elected by what came to be known – for fairly self-evident reasons – as the Rump Parliament, and then by military dictatorship. With the Restoration in 1660 came a revival of traditional institutions: there was a deliberate attempt to revert, unconditionally, to the position as it had been at the beginning of 1642.

Further tension between Crown and Parliament ensued, resulting in the clash between James II and a Parliament resistant both to his claims to the divine right of kings and to his Roman Catholic faith. In 1685 the Commons refused to grant the King money to maintain a standing army. It also refused to repeal the Test Acts which restricted public office to Anglicans. James prorogued – that is, dissolved – Parliament and began to rule by prerogative powers, variously 'suspending' laws, including the Test Acts. Various leading politicians invited the Protestant Dutchman, William of

Orange, James' son-in-law, to bring a military force to England. He did so and James fled the country.

On the invitation of peers and former members of the Commons, William summoned a convention which proceeded to offer him and his wife Mary the throne which it declared James to have abdicated. However, the offer was conditional. The convention promulgated a declaration of right, embodying thirteen articles affecting the rights of Parliament. The suspending of laws without the approval of Parliament was declared to be illegal; the dispensing power – to exempt individuals or groups from the provisions of particular acts – was forbidden; and the levying of taxation without the assent of Parliament was prohibited.

On 13 February 1689, William and Mary accepted both the throne and the declaration of right. The declaration was subsequently embodied in statute as the Bill of Rights and the convention turned, retrospectively, into a Parliament. According to G. M. Trevelyan (1938), James II had forced the country to choose between royal absolutism and parliamentary government. It chose parliamentary government.

The dependence of the monarch on Parliament was thus established. Increasingly, the monarch withdrew from the tasks of parliamentary management. Those tasks were assumed by the King's ministers and the eighteenth century witnessed the emergence of a Cabinet and a Prime Minister. That century witnessed a powerful but not overly assertive House of Commons. Many MPs sat for rotten boroughs controlled by members of the aristocracy. The combination of aristocratic control and royal patronage was usually sufficient to ensure a majority for the King's ministry.

The nineteenth century

During this period, parliamentary politics were confined to a political elite. The aristocracy and the landed interests had a political voice. Few others had. Industrialization, as we noted in the preceding chapter, created powerful pressures. There were demands for reform and at the beginning of the 1830s, the Whigs – who had been the 'outs' in politics for a quarter of a century – found themselves in power and in a position to introduce a reform bill. The 1832 Reform Act enlarged the electorate by 49 per cent. In so doing, it helped loosen the grip of the aristocracy on the Commons but did not enlarge the electorate to such an extent that large scale party organization was necessary to contact and mobilize electors. The consequence was a greater scope for independent action by Members of Parliament. The Act thus heralded what has been described as a 'golden age' of Parliament. MPs turned governments out and put new ones in (Bagehot's elective function) and variously overruled government policy. 'There was always a possibility that a speech might turn votes; the result of a division was not a foregone conclusion' (Campion 1952: 15).

Too much should not be made of this golden age. The domain of public policy was very limited – most bills passed were private, not public, bills – and defeats were not excessive in number. Furthermore, the period was a short-lived one. Pressure from a burgeoning urban middle class and from artisans contributed to a further major Reform Act in 1867. This was followed by measures to restrict corrupt practices and to introduce secret ballots. With the passage of the Representation of the People Act in 1884, a majority of working men had the vote. The measures transformed the political landscape. Mass parties developed in response to the new situation. In the words of Richard Crossman (1963: 39), 'organized corruption was gradually replaced by party organization'.

The consequences for the House of Commons were profound. On the one hand, its superiority over the unelected Upper House was established. On the other, it effectively lost two of the functions ascribed to it by Bagehot. The elective function passed to the electorate. The legislative function passed, in effect, to the Cabinet. Party came to dominate parliamentary activity. Government achieved control of the timetable. Whips – MPs appointed to keep fellow supporters informed of business and ensure they turned out and voted – became prominent figures in the life of members (Norton 1979: 10–14). By the turn of the century, party cohesion was a well established feature of parliamentary life (Lowell 1924: 76–78). 'The task of the House of Commons became one of supporting the Cabinet chosen at the polls and passing its legislation. . . . By the 1900s, the Cabinet dominated British government' (Mackintosh 1977: 174).

The twentieth century

The party leadership in government was able to utilise its parliamentary majority to ensure that those features of the nineteenth

century House that were to the benefit of government were retained. Those that were seen as a hindrance were diminished or
removed. Hence, the emphasis on an amateur House, with issues
being debated on the floor, was maintained. A majority was easier
to deploy on the floor. A few critical voices could be lost among
the cries of loyal supporters. The use of investigative committees
facilitated critical scrutiny. What use there had been of select committees was drastically reduced.

However, the use of standing committees for taking the committee stage of legislation was extended. Standing committees
were to the benefit of the government's legislative programme:
more bills could be considered at the same time, avoiding a queue
for detailed consideration on the floor of the House. From 1907, all
bills were referred to standing committee unless the House voted
otherwise. Government was able to deploy its majority in standing
committee. Before the 1940s, a minister's parliamentary private
secretary (an MP who was a minister's unpaid helper) used to act
as an unofficial whip. After 1945, it became standard to appoint
whips to standing committees.

Government also became less willing to divulge information to
the House. Increasingly, MPs were expected to defer to the superior
knowledge of government. As government bills came to dominate
the legislative agenda, and as those bills became more complex, the
House failed to generate the resources to keep pace with those
developments. Hence, in its relationship with government, the
House exhibited the limitations mentioned in the introduction. It
lacked both the political will and the institutional resources to challenge the measures formulated by government.

In terms of the relationship with citizens, the century has witnessed some significant developments. One has been the enlargement of the electorate. The franchise was extended to women aged
30 years and over under the provisions of the Representation of
the People Act in 1918. It was extended to encompass those aged
21 and over – thus bringing the female franchise in line with the
male – in 1928. The voting age was lowered to 18 years by the
Representation of the People Act of 1969.

However, for much of the century, an increased electorate did
not entail a significant increase in the demands made of the local
MP. MPs were frequently amateurs for whom parliamentary
service was not a career occupation (see King 1981). For many

Conservatives, it was a public duty and something often to be combined with other activities, such as practising at the bar or serving as a company director or landowner. For some Labour MPs, it was essentially an end-of-career activity, a reward for long service to the cause of the party or trade unions. Even if many had wanted to be more active in dealing with their constituencies, there was the problem of limited resources. Payment for MPs was introduced only in 1912 (the princely sum of £400 a year) and saw few increases thereafter. Indeed, it was actually reduced for three years in the 1930s because of the depression.

For many MPs in post-war Parliaments, service was not always particularly rewarding. For some without independent means, it was difficult to survive.[2] For those achieving ministerial office, and those amateurs who took some delight in watching – as one put it in the title of her autobiography – 'from the wings' (Cazalet-Keir 1967), parliamentary life had some purpose. For others, Westminster offered little more than 'corridors of frustration' (Teeling 1970).

Recent changes

Recent years have seen a number of changes which have relevance for our later analysis. They may be briefly summarised under five headings: background, resources, behaviour, structures and visibility.

Background

Members of Parliament have become more middle class in background (Mellors 1978). Since 1945, the Conservative Party has lost some of its upper and upper-middle class contingent. The proportion of Conservative MPs educated at public school and Oxford or Cambridge universities has declined, most notably so in the recent years. Less than one in three of all new Conservatives elected in 1979 had such a background; in the following election, the proportion was one in four. Whereas in 1945, half of all Conservative MPs had such an education, by 1983 the proportion was just over one in three.

The proportion of manual workers in the ranks of the parliamentary Labour Party (the PLP) declined from 1945 to 1979 –

from approximately one in four to one in ten – though showed a slight increase thereafter. The number of university-educated MPs on the Labour benches increased – from just over one-third in 1945 to over half by 1970 – as did the number drawn from professions such as teaching and journalism (Burch and Moran 1985). In 1987, seventy per cent of all Members of Parliament were drawn from professional or business backgrounds (Rush 1988).

Allied to this has been a change in career attitudes among MPs. Amateurs, looking upon service as not necessarily a full-time and long-term activity, have been displaced by career politicians, for whom parliamentary life is long-term and more important than any other pursuit (Buck 1963; King 1981).

Resources

Until the 1960s, MPs had few resources other than their salary and, for most, a school-like locker in which to keep their papers. In 1969 a secretarial allowance of £500 a year was introduced. Members were also allowed to make free telephone calls within the UK. The secretarial allowance evolved into an 'office equipment, secretarial and research assistance allowance' and is now known as the office cost allowance. It was variously increased until in 1992 it was almost £30,000 a year, almost the same as the member's salary. In July 1992, the House voted to increase the amount by forty per cent. Members also receive now accommodation allowances (see Rush 1983: Chapter IX; Batty and George 1985).

Physical resources have expanded. Extra office space has been created in the Palace of Westminster. The old Scotland Yard buildings – on the Victoria embankment a hundred yards from the Palace of Westminster – have provided more extensive office space. The opening in 1991 of a new building in Parliament Street – phase one of a new building project – has further extended office space for MPs and the Commons' Library. Each MP now has a desk space and when phase two of the new building is completed, every MP will actually have an office. Library and computer-retrieval facilities have also been expanded. By international standards, office, secretarial and research facilities remain poor. By comparison with preceding decades, they have developed considerably.

Behavioural changes

The behaviour of MPs has changed in recent decades. There have been some changes in behaviour on the floor of the House. Given the rise of the professional politician, there is far more competition to catch the Speaker's eye. There is far greater demand to take part in question time (Franklin and Norton 1993). Most significantly of all, though, has been the change in behaviour in the division (voting) lobbies. Members have proved relatively more independent in their voting behaviour. As we have seen, cohesion was a marked feature of parliamentary life by the turn of the century. That cohesion has been maintained throughout the twentieth century, reaching its peak in the 1950s. In the 1960s, one distinguished American commentator was able to declare that cohesion had increased so much 'until in recent decades it was so close to 100 per cent that there was no longer any point in measuring it' (Beer 1969: 350–1). Shortly afterwards, it did become relevant to measure it.

The early years of the 1970s saw a significant increase in cross-voting by Conservative MPs (Norton 1975; 1978a). They voted against their own leaders more often than before, in greater numbers and with more effect. On six occasions, cross-voting resulted in the government being defeated. Cross-voting also became a feature of Labour MPs after the party was returned to office in 1974 (Norton 1980) contributing to most of the forty-two defeats suffered by the government in the 1974–79 parliament.[3] The number of defeats on the floor of the House, combined with defeats in standing committee, ran into three figures (see Norton 1980; Schwarz 1980). Some degree of independent voting has been maintained in succeeding Parliaments (Norton 1985; Saalfeld 1988; Griffith and Ryle 1990: 128–30). In 1986, the government lost the second reading of the Shops Bill (Regan 1988; Bown 1990), the first time in the twentieth century a Government with a clear overall majority had lost a second reading vote.

The cause of this behavioural change has been the subject of considerable debate (see, for example, Franklin, Baxter and Jordan 1986; Norton 1987a). This writer has advanced the 'poor leadership' thesis, ascribing the triggering effect for the dissension to Edward Heath's style of prime ministerial leadership (Norton 1978a). Once triggered, such behaviour developed a momentum, ensuring that it outlived the Prime Minister responsible for unleashing it.

But what were the consequences? As MPs began to realise what they could achieve by voting against their own side, many began to change their attitude toward government. According to Samuel Beer, their old deferential attitude was replaced by a more participant attitude (Beer 1982). They wanted to be more involved in influencing public policy and the actions of government. This new attitude also spurred greater demands for new structures and improved resources.

These behavioural changes should not be exaggerated. Cohesion remains a very marked feature of parliamentary behaviour (Rose 1983). The change is relative. Whereas prior to 1970, a government with an overall majority was guaranteed a majority if it pressed ahead with a measure, today it is usually assured a majority but cannot quite take it for granted.

Structures

The late 1970s and 1980s saw some MPs flexing their new-found political muscle in order to extend their resources and to create a more specialized infrastructure. In 1986, MPs voted – against government advice – to increase their secretarial and research allowance by fifty per cent; they repeated the exercise six years later. The House also variously approved new procedures and new structures (Norton 1986). Among the latter was the National Audit Office, to undertake efficiency audits of government departments, and – within the House itself – a series of departmentally-related select committees.

The committees marked a radical departure in that they covered virtually all government departments. Fourteen were established in the 1979–83 Parliament. In the new 1992 Parliament, their number increased to sixteen. Each now has eleven members. The practice is for each to meet once a week, to investigate particular topics through a series of evidence-taking sessions, and to issue reports embodying – where they deem it appropriate – recommendations for action. Since their creation, the committees have been industrious and prolific in output (see Downs 1985; Drewry 1989). As we shall see, they have fulfilled a variety of functions.

Visibility

The other major change is the televising of proceedings. The House of Lords admitted the television cameras in 1985. The House of Commons lagged behind, voting to admit the cameras in 1988 and with the cameras actually transmitting proceedings from 21 November 1989. The cameras record proceedings not only on the floor of the House but also in committee, both select and standing. The television coverage has proved both more extensive than had been anticipated and also popular, both with MPs and with the viewing public (see Chapter 12). What had started out as an experiment was soon made permanent.

These various changes are essentially changes to have taken place within the House. The House has also been operating within a changing political environment and one in which greater demands have been made of it (Norton 1992a). The continuing demands made of government have ensured that the volume of legislation has continued to grow. The consequences of membership of the European community have included EC business occupying parliamentary time, either on the floor of the house or in committee. Pressure groups have lobbied MPs (and peers) on a more extensive basis than before. As government sought more of an arms-length relationship with many groups after 1979, so the House of Commons – with somewhat greater independence and with more specialized structures – began to appear relatively more attractive than before (Norton 1991b). Constituents have also proved more demanding, writing more often to their MPs and having greater expectations – or appearing to local parties and to members to have greater expectations – of members spending more time than before in their constituencies (Norton and Wood 1990; Wood and Norton 1993). These changed conditions have significant consequences both for the activity of Members of Parliament and for the various functions of the House.

The House of Lords

The House of Lords can claim to have its origins in the Anglo-Saxon *Witenagemot* and its successor, the Norman *Curia regis* of the twelfth and thirteenth centuries, summoned by the King to help discern and declare the law and to proffer advice before the levying of new taxes. The *Curia* comprised the leading barons and churchmen of the kingdom. If a baron regularly attended, it became common for his heir to be summoned following his death. The court thus acquired a body of attenders there by virtue of being their fathers' sons rather than in their own right as tenants of the king.

In the thirteenth century, as we have seen, the King summoned knights and later burgesses to court. In the fourteenth century, the barons and churchmen started to deliberate separately from the knights and burgesses, thus creating the two bodies that we now recognise as the House of Lords and the House of Commons.

Formally, the two Houses were co-equal, though the principle of the Commons being responsible for initiating taxation was soon conceded. Henry IV affirmed the position in 1407 and the Commons defended it after the Restoration when the Lords attempted to initiate bills to raise taxes. Indeed, the Commons extended its privilege, denying the right of the Lords to amend money bills (McKenzie 1968: 70). In other matters, the Lords was equal to the Commons.

Indeed, in political terms, their lordships came to exert considerable influence over members of the Commons, not formally but through their control of parliamentary seats. Most, though not all, of the MPs returned for 'pocket' boroughs owed their positions to the patronage of peers. A table compiled about 1815 showed that 471 parliamentary seats were controlled by 144 peers and 123 commoners (Ostrogorski 1902: 20). Some members of the Lords preferred to make their political presence felt through their surrogates in the Commons rather than through their own House. In the Lords, each had one voice. In the Lower House, they might control several.

Franchise and boundary reforms undermined this control. The House of Lords, though, remained a powerful body. It used its powers to initiate and, perhaps more importantly, to vote down bills. It continued to use this power despite the fact that its legitimacy as a co-equal body was undermined by the widening of the franchise. An unelected chamber had difficulty withstanding the claims of an elected chamber. As Lord Shaftesbury noted during the passage of the 1867 Reform Bill, the House might get away with voting down a particularly unjust or coercive bill, but to do so more than once would not be permitted. 'It would be said, "The people must govern, and not a set of hereditary peers never chosen by the people" (Norton 1981: 21). The House – Conservative dominated, as it had been since the late eighteenth century[4] – did vote down more than one contentious Liberal bill and the cry that Shaftesbury anticipated was heard. The latter half of the nineteenth century saw calls for the reform or even the abolition of the Upper House. The policy of 'mend or end' became popular in Liberal circles. In 1893, the Lords threw out the Home Rule Bill. The following year, the Liberal Party conference voted in favour of abolishing the Lords' power to veto bills.

The most significant clash occurred in the first decade of the twentieth century. The Liberal Government of 1906 introduced a number of measures that proved too radical for the tastes of the Conservative majority in the Upper House. The Lords threw out or emasculated several major bills, including an Education Bill, before finally rejecting the Budget in 1909 'until it had been submitted to the judgement of the country' (quoted in Norton 1981: 22). The government called an election on the issue not of the budget but of the House of Lords. The result, after two elections, was the passage of the Parliament Act of 1911. The King had agreed to create a sufficient number of new Liberal peers should that be necessary in order to ensure a majority for the bill. In the event, it was not necessary: the number of Conservative 'hedgers' outnumbered the 'ditchers', those who wanted to make a last-ditch stance against reform.

The 1911 Act provided that a non-money bill could be delayed by the Lords for a maximum of two successive sessions, the bill being enacted if passed by the Commons in the next session. Money bills, those dealing exclusively with money and certified as such by the Speaker, were to become law one month after leaving the Commons, whether approved by the Lords or not. The subordinate position of the House was thus enshrined in statute. In succeeding decades, the House essentially acknowledged its position as a politically inferior chamber and rarely challenged the principle of measures sent to it by the Commons.

Subordination and reform: 1945 to 1970

The subordinate position of the House found further confirmation during the period of Labour Government from 1945 to 1951.

Under the Parliament Act of 1949 the two-session veto on non-money bills was reduced to one session. The two party leaders in the Lords, Salisbury (Conservative) and Addison (Labour), also agreed that the House should not reject the second reading of a bill promised by the government in its manifesto. The Salisbury-Addison agreement has remained in force ever since.

The inferior position of the House appeared to limit peers' interest in taking part in its activities. In the 1940s, the House had a membership of over 800, but of those 'only about 100 attend regularly and of these perhaps sixty of them take an active part in its business' (Gordon 1948: 139). The House rarely met for more than three days a week and on those days would often not sit for more than three hours. Votes were rare and when they were taken peers voted on party lines (Bromhead 1958). Limited powers and limited activity led to little outside interest in the House. Even MPs gave it little attention, some looking upon it as providing, through its gallery, no more than a convenient place for depositing unwanted guests. When it did attract attention it was from critics who wanted to reform it or – the preference of some Labour MPs – do away with it altogether.

In the event, some reform did take place. The 1958 Life Peerages Act introduced the provision for peerages to be held solely for the lifetime of the holder. This allowed for the elevation to the peerage of many, such as trade unionists and other Labour supporters, who objected to the hereditary principle. It also meant that the membership could be enlarged without contributing to its enlargement in future generations. Having introduced an Act to enable new peerages to be created, the same Conservative Government was responsible also for an Act – the 1963 Peerages Act – that allowed members of the Upper House to renounce their peerages.

The measure had been championed for some years by the second Viscount Stansgate – Tony Benn – who wanted to give up his peerage in order to return to the House of Commons. However, the act also served to the advantage of two Conservative peers (Lords Home and Hailsham) who, given the facility to renounce, could then seek the Conservative leadership following Harold Macmillan's resignation in 1963. Lord Home was the successful candidate for the succession and renounced his peerage in order to contest a seat for the elected House.

However, comprehensive reform of the Lords was to prove unsuccessful. In 1969, a bill – the Parliament (No. 2) Bill – designed to phase out the hereditary principle and give the government of the day a working majority, failed to achieve passage in the House of Commons. A combination of right-wing Conservatives led by Enoch Powell, who felt the bill went too far, and left-wing Labour MPs led by Michael Foot, who felt it did not go far enough, kept debate going on the bill until the government decided to withdraw it. The assumption, in the wake of the bill's failure, was that reform was dead and that the Upper House would basically lumber on in the way it had for the past few decades.

Recent changes

In the event, expectations of a relatively moribund House were to prove unfounded. Rather like the Commons, the House of Lords has experienced a number of significant changes in the years since 1970. These changes can be considered under three principal headings: behaviour, structures and visibility.

Behaviour

The House of Lords has seen something of a revival in terms of attendance and activity. Over the past twenty years, the daily attendance has increased. By the end of the 1980s, the average daily attendance exceeded 300. More than 700 peers attended one or more sittings each year and, of those, more than 500 contributed to debate (Shell 1988). In other words, well over half of all peers made the effort to turn up once or more each session. The House now sits on more days, and for longer hours, than it did in previous decades. In the 1985–86 session, for example, the House sat after ten o'clock in the evening on ninety-three occasions. Votes have also become more frequent, as have government defeats. Relations between the Conservative House and a Labour Government from 1974 to 1979 were often poor, and the Government suffered 347 defeats. Equally remarkable has been the subsequent relationship between the Conservative House and a Conservative Government (see Baldwin 1985a). From 1979 to 1990, the Thatcher Government suffered just over 150 defeats at the hands of their lordships.

Structures

Most business in the Lords, including the committee stage of bills, continues to be taken on the floor of the House. However, the House occasionally employs select committees for *ad hoc* enquiries and uses two permanent select committees to consider European Community draft legislation and science and technology. The European Communities Committee works through subcommittees and each session draws on the service of about eighty peers. It has established a formidable reputation for its work (see Chapter 7) and is regarded as far superior to the equivalent committee in the Commons. The Science and Technology committee has also established a considerable reputation for its extensive, and informed, enquiries (see Chapter 6); its 1986 report on civil research and development in the UK constituted a major reference work on the subject and spurred the Prime Minister to reorganise the Government's handling of the subject. In 1992, a select committee of the House recommended a widening of the scope for select committee activity and for some experimental use of committees in considering bills (Select Committee on the Committee Work of the House 1992).

Visibility

The other major change is that of the televising of proceedings. As we have noted already, the Lords admitted the cameras in 1985, four years ahead of their entry to the Commons. In the first four years, Lords' debates received late-night coverage but, despite the timing, relatively good viewing figures. The coverage was largely squeezed out once the cameras started recording proceedings in the Commons.

The reasons for these changes have also been the subject of academic debate. According to Nicholas Baldwin (1985a), they are the product of the Life Peerages Act, bringing new blood into the House, and a realization that if reform was unlikely then peers had to make the existing House work. A further impetus was provided by large government majorities in the Commons in the 1980s. Many peers viewed this as producing a Lower House incapable of providing effective critical scrutiny of government and hence took upon themselves the task of providing that scrutiny (Baldwin

1985a: 111). Though Conservative peers dominated in the House, there were not necessarily supportive of Thatcherite policies. Party loyalty was not sufficient to ensure their consistent loyalty in the lobbies.

Conclusion

Both Houses of Parliament have a history spanning several centuries. They have had significant consequences for the political system. At times, they have been important allies – and on occasion adversaries – of the King. In the seventeenth century, Parliament was a major actor in shaping the nation's constitution.

Though the institution, like other western legislatures, has not been able to withstand the forces identified in the introduction, it remains a central part of the body politic. It is not, and never has been for any continuous period in its history, a policy-making body. It continues, though, to have important consequences for the political system. Neither House is a static body. Recent years have seen remarkable changes in both Houses. Those changes have affected significantly the functions they perform. It is to those functions that we now turn.

Notes

1. The number of MPs has been 651 since the general election of April 1992. From 1983 to 1992, there were 650. The number has varied during the century. At one point (from 1918 to 1922) there were 707 seats, reduced thereafter because of the loss of most Irish seats.
2. For example, one Conservative MP recounted to this writer his experience in the 1950s when he encountered, on a train, a Labour MP who admitted to travelling back and forth to his constituency during the night as often as possible because he could not afford to stay in London.
3. Twenty-three of the defeats were caused by Labour MPs voting with the opposition. The other nineteen were the result of the other parties in the House voting against the Government after it slipped into minority status in the House in April 1976 following by-election losses and one defection. See Norton (1980).
4. There was a small Whig majority in the House at the beginning of the eighteenth century. Some new creations tipped the balance in favour of the Tories before the Whigs again acquired a majority. However, after

Pitt the Younger became Prime Minister, creations took place on an unprecedented scale. During the seventeen years of his premiership, no less than 140 new peers were created, 'providing the Tories not merely with a majority, but placing them in a position of ascendancy in the House of Lords' (Baldwin 1985a: 96). The Tory Party evolved into the Conservative party in the 1830s.

Part I
Parliament and Government

3

Recruiting and Training Ministers

Government ministers are drawn from, and remain in, Parliament. The significance of this well-known fact is often overlooked. It has fundamental implications for the ways in which government and Parliament function.

Ministers in Parliament

There is no legal requirement that ministers must be appointed from among MPs or peers. It is possible, and has occasionally happened, that a minister has been appointed while a member of neither House. Normally, such a minister has been elevated to the peerage or found a seat in the Commons through a by-election. On occasion, the Solicitor General for Scotland – one of the Scottish law officers – has been drawn from, and been made a member of, neither House. This was the case, for example, following the 1992 general election, when a Scottish lawyer, Thomas Dawson, was appointed to the post and remained outside Parliament.

Such occasions are relatively rare. Though there is no legal requirement, it is a convention of the constitution that ministers must normally be drawn from Parliament.[1] That is a well established convention and derives from the circumstances of Parliament's history (see Chapter 2). The monarch needed the support of Parliament and it was therefore prudent to have his ministers in a position to marshal and contribute to that support.

An attempt was made through the Act of Settlement of 1701 to sever the link between ministers and Parliament by making 'placemen' – holders of office of profit under the crown, a category that includes ministers – ineligible for membership of the Commons. The provision, though, was not to come into effect until the death of Queen Anne and was modified before Anne's demise by an Act of 1706. This allowed ministers to retain their seats provided they sought re-election.

> Though this put them to trouble and expense and was not repealed until as late as 1926, only very occasionally did it result in the office-holder's defeat, since the convention was soon established that it was ungentlemanly to oppose a member seeking re-election.
>
> (Cannon and Griffiths 1988: 441)

The succession to the throne of the Hanoverians added enormously to the King's dependence on ministers to manage Parliament. The most stable administrations proved to be those led by ministers who enjoyed the confidence of both monarch and the House of Commons.

The practice of ministers being drawn from, and remaining in, Parliament thus pre-dates the twentieth century. What has been noteworthy about this century has been, first, a decisive shift to the Commons as the pool from which ministers are drawn and, second, the increase in ministerial numbers. Ministers have become less aristocratic and more numerous.

The shift to the Commons

As the franchise was extended and the Commons became the predominant of the two chambers, so the greater the emphasis on having ministers in the Lower House, answerable to elected representatives. In the nineteenth century, it was not uncommon to have a preponderance of peers in the Cabinet and, indeed, for the Prime Minister to be a peer. The twentieth century opened with the third Marquess of Salisbury still occupying the premiership. Since then, there has been a decisive, but not necessarily rapid, shift of emphasis to the Commons.

In 1923, George V had to choose between Viscount Curzon and MP Stanley Baldwin for the premiership. He chose the latter. The King's action has been taken as establishing the convention that the Prime Minister must be drawn from the Commons.[2] It was, in effect, confirmed in 1940 when Lord Halifax, favoured by some Labour members for the premiership, recognized that his membership of the Upper House precluded him from the post.

We have already noted the events of 1963 (see Chapter 2) when the Queen sent for the fourteenth Earl of Home to ask him to form a government: he relinquished his title and, as Sir Alec Douglas-Home, was returned to the Commons at a by-election (see Shepherd 1991: 149–59). The occasion was exceptional and only made possible by the passage of the Peerages Act. Lord Home was eligible to renounce his peerage within the time limit stipulated. He was also the beneficiary of the fact that the Conservative Party had no formal means of electing a leader, with the choice being left to the monarch in the event of no obvious leader emerging. Today, election of the leader is by Conservative MPs, and peers – except recently ennobled ones – would not be eligible to renounce their peerages. The choice of leader, in other words, must fall on a member of the Lower House.

The emphasis on being answerable to an elected House has resulted also in fewer peers serving in the Cabinet. Churchill included six peers in his first peacetime Cabinet in 1951. Harold Macmillan, a member by marriage of the family of the Duke of Devonshire, included five in his Cabinet in 1957. He was the last premier to have a duke (his own nephew-in-law, the Duke of Devonshire) in his government as a junior minister. In both cases, the numbers were actually quite generous and included a qualitative dimension: a number of peers were given senior positions. Since then, no Prime Minister has drawn as heavily on the Upper House for members of the Cabinet.

Two members of the Cabinet are necessarily drawn from the Lords – the Lord Chancellor and the Leader of the House of Lords – but the number of peers in the Cabinet now rarely exceeds four. The Cabinets of Margaret Thatcher occasionally contained a senior departmental minister who was in the Lords – Lord Carrington as Foreign Secretary (1979–82), Lord Cockfield as Trade Secretary (1982–83) and Chancellor of the Duchy of Lancaster (1983–84), and Lord Young as Employment Secretary (1985–87) and Trade and Industry Secretary (1987–89). However, after Lord Young's departure, the Cabinet had only the Lord Chancellor and Leader of the House, a position maintained by Mrs Thatcher's successor, John Major.

Below Cabinet level, peers are more numerous in ministerial ranks. It is useful for Prime Ministers to appoint a peer as one of the ministers in a department as it means that there is then a minister free of constituency duties and someone who can carry most of the routine ministerial tasks during an election campaign, when the other ministers are busy campaigning. Nonetheless, as we shall see, peers still constitute a minority – usually about one-fifth – of government ministers.

Growth in numbers

During the twentieth century, the size of the Cabinet has not changed significantly, usually comprising twenty or so senior ministers. In 1901, the Cabinet had nineteen members. In 1992, it had twenty-two. There have been some variations, partly reflecting a variation in the number of government departments (see Clarke 1975: 65), and conditions of war have seen the formation of an Inner, or War, Cabinet, but the basic membership has shown no significant increase. Where there has been an increase has been in the number of ministers outside the Cabinet.

At the beginning of the century, the number of ministers of Cabinet rank (senior ministers not in the Cabinet, such as the Paymaster General) and junior ministers (such as the parliamentary secretary to the local government board) was not much larger than the number of ministers in the Cabinet; indeed, the number was only larger because of the inclusion of Commons' and Lords' whips. Since then, the growth in government responsibilities has resulted in a significant increase in the number of ministers. The growth has been pronounced especially in the years since 1945. In 1945, there were – excluding the whips – thirty-two junior ministers; following the 1979 general election there were fifty-eight (Theakston 1987: 42–43) and following the 1992 election there were sixty-three.

The number of ministers, in total and by rank, in the Conservative Government returned in the 1992 general election is given in Table 3.1. In two departments – Environment and Trade and Industry – there were actually six ministers in addition to the Cabinet minister: each department had three ministers of state and three under-secretaries. In 1901, no department had more than one junior minister attached to it.

Table 3.1 Number of government ministers in Parliament, October 1992

Rank	House of Commons	House of Lords	Total
Cabinet ministers (including PM)	20	2	22
Ministers of state[1]	23	5	28
Law officers	2	1	3[2]
Under-secretaries of state	24	8	32
Whips (including chief whip)	14	7	21
Total	83	23	106[2]

Notes: [1] includes the Paymaster-General and the Financial and Economic Secretaries to the Treasury.
[2] This figure excludes the Solicitor General for Scotland (Thomas Dawson) who is not a member of either House.

Consequences for ministers

The fact that ministers are drawn from, and remain within, Parliament – and are drawn predominantly from the House of Commons – has a number of consequences in terms of the recruitment and training of those who are to form the Government of the United Kingdom.

Ministerial recruitment

Politicians seek membership of a legislature because they believe that such membership will be of value to them. 'Membership may have immediate political value, long-range career value, and financial value, as well as value calculated in less tangible ideological and psychological terms' (Mezey 1979: 224).

Of these, the long-range political career is the most important for our purposes. It is also distinctive. For anyone seeking to undertake public service, there are alternatives to serving in Parliament. For anyone seeking financial gain, there are far more remunerative positions to pursue than that of being a Member of Parliament or, indeed, a minister. (One minister, Lord Gowrie, resigned in 1985 claiming that his ministerial salary was not enough to live on.) For anyone seeking to have some influence on public policy, there are again alternatives to being an MP: for example, a senior civil servant, policy adviser (in, for example, the No. 10 Policy Unit) or head of an influential pressure group. For anyone seeking to find a platform for a particular ideological view point, there are again alternatives: journalism, or serving in a policy research body or think tank. However, for anyone wishing to become and make a career as a government minister, there is only one route. Parliament, in effect, enjoys a virtual monopoly in terms of recruitment.

As we have noted, someone – usually not a politician – may be elevated to ministerial office without being in either House at the time of appointment. However, such instances are exceptional and – equally important in this context – unpredictable. In other words, anyone actually *seeking* a career as a minister cannot plan to do so through a route other than membership of the House of Commons.

The House of Commons thus serves as a magnet for those wanting to exercise political power as ministers. As one American observer noted, 'the British House of Commons may play an insignificant role in policy-making . . . [but] as the only channel to top executive office it has the special attractiveness of 'the only game in town' for the politically ambitious' (Matthews 1985: 22).

This thus distinguishes Parliament from political systems where the executive and legislature are separately elected. In the United States, for example, there are multiple career lines. For anyone seeking the presidency or a Cabinet post there is no single and predictable career course to follow, but rather a range of options: state politics (primarily the governorship), the federal legislature (House or Senate), public service, education or business. Congress, therefore, does not constitute the exclusive pool from which Cabinet officers or presidential candidates are drawn. Nonetheless, members of the House or Senate may be chosen for such positions. In the European Parliament, there is no such likelihood. '[T]he European Parliament's situation has remained unchanged since 1979; it offers no links to 'external' governmental opportunities for upward mobility. . . . the only way up is out' (Westlake 1992: 26). Consequently, the Parliament has not been able to retain a body of long-serving members able to form a clear and cohesive political elite (Westlake 1992).

The first act of a politician in Britain wanting ministerial office is therefore to obtain a parliamentary candidature. In order to stand any chance of election, that means getting selected as a candidate for one of the main parties. That is the first but not the only step to take, for election by itself is rarely sufficient. Exceptionally, a new

Member of Parliament – whose reputation for particular qualities has preceded him (never, as yet, her) – may be offered a ministerial post straight away. In practice, most members have to serve an apprenticeship in the House before being offered a government post.

There are more Members of Parliament on the government side of the House than there are posts to be filled: the ratio is usually at least four to one. Consequently, there is competition for places on the treasury bench (the traditional name for the government front bench). The House serves as an arena in which ambitious members seek to get themselves noticed by those with the capacity to influence their promotion to office. This means the Prime Minister, senior ministers and – most importantly of all for getting a foot on the first rung of the ministerial ladder – the whips. There is always a whip present in the chamber and the Chief Whip is the Prime Minister's principal adviser on junior ministerial appointments. During Margaret Thatcher's premiership, for example, one new MP that she wanted to appoint to ministerial office straight away had his promotion delayed for two years on the insistence of the Chief Whip (see Norton 1992c).

To establish a reputation in the House, members may focus on the chamber – making speeches, tabling oral questions and generally making themselves visible. Occasionally, a member may get noticed and promoted on the basis of a particular speech.[3] More usually, reputations – and contacts – are made over a period of time.

Apart from activity on the floor, there are two other principal avenues to be pursued. One is to serve as an officer of a back bench party committee. This provides the member with some status and helps establish some degree of specialization. The other is to serve as a parliamentary private secretary (a PPS), that is – as we noted in Chapter 2 – an unpaid assistant to a minister. A PPS can acquire some knowledge of how a department is run and at the same time acquire a ministerial champion who can mention his or her particular qualities to the whips and the Prime Minister. Of the two, the latter route is the one seen by new members as being the more effective (see Norton 1993b). Of junior ministers serving in 1989, almost three-quarters had served as PPSs (Norton 1989a: 235). Both routes require obtaining the confidence of others: fellow members in the case of committee officership and a minister in order to become a PPS.

A training ground

The fact that ministers are drawn from the ranks of parliamentarians ensures that Parliament serves as the recruiting agency for ministerial aspirants. However, equally significant is the fact that ministers remain within Parliament. A consequence of this is that Parliament is important not only for nurturing future ministers but also serving as a training, or testing, ground for ministers.

The fact that ministers will remain within Parliament may itself be a significant factor in influencing the choice of backbenchers for ministerial office. Skills that are appropriate to handling oneself in the House may take precedence over other qualities. A good speaker or someone who in committee has demonstrated a good grasp of detail may hold an advantage over a colleague who may be a good administrator but who cannot hold the House during debate or has a poor grasp of what is being discussed in a standing committee.

Once in office, a minister is expected to be able to perform competently at the despatch box during debates and at question time. A good performance can contribute to a minister's standing and future career prospects. A poor speech can mar future advancement. On occasion, it can contribute to a minister's downfall. Nicholas Fairbairn, for example, ceased to be Solicitor General for Scotland in 1982 after his disastrous handling of a Commons' debate on a controversial legal case.

The chamber provides an arena in which ministers seek to make and defend their reputations, and those of their respective parties. The clash between the Prime Minister and the Leader of the Opposition, especially at question time, provides an occasion that attracts much media attention. A poor performance can undermine party confidence. The first speech of John Smith at the despatch box as Leader of the Opposition was on 24 September 1992, when Parliament was recalled to discuss the economy, following a sterling crisis and Britain's withdrawal from the European exchange rate mechanism (ERM). He was widely recognized as having made a brilliant speech in response to a poor performance by the Prime Minister. The effect was to boost Smith's own authority and to undermine morale on the Government side of the House at a time when the Government was in economic and political difficulties.

Performance outside the chamber is also important. It is to a minister's advantage to maintain good relations with his own supporters. An ability to mix easily – to be clubbable – is not a prerequisite for achieving and retaining office, but it is an advantage. A poor standing with backbenchers can make a minister vulnerable in the event of a policy or administrative mistake. If a minister loses the confidence of his parliamentary party, it is difficult to continue in office.

On the Conservative side of the House, in the ten years between 1982 and 1992 five ministers resigned after losing the support of backbenchers. One was the Prime Minister, Margaret Thatcher, in 1990 (see Norton 1992c). Lord Carrington resigned as Foreign Secretary in 1982 over policy on the Falkland Islands (two other Foreign Office ministers resigned with him), Leon Brittan as Trade and Industry Secretary in 1986 over the Westland affair (see Marshall 1989), Edwina Currie as a health minister in 1988 over comments made over salmonella in eggs, and David Mellor as National Heritage Secretary in September 1992 following press stories about his private life. All had their detractors on the backbenches prior to the event that precipitated their departure. In the case of David Mellor, for example, he had 'never been widely popular at Westminster. . . . His style has irritated conformist MPs who have regarded him as too bumptious, too tactless, too keen on personal publicity and perhaps rather too dilettante for a Tory minister' (Riddell 1992: 3).

Conversely, some ministers have managed to maintain the support of members. In 1991, for example, the Northern Ireland Secretary, Peter Brooke, faced calls for his resignation after he lightheartedly sang on an Irish television programme a few hours after several people were killed in a terrorist bombing in Northern Ireland. His standing with members on both sides of the House – coupled with a desire by Labour and Conservative MPs not to allow the minister to give in to pressure from Unionist politicians such as Democratic Unionist leader Ian Paisley – helped ensure that he remained in office, at least until the 1992 general election. His popularity with members also facilitated his return to government as National Heritage Secretary, in place of David Mellor, six months after the election.

Remaining as members of a body which may not choose them but can influence their future has, then, a significant influence on ministers. The resignations we have mentioned are few in number but serve as a salutary reminder to other ministers. It is an exceptionally thick-skinned minister who is unconcerned about parliamentary reputation. It is a rare, and usually imprudent, minister who neglects government backbenchers. For ambitious ministers in Conservative Governments there is a particular incentive to be attentive to one's parliamentary party: it constitutes the body that chooses the party leader. As it can now also vote the incumbent out of the leadership (and twice has – in 1975 as well as 1990), the parliamentary party is a body that also can demand the attention of the party leader.

Parliament is thus a vital training ground or, to put it perhaps more accurately, an environment in which ministers have to learn to survive. Most do so without undue difficulty. But knowing they have to survive in that fairly closeted environment influences both their perceptions and their behaviour.

Wider consequences

The fact that ministers are drawn from and stay within Parliament also has other consequences for Parliament and for government. For Parliament, or rather in this context the House of Commons, there are what may be seen as essentially beneficial consequences in terms of career attractiveness, stability in membership, proximity to ministers, and socialization. For government, there are important consequences in terms of control, ministerial selection and legitimation.

Parliament

Career attractiveness

As we have seen, for anyone seeking to make a career in politics, there is little or no alternative to seeking a seat in the House of Commons. As David Marquand observed in the context of the European Parliament, a Parliament 'of aging party warhorses put out to grass would clearly be a different proposition from a Parliament of sharp and ambitious Turks' (Marquand 1979: 67). The House of Commons has attracted the young Turks. The House of Lords is the chamber for those who have already seen service in other careers.

Given a rise in the number of aspiring young politicians (the explanation for which we shall explore later), the competition for party candidatures has become greater. In a safe Conservative seat, for example, the number of names submitted to the local party can now run into several hundred. The result is a much larger pool from which parties can choose in selecting candidates for parliamentary elections. (The parties have also changed their selection procedures.)[4] The outcome of these developments has been a Commons with a much more career-oriented membership. The result, as we shall see, has been a more active House.

Stability in membership

A stable membership allows for some degree of continuity. Experience can be drawn on. There is the potential for a corporate spirit to develop. There would thus appear to be some advantage to the House in having some measure of continuity in its membership.

Given that those intent on a political career have no alternative path to pursue, the Commons loses relatively few members as a result of competing job opportunities. Some younger members have left the House because they felt there was little prospect of promotion from the back benches – such as Conservative Matthew Parris who left the House in 1986, seven years after first being elected, in order to pursue a career in the media – but they are few in number. The injection of new blood into the House is achieved predominantly through a change in electoral fortunes and in the retirement of members at the end of their political careers. Between 1900 and 1974, two-thirds of the MPs who left the House did so through retirement or electoral defeat; a further fifteen to sixteen per cent died in office (Rush 1979: 93).

A massive swing in political fortunes at a general election affects membership stability. In the twentieth century, the general elections of 1906 and 1945 resulted in a large body of new MPs. Other elections have not had such a dramatic effect. Consequently, members wanting to make a career in the House have usually had an opportunity to do so. The greater career orientation of members appears to have contributed to longer parliamentary careers, with an increase since 1945 in the age at which members have retired (Rush 1979: 94).

The result is a House of Commons with a stability in membership that is relatively high by international comparison. There is some turnover in membership at each general election, thus allowing for the injection of some new members, but at least eighty per cent of members will usually continue from one Parliament to the next.

Ministerial ambition is not the sole explanation for such stability. Many ex-ministers remain in the House, as do some backbenchers who know their chances of promotion to office are slight. The fact that ministers remain in Parliament may contribute a partial explanation for the presence of those not destined for future office. They remain close to those who are in office.

Proximity to ministers

The fact that ministers remain in Parliament is valuable to other members in that it ensures a closeness that can be utilised by each House collectively and by members individually. Ministers take part in debates and answer questions. They will also variously be present to listen to other ministers in debate. Given that they are members, they are also entitled to vote. They are thus present during divisions. As the process of voting takes several minutes – on average, about twelve minutes each division – ministers spend some time rubbing shoulders with backbench supporters in the division lobbies. This presents an opportunity – a much-used one – for backbenchers to talk to ministers and put over particular points. Conversely, ministers often utilise the opportunity to track down particular members they want to see. Such opportunities for face-to-face contact are recognised by members as invaluable for increasing the likelihood of a positive response to a request: a minister finds it more difficult to say no when facing the member making the request.

Ministers also have offices in the Palace of Westminster. Some will also spend time meeting members in the tea, smoking and dining rooms, not least for reasons of increasing their profile among potential backbench supporters.

Socialization

The fact that ministers start life as members of Parliament and remain as members ensures – or is likely to ensure – that they are familiar with parliamentary norms and expectations. Aspirant ministers have to know their way round the institution. A survey by the Study of Parliament Group of new MPs first returned in the 1992 general election found that approximately half of them regarded themselves as 'very familiar' or 'somewhat familiar' with parliamentary procedure. Once elected, they face the same demands and pressures as their other colleagues. And once elevated to ministerial office, those demands do not necessarily cease. Ministers in the House of Commons retain constituency responsibilities (see Chapter 9). They have to carry out tasks as members of Parliament and not solely as ministers.

There is thus a socialization of those who are to form the political elite into the parliamentary process. Though ministers are answerable to Parliament, they are also members of the very institution to which they are answerable. They are themselves likely to return to the backbenches at some stage, be it by choice or prime ministerial diktat. This reduces the likelihood of ministers ignoring and not understanding Parliament's needs and expectations. This contrasts with those political systems where there is a separation of executive and legislature, increasing the potential for misunderstanding between the two.

Within Parliament there is nonetheless some potential for misunderstanding. This was demonstrated in 1982 when Lord Carrington resigned as Foreign Secretary. As a member of the House of Lords, he had some sense of what peers might be expecting of him. However, he failed to appreciate the strength of feeling on the Conservative backbenches in the Commons on the issue of the Falkland Islands. The policy he had pursued had not been as resolute in defence of the sovereignty of the islands as many Conservative members had wanted. If ministers were members of neither House, the potential for them to fail to appreciate likely parliamentary reaction would be significantly greater.

Government

Control

Party dominates Parliament and political behaviour. We have seen the conditions that made this possible (see Chapter 2). For its continuance in office, government is dependent on a parliamentary majority. Formally, this should ensure parliamentary control of the executive. In practice, the flow of control is the other way. In the eighteenth century, control could be achieved through royal patronage and placemen in the Commons. Since the last third of the nineteenth century, it has been achieved through party.

The presence of ministers in Parliament is not the cause of party control (see Crowe 1986) but serves rather to facilitate it. Being in Parliament means ministers have a platform to lead and to persuade their supporters. Ministers can serve as an important reference group for loyal and ambitious backbenchers. 'Some MPs model themselves after the frontbench group, especially those backbenchers who seek higher office themselves' (Crowe 1986: 164). Ministers alone can introduce bills making a charge on the public revenue. In debate, frontbenchers are the focus of attention. And ministers collectively constitute a significant block vote.

Ministers are bound by the convention of collective responsibility. This convention requires that ministers do not oppose a policy once it has been agreed. Some uncertainty existed in the nineteenth century as to whether the convention applied to junior ministers. In the twentieth, there has been no such ambiguity (Norton 1989b: 34–35). It encompasses all ministers and in recent years has been employed to constrain the activities of parliamentary private secretaries (Norton 1989a: 234–6; 1989b: 35–36); PPSs voting against the Government lose their posts.[5] The result is a block vote at the disposal of government. Given the increase over the century in the number of ministers, and the increase in the years since 1979 in the number of PPSs (from twenty-nine in 1979 to forty in 1989), it is now a sizeable block vote. In the parliament returned in 1992, it constituted more than one-third of the Conservative parliamentary party. In the event of a difficult vote, with some Conservative backbenchers expected to cross-vote, the 'payroll vote' is normally much in evidence.[6]

Ministerial selection

The fact that ministers have to survive within a parliamentary environment has some effect on ministerial selection. An ability to handle oneself in the House is an advantage for anyone keen to become a minister. A Prime Minister is also not infrequently influenced by the extent of support – or lack of it – a potential or existing minister has on the back benches in deciding the distribution of ministerial portfolios.

Sacking a minister with a significant body of back bench support causes more problems for a Prime Minister than dispensing with the services of one who has few friends in the party. In the first Parliament of her administration, for example, Margaret Thatcher singled out for dismissal those 'wet' members of her Cabinet with no substantial body of parliamentary supporters (such as Norman St. John-Stevas and Sir Ian Gilmour), retaining those with some backbench support (such as James Prior and Francis Pym) until a more opportune time came to remove them (Pym) or transfer them to another post (Prior). A failure to promote to office able and popular backbenchers can also prove problematic. Edward Heath's failure to promote backbench critics such as John Biffen resulted in his policies being subject to effective criticisms from such members as well as undermining morale within the parliamentary party (see Norton 1978a).

The fact of ministers remaining in Parliament is an influence in their appointment. Arguably, it may be a too significant influence. There is the danger that parliamentary skills may be prized over skills that may be as necessary to control and lead a government department. A minister capable of strategic thinking, with a good grasp of future policy requirements, and a capacity for hard work and administration, may make little progress – indeed, may lose office – if these are not matched by a capacity to handle oneself in debate and in one's relations with backbenchers.

The shift in April 1992 of William Waldegrave from the post of Health Secretary to Chancellor of the Duchy of Lancaster, with responsibility for the Citizen's Charter, was seen by many observers as a consequence, in part, of his poor performance at the despatch box. There was general recognition that the minister was bright and hard working, with a good intellectual grasp of his brief, but he lacked a strong and confident manner in the chamber, and failed to shine against an abrasive shadow Health Secretary, Robin Cook.

On this analysis, therefore, it is possible to argue that far from lacking power, Parliament is too powerful. Ministerial membership in Parliament imposes constraints in ministerial selection, with a Prime Minister unable to exploit alternative avenues – because none exists – in ministerial recruitment.

Legitimation

The fact that ministers are drawn from the ranks of parliamentarians and remain within Parliament contributes to the legitimation of government. Membership of the legislature confers some status on ministers, over and above that accruing from being ministers. That ministers in the Commons have fought elections to be returned to Parliament as MPs gives them a particular status, the knowledge that they are subject individually to re-election as members adding to their presumed sensitivity to electors' opinions. Remaining within Parliament means ministers are available to be questioned by members, and this adds to what Packenham has characterised as a form of latent legitimation (see Chapters 1 and 8).

Remaining within Parliament also adds a particular burden to the workload of ministers (see James 1992: 19–29). They have variously to be present, not just to take part in question time and debates, but also to vote and to support fellow ministers in important debates. As MPs, they have to pursue constituency casework. The burden on individuals is heavy and they may therefore have mixed feelings about having to shoulder the twin burden of ministerial office and parliamentary membership. However, from the perspective of government, the balance of advantages clearly favours the present integration of ministers in Parliament.

Conclusion

The Act of Settlement of 1701 almost resulted in a formal separation of ministers from Parliament. That was avoided and ministers continue to be selected from and remain within the ranks of MPs and peers. Parliament enjoys a hegemony as the recruiting ground for ministers. It creates an environment in which ministers have to learn to handle themselves competently in order to survive. It also results in an environment in which backbenchers have some personal access to ministers and in which ministers can be empathetic to parliamentary norms and expectations.

Government for its part is given a powerful tool of parliamentary leadership and management. Being drawn from and remaining within Parliament also enhances its legitimacy. As we shall see, the inter-locking relationship is one that both facilitates and limits Members of Parliament in attempting to have some impact on public policy and the administration of government.

Notes

1. Conventions constitute rules of behaviour that have no legal force but which are treated as binding by those at whom they are directed in order to make the formal, legally binding provisions of the constitution mesh with the prevailing political reality. Thus, for example, it is a convention of the constitution that the monarch assents to all bills passed by the two Houses of Parliament, even though she has the legal right to refuse her assent. See Norton (1982a: 7–8).
2. The King's action gave rise to the convention even though it appears the reason for his choice was not that Curzon sat in an unelected House but that the House contained no Labour peers. Following the 1922 general election, Labour had become the official Opposition.
3. Iain Macleod in the 1950s, for example, was believed to have been given office after a devastating speech he made attacking an opposition front-bencher (Aneurin Bevan) impressed the Prime Minister (Winston Churchill) and, more recently, Francis Maude was given office in 1985 – two years after being elected to Parliament – reputedly because he made a speech that was noticed by Margaret Thatcher, who happened to be in the chamber at the time.
4. The Labour party in 1981 adopted a policy of compulsory re-selection for sitting Labour members, requiring them to go through a full re-selection process during the lifetime of a Parliament. Later in the decade, the party's National Executive Committee took a more active role in candidate approval, on occasion imposing candidates in by-elections. Where incumbents failed to achieve re-selection, they were replaced by younger and usually constituency-active candidates. On the Conservative side, and more germane in the context of this discussion, the selection process was made more professional, with those wanting to go on the Party's candidates' list having to go through a rigorous weekend selection course, a practice developed from management training.
5. In October 1992, for example, Elizabeth Peacock, Conservative member for Batley and Spen, was sacked as PPS to the minister for social security after she voted against the Government on the issue of closure of coal mines.
6. The 'payroll vote' is a term in common usage but is inaccurate, given that it encompasses PPSs, who receive no payment for their services.

4

Policy Making:
The Early Stages

The capacity of legislatures to affect the content of public policy is a central concern of legislative scholars (see Olson and Mezey 1991). From empirical observation, it is clear that the capacity to affect policy varies from one legislature to another.

In terms of their impact on public policy, three types of legislature can be identified: policy-making, policy-influencing, and those with little or no policy affect. The essential characteristics of each are identified in Table 4.1. Policy-making legislatures can involve themselves in the drawing up, the making, of policy. Policy-influencing legislatures have the formal capacity to amend, even reject, measures of public policy placed before them, but they are

Table 4.1   Types of legislatures

Policy-making legislatures
Have the capacity to amend or reject policy brought forward by the executive, and the capacity to formulate and substitute policy of their own.

Policy-influencing legislatures
Have the capacity to amend or reject policy brought forward by the executive, but lack the capacity to formulate and substitute policy of their own.

Legislatures with little or no policy affect
Lack the capacity both to amend or reject policy brought forward by the executive and to formulate and substitute policy of their own. They confine themselves to assenting to whatever is placed before them.

essentially dependent on government to put those measures forward. Even if they reject a measure, they look to government to
formulate and bring forward a replacement. The legislature itself
does not seek to generate, to make, policy. It lacks the political
will, the institutional resources or even, in some cases, the constitutional power to do so.

For most of its history, Parliament has not been a policy-making
body. The monarch came to depend on Parliament for assenting
both to supply and to legislation (see Chapter 2). Demanding a
redress of grievance before granting supply could be construed as
initiating some change in the King's policies. But for most of the
centuries of its existence, Parliament has looked to the executive –
first the monarch, then the King's government – to bring forward
measures for it to consider. Even in the wake of the Glorious
Revolution of 1688, those responsible for the Bill of Rights wanted
'a real, working, governing King, a King with a policy' (Maitland,
in Wiseman 1966: 5).

The position has been exacerbated by the growth of party. The
rise of party in the nineteenth century heralded the consolidation
of policy-initiating power in the hands of the executive. Increasing
demands on government by organized interests resulted in more
public legislation and an increasing domination by government of
the parliamentary timetable.

This development has not been peculiar to Britain. In the
typology of Table 4.1, Parliament is a policy-influencing legislature. So too are most legislatures of western Europe (Norton
1990b) and of the Commonwealth. The category, in fact, is the
most crowded of the three. The number has been swelled by the
new legislatures of central and eastern Europe, but even prior
to their emergence it was the most populous category. What is
noteworthy, but not altogether surprising given the effects of
industrialization, is that the first category – that of policy-
making legislatures – is almost empty. The only major national
legislature to have occupied the category on any consistent basis
is the U.S. Congress. It is joined by the state legislatures of the
United States (see Mezey 1979: Chapter 2). The separation of
powers in the USA, combined with an ideological consensus
that has militated against the emergence of strong parties (Norton 1993a), has resulted in a legislative system that stands apart
from others.

The policy-making process

The process by which a proposal is translated into public policy is often a complex and lengthy one. Four principal stages in the process can be identified: those of initiation, formulation, deliberation and approval, and implementation.

Initiation is the first stage of a formal process. Proposals for changes in public policy emanate from different sources, such as individuals, pressure groups and companies. The National Society for the Prevention of Cruelty to Children (NSPCC), for example, may feel that laws against child abuse need strengthening. A twenty-year-old active in politics may feel that the law should be changed to allow those aged eighteen to twenty-one to stand for election to public office. Depositors who have lost money in a particular venture may want new laws to restrict who can set up in business. For these proposals to end up as public policy, they have to find their way on to the agenda of debate within the policy-making process itself. Private bodies cannot themselves introduce public bills or, for that matter, place a proposal before the EC Council of Ministers. Proposals for public bills have to come from – be initiated by – ministers or by private members. Our principal concern is the extent to which Parliament determines the agenda for the deliberation and determination of public policy in the United Kingdom. In terms of legislation, that means to what extent does Parliament set its own agenda?

In terms of *formulation*, we mean putting the flesh on the bones of a particular proposal. The proposal may be that, in the interests of safety on the roads, lorries must have more powerful rear lights in poor visibility. But what categories of lorry are to be included? What form is this extra lighting to take? What penalties are to be imposed for not having such lighting? Translating the principle into practical detail constitutes the formulation stage. There are two elements to this stage.

First, those responsible for introducing the measure have to agree the detail. In the case of a government bill, for example, that will be the ministers in the relevant department and, subsequently, the appropriate Cabinet committee. Second, there is the formal construction of the document. In the case of legislation, that means drafting a bill. For government (and some private members') bills, this task is undertaken by trained lawyers known as parliamentary counsel. Where the proposal does not involve primary legislation, such as a document to be placed before an international body, the formal construction will usually be undertaken by departmental civil servants.

The stages of initiation and formulation may thus be taken to form the essential stages of policy making. They involve the putting together, the crafting, of a coherent proposal that is intended to be applied in a particular community. The remaining stages complete the process from making to application. *Deliberation and approval* entail consideration of the policy by Parliament and the formal giving of assent to it by the Queen-in-Parliament. Without that assent, it cannot constitute an Act of Parliament and be enforced as the law of the land. *Implementation* constitutes the carrying into effect of the policy. The nature of the implementation will vary depending upon the nature of the policy. Some measures can be implemented through administrative action by officials, such as payment of a new kind of benefit; some are implemented through police action, as with enforcing a ban on a particular activity.

The purpose of this chapter is to focus on the first two stages of the process. What role does Parliament play in actual policy making? Our initial assumption, based on history and comparative observation, is that it is a minor one.

Initiation

More detailed study of the contemporary policy-making process bears out the evidence of historical and comparative analysis. Parliament is a marginal, and at best a proximate, actor in policy-making.

The political parties contest elections on the basis of increasingly bulky and detailed election manifestos. Winning parties have a very good record of implementing manifesto promises (Hofferbert and Budge 1992: 151–82). MPs' input into the content of manifestos has varied, but generally they have a limited and at times almost non-existent say in what is included.

On the Labour side, the manifesto is determined formally by the leadership in the House of Commons in consultation with the party's National Executive Committee (Norton 1990a: 145–8). On the Conservative side, the party leader is formally the fount of all policy. In practice, various advisory bodies are used, usually small groups covering particular sectors (Patten 1980: 9–25; Norton and Aughey 1981: 230). The officers of backbench party committees in the Commons are normally included in these groups. Their influence has varied. On occasion they have been important, most recently in 1987, but more often than not they have made little direct contribution (Ramsden 1980; Brand 1992: 46–47). In the formulation of the Conservative Party's 1992 election manifesto, for example, such policy groups were employed, but the key figure in each was usually the relevant minister, with the overall shape and direction of the manifesto being determined by the Prime Minister, John Major, Party Chairman Chris Patten, and the head of the No. 10 policy unit, Sarah Hogg.

The party manifesto provides the basis for the government's 'flagship' legislation during a Parliament. It constitutes only a minority of the legislation to be introduced. Other measures will be introduced in response to particular crises (such as the Dangerous Dogs Bill, following particularly vicious attacks by dogs on a number of people, including children, in 1991), as a result of international agreements reached by government (as with the 1986 European Communities [Amendment] Bill, ratifying the Single European Act), and – most numerous of all – as a result of discussions within government departments. Rose (1980: 70–72) found that at least three-quarters of bills originated in departments. Burton and Drewry (1981: Chapter 7) distinguish between 'policy bills', which implement significant policy changes, and 'administration bills', which tidy up and/or update earlier legislation. Bills promised in the manifesto will tend to fall in the former category and bills originating in departments will tend to fall more often in the latter category. The correlation, however, is far from total.

The opportunities to initiate and achieve passage of government bills, whether policy or administration bills, are substantial. The Government dominates the parliamentary timetable, enjoying precedence in public business on all but a limited number of days each session.[1] Most bills introduced and passed each session are government bills. Table 4.2 shows that of 213 government bills introduced in the 1987–92 Parliament, 202 – ninety-five per cent – were passed. Of 584 private members' bills introduced, most were never debated and 65 – eleven per cent – were passed.

Table 4.2 Bills introduced 1987–92

| | Bills Introduced | | | |
| | Government | | Private Members[1] | |
Sessions	Passed	Failed	Passed	Failed
1987–88	49	0	13	109
1988–89	37	0	9	136
1989–90	34	2	11	120
1990–91	49	3	19	103
1991–92	33	6[2]	13	51
Total	202	11	65	519

Notes: [1] The number of private Members' bills includes bills introduced in the House of Lords but never brought to the Commons.

[2] The high number of government bills failing in this session is because the session was cut short by the calling of the general election.

Source: Figures derived from the House of Commons, *Weekly Information Bulletin*, for each session.

The disparity between the two types of bills is even greater when the length of bills, and not just the number, are compared. The combined number of pages of all private members' bills passed probably amounted to no more than the combined length of four or five major government bills.

Not surprisingly, therefore, for bodies seeking to change public policy, the first and often only port of call is a government department. A 1986 survey of more than 250 organized interests found that ministers and civil servants were judged to be the key actors in policy initiation (Rush 1990: 272). In order to influence ministers, groups placed as much emphasis on the mass media as they did on Parliament. MPs may play a limited role as facilitators, helping introduce representatives of a group or company to a minister, but their intervention is neither essential nor, consequentially, always sought. As one group in the 1986 survey commented: 'We usually go to the minister direct without MPs' assistance. . . . Our comments do bear fruit, there are lots of examples where they have' (Rush 1990: 272).

The essential link for organized interests is thus government departments. The links, as we have noted (Chapter 1), have become extensive and institutionalized. The policy style involved in negotiations between civil servants and representatives of outside groups has been characterised by Jordan and Richardson

(1982) as one of 'bureaucratic accommodation'. It is in the interests of both sides to produce a mutually agreeable proposal, which is then passed upwards for ministerial assent. Such negotiations are geared essentially to achieving incremental change: an adjustment, for example, to some existing regulation. For more substantial change, especially that involving major legislation, the principal figure is the minister.

Bruce Headey's research of civil servants (1974) found that civil servants prefer a minister who can take a decision. Once a minister has 'taken a view', the civil servants set about the task of carrying it out. In terms of legislation, policy bills will often be preceded by a consultative green paper, inviting comments from affected bodies, or – where the government has decided on a measure – a white paper, detailing the government's proposals. White paper proposals will be taken to a Cabinet committee and approved by full Cabinet before publication. They will be drawn up by civil servants on the instructions of the minister. For the education white paper published in July 1992, the Secretary of State for Education, John Patten, actually wrote parts himself.

White papers may be described as finalizing the first half of the formulation stage. The second stage is the legislative drafting. Up to this second stage, the whole process is clearly dominated by civil servants and ministers. There is no regular parliamentary involvement. The foregoing paragraphs are noteworthy for the dearth of references to Members of Parliament.

Sporadic involvement

However, to establish that there is no regular involvement by Parliament is not to establish that there is no involvement at all by Parliament. There are limited opportunities for measures to be initiated by MPs and peers. They are employed and occasionally result in policies being accepted and implemented. There is also the possibility of a negative impact by Parliament, preventing a proposal from being brought forward. This impact is difficult to observe and quantify but is almost certainly rare.

Parliament's involvement in the initiating stage may be classified as sporadic. Given the pressures we have identified favouring the dominance of the executive, it is perhaps surprising that there is any at all. What is equally noteworthy is that the potential for involvement has increased in recent years.

The principal means by which policies may be brought on to the policy-making agenda are several. On the floor of each House they comprise questions, motions, and the second readings of private members' bills. Away from the floor, there are two unofficial routes, those of party committees and all-party groups, and one official route, that of select committees. There is also the opportunity to table early day motions. These means are not mutually exclusive and several or all may be utilised to achieve consideration of a particular policy.

The occasions when these means are likely to prove most effective are when there is no existing policy in the area or when the issue is a contentious but non-party one, with the government preferring to adopt an ostensible hands-off approach. The most notable examples occurred in the latter half of the 1960s on a number of 'conscience issues', notably abortion, divorce, homosexuality, the death penalty, and theatre censorship (Richards 1970). The government was not prepared to initiate a change in policy on these issues. Instead, the initiation was left to MPs and peers.

Questions and motions

Private members in both Houses have an opportunity to table questions for answer by ministers. In the Commons, the number that are now tabled each year, and the number answered in each question time (see Chapter 6), means that by themselves they offer no real opportunity to spark discussion and parliamentary interest in a policy proposal. Their use in this context is as part of a wider campaign. In the Upper House, questions have a greater potential. 'Starred' questions, taken at the beginning of a sitting, each receive more time than a Commons' question, permitting several contributions from peers. 'Unstarred' questions are debatable questions. One is usually taken at the end of a sitting, allowing peers to have a short debate.

Private members also ballot to introduce motions. In the Commons, most private members' motions are taken on a Friday. Private members' business enjoys precedence on a Friday, and each session the Fridays are divided between private members' bills and motions. In the Lords, Wednesdays are normally given over to debates, one Wednesday each month usually being reserved for motions chosen by ballot, the remaining Wednesdays being distributed to the different party groups, each then allocating its slots to individual peers.

These occasions have the potential to excite the interest of parliamentarians in a particular policy and bring it effectively on to the agenda. If a debate reveals strong support, it may then encourage the sponsoring member – or even the government – to introduce a bill to give effect to the policy.

There are various occasions when these devices have had that effect. Of the conscience issues in the 1960s, for example, the measure to legalize homosexual relations between consenting male adults was sparked in large part by debate on a motion tabled by Lord Arran in May 1965. The tenor of the debate was sufficiently supportive for Arran to introduce a bill on the subject two weeks later (Richards 1970: 76). Another motion in the Lords, in 1966, calling for a committee to review the law on stage censorship, was an important part of the movement resulting in the abolition of such censorship.

However, too much should not be made of these examples. They are important but notable for their rarity. Questions and motions are used normally to raise specific issues amenable to administrative redress, to find out what government is doing or intending to do on particular matters, and to give vent to feelings – in the Commons, in particular, partisan feelings. Their relevance is thus greater for some of the other consequences we shall consider in later chapters. By themselves, their part in policy initiating is extraordinarily limited.

Second readings of private members' bills

The second readings – the debates on principle – of private members' bills are more important. In the Lords, peers have an unrestricted right to introduce bills and time is usually found to debate them. Many, though, will go no further because of lack of time to debate them in the Commons. For example, of forty-one private members' bills that started life in the Lords in the 1987–92 Parliament, seventeen never got to the Commons. Of those that reach the Commons, most fail. Of the twenty-four bills in the

1987 Parliament that did make it, sixteen were not passed. The remaining eight, however, reached the statute book. There is thus *some* scope for peers to initiate legislation.

In the Commons, MPs have three routes by which to introduce bills: through the ballot, through the ten-minute rule bill procedure, and through the submission of unballoted bills. Each session, MPs ballot to introduce bills on the Fridays set aside for private members' legislation. Twenty names are drawn and the top half-dozen or so are usually guaranteed a full debate on their bills. This constitutes the principal route for introducing a bill that stands some chance of becoming law. Of the sixty-five private members' bills passed in the 1987–92 parliament, forty-one were balloted bills.

3 ways to introduce bills:
① ballot

MPs also ballot to bring in bills under the ten-minute rule procedure. This allows a member to speak for ten minutes in asking for permission to introduce a bill; a member may rise to speak against for ten minutes. Taken at the beginning of public business on Tuesdays and Wednesdays (that is, immediately after question time), ten-minute rule bills occupy prime parliamentary time and they give MPs, by voting on whether to give leave to introduce the bill, a chance to express a preference on the proposed measure. The procedure is very much geared to initiating policy. Ten-minute rule bills are proposals – not drafted bills. Members hope to show sufficient support for a measure in the hope that the government may be persuaded to introduce a measure of its own. Failing that, there is always a chance that, if the House votes to give leave for a bill to be introduced, the ten-minute rule bill may actually find its way on the statute book.

② 10-min rule

In practice, neither usually happens. Since 1970, a grand total of only six ten-minute rule bills have become law. There are few, if any, known instances of a vote on a ten-minute rule bill, by itself, inducing government action.

Under the third method, an MP can simply introduce an unballoted bill under Standing Order 58. No time is provided for these bills. Their titles are read out at the end of business on a Friday and a simple cry of 'object' by a member is sufficient to block them. Most are so blocked. Such bills, therefore, have little or no utility as mechanisms for initiating significant changes of public policy. If they are short, uncontentious measures, they may pass: in the 1987 Parliament, no less than sixteen did so.

③ unballoted bill

As is clear from Table 4.2, the vast majority of bills introduced by private members do not get passed. More than a third, those introduced under Standing Order 58, do not even get debated. A similar proportion, those introduced under the ten-minute rule, get only a few minutes each. Nonetheless, they have some use for initiating a change in public policy. After all, as the table also shows, a total of sixty-five bills were passed in a five-session Parliament.

However, quantity should not be mistaken for suggesting that they have had a major impact on public policy. Most balloted bills are successful because they are modest proposals enjoying support from a wide body of members and from the government. Indeed, a significant proportion come from government departments in the form of what are now known as 'handout bills'. To increase the chances of getting a bill through, MPs successful in the ballot will sometimes select bills prepared by government departments, for which no time is available in the government's timetable. Marsh and Read (1988: 45–6) found that eighteen per cent of bills introduced in the sessions from 1979–80 to 1985–86 originated in departments, a larger proportion than in any previous post-war period.[2] The practice is a continuing one. The MP coming top of the ballot in the 1992–93 session, for example, selected a bill on offer from the Department of the Environment. Furthermore, as we have just noted, unballoted bills are likely to be even more modest, since they need to avoid the vocal opposition of even a single MP.

Nonetheless, private members' bills have some significance. On occasion, they have initiated major changes in the law on social issues. The most notable examples we have already mentioned, those of the 1960s on issues such as divorce, abortion and homosexuality. They have, on occasion, had an effect not apparent from the raw figures in Table 4.2. That is, they have prompted government to take action. One example is that of the House Buyers Bill introduced in 1983 by Labour MP Austin Mitchell to remove the monopoly of solicitors on house conveyancing (Mitchell 1986). After MPs gave it a second reading, against ministerial advice, the Government announced it would take action of its own. Such occasions are rare but nonetheless important. Finally, there is the impact of the modest measures that get passed each session. Table 4.3 lists the eighteen successful measures of the 1990–91 session, introduced under either the ballot or Standing Order 58 procedure. (There was one other successful bill, introduced in the Lords.) The titles give some idea of the range of policies implemented.

Table 4.3   Private members' bills passed, 1990–91 session

Bills introduced under the ballot or standing order 58 (unballoted bills) procedure[1]	
Title of bill	*Bill's sponsor*
Badgers	Roy Hughes (Lab)
Children and Young Persons (Protection from Tobacco)	Andrew Faulds (Lab)
Criminal Procedure (Insanity and Unfitness to Plead)	John Greenway (Con)
Crofters Forestry (Scotland)	Calum Macdonald (Lab)
Local Government Finance (Publicity for Auditors' Reports)	Michael Mates (Con)
Motor Vehicles (Safety Equipment for Children)	Michael Jopling (Con)
Property Misdescriptions	John Butcher (Con)
Radioactive Material (Road Transport)	Dudley Fishburn (Con)
Registered Homes (Amendment)	John Butterfill (Con)
Road Traffic (Temporary Restrictions)	William Cash (Con)
Wildlife and Countryside (Amendment)	Donald Coleman (Lab)
Age of Legal Capacity (Scotland)	Sir Nicholas Fairbairn (Con)
Badgers (Further Protection)	Alan Meale (Lab)
Breeding of Dogs	Alan Williams (Lab)
Football (Offences)	Sir John Wheeler (Con)
Forestry	Sir Hector Monro (Con)
Smoke Detectors	Conal Gregory (Con)
Welfare of Animals at Slaughter	Sir Richard Body (Con)

[1] In addition, one private member's bill introduced by a peer passed in this session.

Though many, indeed most, of the private members' bills that are successful have their genesis in government departments, official reports or pressure groups (Marsh and Read 1988), private members are nonetheless responsible for initiating those measures, for actually bringing them before Parliament for deliberation and approval. As such, private members' legislation is important as an initiating mechanism. As we shall see, it is not as

significant as it is in fulfilling other tasks, but it is the most important of the various mechanisms available to MPs and peers to initiate a change in public policy.

Party committees

Off the floor of the House, there are various means by which MPs
can seek to initiate policy, though essentially indirectly: that is, by
raising it in the hope that it will be taken up by government.

Party committees constitute one such potential source. Both the
Conservative and Labour Parties have backbench committees.
(On the Labour side, they are known as departmental groups.) In
the areas they cover, they tend to mirror government departments
– agriculture, foreign affairs, environment and so on. They offer a
means for backbenchers interested in a particular subject to gather
and discuss it, to listen to invited guests, and to meet the relevant
minister (or shadow minister, if in opposition) to discuss policy and
forthcoming legislation. As a private party gathering, each committee offers an opportunity for straight talking. If government
backbenchers do not like a particular proposal, they can say so
without the constraints imposed by debates in a public forum.

Committees on the Conservative side have tended to meet
more regularly than Labour groups and have enjoyed a reputation
for being more influential (Norton 1979; 1983). Disquiet expressed
by a committee has some effect. As one MP once put it, 'if a
committee really blows off steam, it's in Cabinet the next day'
(King 1974: 49). The committees covering the more important
subjects, such as finance and foreign affairs, are regarded as influential bodies and their officers will be accorded some deference
within the party.

Committees have the potential to initiate policy as well as influence proposals brought forward by their leaders. In practice, influence is more frequent than initiation (see Norton 1983, 1993b).
Though difficult to quantify, given the privacy of the meetings,
there are few known occasions of committees initiating policy.
More frequently, they have served as conduits for the expression
of backbench disquiet on government policy which, on occasion,
has induced a government response. In the period of Conservative
government in the 1970s, they had some sporadic influence, delay-
ing the introduction of a bill (the Maplin Development Bill) and

achieving some modification to the Industry Bill in 1972 (Norton 1978a). Some committee meetings have also proved important in the years of Conservative government since 1979. In 1984, for example, criticism of the Education Secretary's proposals for student grants expressed at a meeting of the education committee appeared to be a contributory element in the decision to withdraw them (Silk 1987: 49). In October 1992, a crowded meeting of the Trade and Industry Committee – with more than 150 members present – was used to demonstrate backbench dissatisfaction with the decision announced by the President of the Board of Trade, Michael Heseltine, to close thirty-one coal pits. The meeting helped convince the Government of the need to modify the policy.

Such examples are important. They suggest that committees serve as vehicles of influence and constraint. In terms of influencing frontbench thinking, that influence may be largely unseen but pervasive (see Norton 1983). However, known examples of influence are not numerous. There is little or no evidence of committees influencing significant changes to policy on a regular basis. The committees serve several purposes, but initiating policy does not figure as one of the principal ones. On the basis of existing evidence, it can hardly be said to figure at all.

Furthermore, the opportunity for influencing, let alone initiating, policy is declining rather than increasing. The growth of demands on MPs' time – from constituents, pressure groups and select and standing committees – has meant that backbenchers are spending less time attending backbench committee meetings (Norton 1993b). Large attendances are the exception to the rule. Small attendances and less regular meetings reduces the likelihood of committees having a major influence on front bench thinking. 'It cuts little ice in my department' was how one minister characterized the party committee covering his responsibilities in 1991 (quoted in Norton 1993b). He was untypical but not the only minister to take such a view.

All-party groups

All-party groups, as the name implies, have none of the partisan connotations that attach to party committees. They meet to discuss and promote a subject of interest to parliamentarians of different parties. (As with party committees, peers can participate in their

[handwritten margin notes: "Same as U.S. caucus? Yet more Specified?"]

work.) There are just over one hundred all-party country groups, each bringing together those MPs and peers with an interest in a particular country. They generally seek to foster contact and good relations with the countries concerned and are rarely involved in seeking to influence or initiate legislation. More importantly for our purposes, there are just under one hundred subject groups. Some of these are confined to a parliamentary membership; some (known as registered groups) have a membership that includes non-parliamentarians.

The subjects covered by the groups are diverse, including AIDS, book publishing, industrial safety and football. Some tend to exist in name only and some have no particular interest in initiating any change in the law. Some, however, are concerned to promote a cause and to press for a change in public policy in order to further that cause. Among the more active and influential has been the long-established Parliamentary and Scientific Committee (PASC), and the Disablement Group, chaired for many years until his retirement from the House by Labour MP Jack Ashley. In recent years, the Football Group – with over 100 members – has been an active body in influencing government on such issues as identity cards and alcohol consumption at football matches.

Such groups suffer from the same problem as party committees in trying to maintain a reasonable attendance, though there is some evidence that MPs committed to a particular cause will main-tain their attendance at the appropriate all-party group meeting rather than going to a party committee. Where there is some com-mitment on the part of members, there is some potential for influ-ence. A government whip will normally try to attend meetings and will note what is said. Ministers cannot dismiss the groups on partisan grounds and, as with groups such as the Disablement Group, will often be willing to receive a delegation to listen to proposals for changes in public policy.

Given this, all-party groups often attract the support of, indeed may even owe their existence to, sympathetic outside groups. The pressure groups may provide administrative and secretarial sup-port. The Animal Welfare Group, for example, is serviced by the RSPCA; the Social Science and Policy group by three outside organizations committed to the social sciences. Such pressure groups are likely to have somewhat more contact with all-party groups than party committees and generally to regard them as more useful, especially so in the case of 'outsider' groups wary of the taint of partisanship (Jones 1990: 129–33). For such 'outsider' groups, an all-party group can provide an important access point to policy makers. 'At the very least', as Barry Jones notes (1990: 126), 'organized interests look to the all-party groups to stimulate parliamentary interest, to raise the political salience of particular issues, and, ultimately, to place them on the political and parliamentary agenda'. Out of all the all-party groups that exist, most never achieve such a result. A few, though, do manage it on occasion.

Select committees

Select committees constitute the area where there has been a growth in parliamentary opportunity to initiate policy, simply by virtue of the increase in the number of such committees. As we briefly noted in Chapter 2, the Commons witnessed the introduction of a series of departmental select committees in 1979.

However, the potential is greater than the reality, at least to date. The committees are multi-functional. They are empowered by their terms of reference to examine 'the expenditure, administration and policy' of their particular departments and associated related bodies. An eleven-member committee meeting once a week has to be selective in what aspect of departmental activity it covers. Some will go for long-term enquiries, others short-term (see Chapter 6). The focus will tend to be some aspect of administration or a particular, usually not overly partisan, policy. Expenditure tends to be the poor relation in terms of the committees' interests.

By their nature, committees are reactive bodies. Those covering long-established departments, with fairly well developed positions on policy, have no new canvass on which to paint. A committee covering a new department, such as the National Heritage Committee established in 1992, has greater scope to initiate policy proposals, but such a committee is exceptional. Given this, and the impetus to avoid overly contentious partisan issues, committees principally look at means of improving existing policies, of making some adjustment here, some modification there.

Most of the recommendations contained in committee reports may be termed humdrum rather than major in policy terms. The number accepted by government is significant, though not excessive. In a parliamentary answer in 1986, for example, the Prime Minister revealed that in the calendar year from March 1985 to March 1986 the government had accepted no less than 150 recommendations that had emanated from select committees. However, the number constituted a minority of the recommendations made by committees and hardly any could be defined as major policy recommendations.

Even so, the cumulative effect of these recommendations is important, not least for those affected by the recommendations. And committees do have the potential to initiate more substantial policy changes. In the first Parliament of the committees' existence, for example, the Foreign Affairs Committee influenced Canadian as well as British policy on the patriation of the Canadian constitution; the Energy Committee influenced a shift of policy on the fiscal regime for North Sea oil; the Employment Committee persuaded the Manpower Services Commission to treat the long-term unemployed as one of its priorities; the Home Affairs Committee was instrumental in persuading the Government to abolish the law allowing detention of suspects on suspicion of being about to commit an offence; and the Education Committee influenced policy on a range of issues, including the rebuilding of the British Library (Liaison Committee 1982; Englefield 1984: 70–71; Drewry 1989, Chapter 20). The cases, though, are not numerous and do not affect matters of high policy. On the whole, then, committee recommendations are important but neither major nor consistent influences.

In the Lords, the potential and the reality are less separated. The Select Committee on Science and Technology, to which we referred briefly in Chapter 2, undertakes substantial enquiries, each enquiry usually lasting at least a year; its membership includes a number of scientists and ex-ministers with experience in the area (Hayter 1991; Grantham 1993) and its reports tend to carry some political clout. Its enquiries are wide-ranging (see Chapter 6). It has influenced government thinking and actions, and basically helped influence the policy agenda, on a range of issues, including space policy, marine science, occupational health and hygiene, hazardous waste disposal, forestry and disclosure of spending on research and development (Hayter 1991). The European Communities Committee is also considered highly influential but by its nature, dealing with draft EC legislation, its capacity for initiating policy is restricted (Bates 1983: 34), though – as we shall see (in Chapter 7) – less restricted than its Commons' counterpart.

Select committees thus have the potential to influence and occasionally propose policy. The potential is occasionally realised. However, rather like party committees, initiating policy is not the principal task carried out by select committees. They are extremely important, as we shall see, in fulfilling other functions.

Early day motions

Early day motions (EDMs) need not occupy too much of our time. Members may table motions for debate 'on an early day'. In practice, time is virtually never available. However, other members may add their names to an EDM and so a motion may serve to indicate the strength of parliamentary feeling on an issue. If a large number of MPs sign a motion, the Government may take notice. Sponsors of motions will often ask the Leader of the House at Thursday business questions if time can be found to debate their particular motions. The answer is invariably 'no' but the occasion provides an opportunity to mention the motion in the chamber.

In practice, little attention is paid to such motions. Many do not embody policy proposals: for example, congratulating a particular figure or sporting team on some success, expressing surprise or outrage at some event, condemning a speech or policy of one's political opponents. Most do not attract a great many signatures. Some do not get more than the signature of the sponsoring member. Furthermore, the numbers tabled have increased dramatically in recent years. Now, more than 1,000 are tabled each parliamentary session. It is difficult for one to stand out from among the rest.

However, MPs will occasionally use EDMs as a means of signalling their desire for a change in policy and on even fewer occasions they may have some impact. Thus, for example, in 1988 one EDM sponsored by two senior Conservatives, Michael Heseltine and Norman Tebbit, demanding the immediate abolition of the Inner London Education Authority (ILEA), attracted so many signatures from Conservative backbenchers that the Education Secretary, Kenneth Baker, decided to amend the Education Reform Bill in order to implement the backbenchers' wish. In 1992, EDMs were used as an important means of signalling backbench sentiment on the issue of Europe and, in effect, attempting to put a shot across the government's bows by Conservative members opposed to European economic and monetary union.

Such occasions are notable for their rarity. Nonetheless, rarity is not the same as non-existence. EDMs can be employed to induce some new policy. Knowing that, backbenchers will variously attempt to use them for that purpose.

Combined effect

These several means are often most effective when used in combination. As we have seen, by themselves they may prove sufficient to induce a policy change. However, MPs keen to promote a new policy will exploit the different avenues available. Conservative backbenchers in the 1950s organized themselves and used the then limited means available to get government to accept the introduction of commercial television (Wilson 1961). As we have seen, some of the social reform of the 1960s was pursued through debates and private members' bills. In 1991, Sir John Wheeler, chairman of the Home Affairs Committee, introduced a private member's bill – successfully – to give effect to the committee's recommendations supporting changes in the law, proposed by Lord Justice Taylor, on offences at football grounds.

The means are thus available but what is also clear is that they are used sporadically. Back-benchers lack the resources and the parliamentary time to initiate policy on a regular basis. Select committees have no sanctions they can employ. Private members' bills cannot make a charge on the public revenue. The limitations are formal as well as political.

Formulation

In the formulation, that is, drawing up, of measures, Parliament plays little part. In so far as it has an input, it is in the determination of what a bill should include rather than in the formal drafting of the measure.

In terms of agreeing details, government bills are determined by ministers after considerable discussion. Ministers can consult on the provisions and they have their officials to assist in preparing white papers and Cabinet submissions. MPs and peers, as such, have no formal involvement, though ministers' parliamentary private secretaries (see Chapter 3) may participate in the preliminary discussions and, along with the relevant whip, give some advice on what backbench reaction is likely to be. Anticipated reaction may thus prove important. Given the privacy of discussions, and the fact that anticipated reaction may lead to a provision being deleted rather than inserted, it is difficult to quantify or even generalize about the extent of such anticipation. On the basis of available evidence from ministers and their advisers, parliamentary reaction does not figure largely in determining the provisions of a bill. If adverse comment is anticipated, steps are taken to address it (meetings with disaffected members, for example); more generally, if it is a major bill, steps are taken to mobilize backbenchers to support it. Partisan loyalty normally ensures that ministers anticipate no difficulties in getting a measure through.

The potential impact of anticipated reaction, though, should not be dismissed. Ministers do not want to alienate their own supporters and would prefer to take through Parliament a bill that earns them plaudits rather than condemnation from their own supporters. An ambitious minister may thus be influenced, sometimes certainly consciously by anticipation of parliamentary reaction, sometimes probably subconsciously. As such, parliamentary opinion, especially opinion on the government benches, may have some impact, though MPs and peers are not themselves prime movers in initiating change.

In the first part of the formulation process, then, parliamentary opinion *may* have some effect. In the second stage of the process, though, parliamentary involvement is very much at the margins.

Drafting bills 'is a highly specialized art. It is a mystic rite understood only by the limited band of official practitioners' (Richards 1970: 33). Government bills are drafted by parliamentary counsel, the 'official practitioners'. The counsel are highly trained; it takes about eight years to become qualified. There are now just under thirty such counsel, working essentially as an independent unit within the Cabinet Office. Normally they work in teams, a team of two usually dealing with each bill, though a slightly larger number will work on measures such as the annual Finance Bill. Bills are drafted on instructions from the sponsoring department. The instructions within a department are usually prepared by lawyers.

Counsel are important figures in that they have the power to tell departments that a particular principle cannot be embodied in legal form. They will also advise on the best way to achieve a particular intention (Engle 1983). In drafting bills, they will bear in mind the parliamentary rules governing such matters as scope and hybridity (a hybrid bill is a public bill affecting private interests). If in doubt, discussions take place with the clerks in both Houses.

The clerks, in fact, could be described as more relevant actors in the formulation stage than MPs and peers. Members have some opportunity to engage in drafting when presenting a private member's bill. In practice, though, bills will often have been drafted by the bodies that lobby MPs and peers to introduce them. Many organizations, such as the Consumers Association, have become adept at drafting bills. Furthermore, the first ten members whose names are drawn in the ballot are eligible now to claim up to £200 towards expenses in drafting. If the bill finds favour with the government, or – in the event of adopting a neutral stance – the Chief Whip believes that the bill stands a chance of passing, it will be reviewed by parliamentary counsel; 'otherwise it is for its sponsor to make such drafting arrangements as he can' (Miers and Page 1982: 134).

Those members who rely on their own skills or those of sympathetic bodies run a high risk of finding the bill technically flawed. Where drafting is deficient, sponsors will often concede that they will accept amendments to remedy the problem.

Formulation is thus not a stage in the policy-making process in which MPs and peers play a significant role. The bulk of the measures debated and passed by Parliament are drafted by trained counsel. The exceptions are some private members' bills, usually short measures not requiring the complex construction of major bills; and even then drafting is often poor.

Conclusion

Parliament looks to government to bring measures forward. It is a 'reactive' legislature. In terms of being proactive, the opportunities are limited. They are, as we have seen, occasionally employed, especially through the medium of private members' bills. The existence of those opportunities is crucial to Parliament's fulfilment of several functions. However, in terms of the making of public policy, their employment is not sufficient to deny the truth of the generalization that the fount of public policy in the United Kingdom is not Parliament, but Her Majesty's Government.

Notes

1. The exceptions are certain Fridays, certain other days when private members' business is taken, twenty opposition days, and three estimates days (see Chapter 6).
2. Griffith and Ryle (1989: 388) put the figure for the 1983–87 Parliament even higher – at just over thirty per cent – but this figure probably includes measures emanating from official reports, which – as Marsh and Read found – boosts the figure considerably.

5

Legislation

The third stage of the policy-making process – that of deliberation and assent – is undertaken, at least for UK legislation, by the Queen-in-Parliament. The Two Houses of Parliament are responsible for the deliberation. The Two Houses plus the Crown are responsible for giving assent. The assent of the monarch is governed by convention (Chapter 2).

Legislative process

A bill has to go through several parliamentary stages before it can be submitted to the Queen for signature and hence become an Act of Parliament. The essential stages are listed in Table 5.1. All bills dealing with finance begin their passage in the Commons. Given the pre-eminence of the Commons, so do most other bills. However, a number each session are introduced first in the House of Lords. This avoids an excessive imbalance in the legislative workload during the parliamentary session. If the Lords only considered bills after they had been first through the Commons, it would have a light workload in the first half of a session and an impossible one in the second half. Among the five bills starting in the Lords in the 1991–92 session were the Charities Bill, the Further and Higher Education Bill, and the Local Government Bill setting up a commission to review local government in England.

Table 5.1 Legislative stages in Parliament

Stage	Where taken	Comments
First reading	On the floor of the House	Formal introduction. No debate.
Second reading	On the floor of the House[1]	Debate on the principle
[Money resolution: Commons	On the floor of the House]	
Committee	In standing committee in the Commons unless House votes otherwise (certain bills taken on the floor of the House); almost invariably on the floor of the House in the Lords	Considered clause by clause; amendments may be made
Report	On the floor of the House[2]	Bill reported back to House; amendments may be made
Third reading	On the floor of the House	Final approval. No amendments possible in the Commons
Lords (or Commons) Amendments	On the floor of the House	Consideration of amendments made by other House

Notes: [1] In the Commons, non-contentious bills may be referred to a committee.
[2] If a bill is taken in committee of the whole House and no amendments are made, there is no report stage.

First and second readings

The typical bill will start its passage in the House of Commons. It is given a first reading. This is a purely formal stage, when the title of the bill is read out and a date for the second reading given; the bill – at this stage in dummy form, merely a long and short title on a piece of paper, with the names of the bill's sponsors – is also ordered to be printed. If the bill was not starting in the Commons, but was coming from the Lords, these formal proceedings would be avoided; it would be scheduled for second reading with no prior proceedings on the floor of the House.

The bill is normally printed within days of first reading and, indeed, in the case of most government bills, within a day. Second reading normally takes place about two weeks later. It is considered desirable for at least two weekends to elapse between first and second reading, though this is not always adhered to. Second reading constitutes the first occasion the House actually has to discuss the measure. If it a non-contentious bill, it may be referred for its second reading debate to a committee,[1] but otherwise – the usual practice – it is taken on the floor of the House.

2nd reading   Second reading constitutes the debate on principle. Some uncontroversial bills are given a second reading without debate. Others will be subject usually to a half-day or full-day debate, in effect, roughly a three-hour (about 4.00 to 7.00 p.m) or a six-hour debate (4.00 to 10.00 p.m.). Bills of great constitutional import may be given two or more days. The 1972 European Communities Bill, providing the legal basis for British membership of the EC, was given three days; the 1976 Scotland and Wales Bill, designed to establish legislative assemblies in Scotland and Wales, was given four days.

Second reading debates are wide ranging. Taken on the floor, any Member can seek to catch the Speaker's eye. On government bills, the minister moves second reading and explains the contents and case for the bill, the minister's shadow on the opposition front bench outlines the opposition's stance, and members from both sides are then called alternately before winding-up speeches from the front benches. At the end of the debate, opponents may divide the House. If a government bill, approval – as we shall see – is usually assured.

Committee stage

Once the House has approved the principle, the bill is sent to committee for detailed consideration. Unless the House votes otherwise, this will be a standing committee. Despite its name, a standing committee is created *ad hoc* for each bill. It can comprise between sixteen and fifty members, though the usual practice is to appoint eighteen members, sometimes a few more. For major bills such as the annual Finance Bill, the committees are larger: the 1992 Finance Bill, for example, was referred to a committee of thirty-four members. The committees are designated by letters of the alphabet – standing committee A, standing committee B and so on – and usually no more than five will be sitting at any one time, though on occasion the number rises to as high as seven or eight. Private members' bills enjoy precedence only in one committee, standing committee C.

The composition of each committee will reflect the party strength on the floor of the House and, indeed, will take the format of the House in miniature, with ministers, a whip, and backbench supporters on one side, and opposition front-benchers, a whip and backbenchers – plus usually a member from one of the smaller parties – on the other. As in the chamber, the two sides sit opposite one another, presided over impartially by an MP drawn from the Speaker's Panel – a panel of senior MPs chosen for their ability to undertake such a task.

Each bill is considered on a clause by clause basis. Amendments are debated before a clause is approved on a 'stand part' motion (that the clause stand part of the bill). The committee is constrained by the decision taken by the House on second reading. It cannot reject the principle of the bill nor consider an amendment that goes against the principle. It is also precluded from considering any amendment that does not fall within the scope of the bill's long title.

Uncontentious bills that are likely to pass without discussion, bills for which immediate passage is sought, and bills of major constitutional significance will usually be taken for committee stage on the floor of the House – that is, in Committee of the Whole House (CWH). The first type is taken on the floor for ① convenience: there is little point in assembling a committee. The ② second is taken to expedite proceedings, avoiding a committee having to be appointed and assembled and then reporting back to ③ the House. The third is taken in order that all members may have an opportunity to deliberate on a matter of great import. Several measures, such as the Mauritius Republic Bill in 1992, fall in the first category; the 1991 Dangerous Dogs Bill, treated by the government as urgent (see Chapter 4), and the 1992 Finance Bill – in attenuated form, rushed through all its stages on 13 March because of the announcement of a general election (the House was dissolved three days later) – are examples of the second category; and the major constitutional bills we have already mentioned are prime examples of the third. There are usually several bills each session falling in the first two categories – thirteen in the 1990–91 session – but constitutional bills are relatively sparse. When they are taken, though, they occupy considerable time. Committee stage of the European Communities Bill in 1972 commenced in March and was not completed until July.

On rare occasions, the House has used its power to refer a bill not to a standing committee, or Committee of the Whole House, but to a select committee. This allows for a more detailed consideration of the merits of the bill and for witnesses to be examined. The bill is then committed to a Committee of the Whole House. This procedure is used for the regular renewal of the Armed Forces Bill but otherwise has not been used since 1975. Since 1980, the House has also had power to refer a bill to a special standing committee. This allows evidence-taking sessions to be held before the committee reverts to a normal standing committee format. Five bills were referred to SSCs between 1981 and 1985, but none since.

Report and third reading

When a bill has completed its committee stage, the committee having gone through it and approved each clause and any new clauses proposed by members, the bill is then reported to the House.

This stage provides an opportunity for all members to consider the bill and further amendments can be, and usually are, made.[2] There is no consideration of each clause and amendments that essentially repeat amendments that failed in committee are not usually selected for consideration. Though the report stage usually occupies only one or two sittings, they can prove to be long sittings because of the number of amendments tabled. For the report stage of the 1986 Financial Services Bill, for example, over 300 amendments were tabled, almost ninety per cent of them by the government (Norton 1990c: 188). About ten per cent of the time of the House – sometimes more – is taken up with the report stage of government bills. In the long session of 1987–88, when the House sat for a total of 1,978 hours, almost 267 hours were taken up with the consideration of bills on report. The report stage is also responsible for generating more late-night sittings than any other single item of business.

After the report stage, a bill is given a third reading. This is the final debate on the measure and more often than not is taken immediately following report. Debate is usually short and does not figure prominently as a drain on the time of the House. Opponents may force a division. Once passed this hurdle, the bill then goes to the other chamber.

House of Lords

In the Lords, a bill has to pass through the same stages as in the Commons. Lords' procedure differs only slightly from the Commons. It is possible for a debate to take place on first reading and it occasionally happens. Amendments may also be made at third reading and again this occasionally happens. However, the biggest difference is in terms of practice.

The committee stage of bills is normally taken by the Lords in Committee of the Whole House. There is provision for bills to be considered by a Public Bill Committee – the Lords' equivalent of standing committee – but this provision has only been used twice in recent years: for the Pilotage Bill in 1986 and the Charities Bill in 1991.[3] Most peers surveyed by a committee of the House in 1991 were against such committees, regarding them as unrepresentative of a non-partisan House and likely to increase the time of the House spent on report (Select Committee on Committee Work of the House 1992: 20). The preference remains to take committee stage in the chamber. The timetable of the Upper House is not under quite the same pressure as in the Commons. As a result, not only is there time to take committee stage on the floor, there is also time to consider all amendments that are tabled.

Once a bill has been considered and passed by the other chamber, it then goes back to the first chamber so that it can consider any amendments made by the second chamber. In the event of an amendment proving unacceptable, it goes back to the other chamber. Potentially the process could be a lengthy one if the second chamber insists on its amendment. In practice, most amendments prove acceptable to the other chamber and, in the event of a clash, the House of Lords usually defers – though not always immediately – to the elected chamber. On occasion, it has refused to concede, most notably in 1976 on the Aircraft and Shipbuilding Industries Bill. As a result, the bill was lost.

Private members' bills

Private members' bills have to go through the same stages listed in Figure 5.1 as government bills. Both categories of bill constitute public general legislation. However, the time for consideration of private members' bills is limited, confined principally to ten, or slightly more, Fridays and taking up less than five per cent of the time of the House each session. Most bills introduced are not debated (see Chapter 4) and those that are face considerable hurdles.

Opposition to the bill by government is usually fatal. No bill which has been the subject of a division on second reading has subsequently made it to the statute book without government time being provided (Marsh and Read 1988: 49). Even government support does not guarantee passage. Opponents may try to talk the bill out. On a Friday, the House sits at 9.30 a.m., and if debate is still continuing at 2.30 p.m. the bill under consideration then falls to the back of the queue on subsequent Fridays, where it is easily blocked (see Chapter 4). To prevent that happening, a bill's sponsor may move a closure motion, a motion that requires the question to be put immediately. However, for a closure motion to be carried, there must be at least one hundred members voting in favour. Achieving that figure on a Friday is notoriously difficult. And if the bill has not been debated for very long, the Speaker will not even allow a closure motion to be moved. Hence, as we saw in Chapter 4, there is a preference on the part of members successful in the ballot to opt for measures that enjoy government or widespread support, thus maximizing the chances of getting them on to the statute book.

Private legislation

There are essentially two types of legislation. Public general legislation, which enacts measures of public policy, and private legislation, which gives specified powers to particular individuals or bodies – for example, to British Rail to acquire and build a railway track on a particular piece of land or to a local authority to undertake a particular activity.

A private bill has to go through analogous stages to public general legislation, but the purposes of the stages differ and the bill itself is not initiated by government or by private members, but by petition from the body sponsoring it. At second reading, the House affirms the principle conditionally. At committee stage, proceedings are quasi-judicial, with counsel representing petitioners. Witnesses are heard under oath. Government sometimes takes an interest in such measures, but normally leaves it for the House to decide. The majority of private bills have no political or, for most MPs, constituency implications. It is therefore a form of legislation that does not impinge much upon the consciousness of MPs (Norton 1977; Silk 1987: 157–8). Where members do take an interest, they can have a powerful influence: a single cry of 'object' is sufficient to force a debate. Most private bills, however, are not debated, with the result that such legislation occupies about three to five per cent of the time of the House each session: a small percentage, though not dissimilar to that given to private members' legislation.

Given that it is, by definition, not concerned with public policy, private legislation will not form part of our analysis. It is mentioned here for the record and in order to distinguish it from private members' legislation, with which it is variously confused.

The effect of Parliament?

Legislation occupies a considerable proportion of the time in both Houses: roughly about a third of the time in the Commons and now almost two-thirds of the time in the Lords. But what effect does Parliament actually have on the bills that it processes?

The fact that ministers come before both Houses to justify measures and respond to speeches from members of the Opposition and their own side, and the fact that the proceedings take place publicly in a formal arena, contribute substantially to Parliament's fulfilment of a number of functions. Those contributions we shall consider in subsequent chapters. Our concern here is with what Jean Blondel and others (1970) called Parliament's 'viscosity', in effect its capacity to change the content of bills placed before it. Does Parliament exercise an independent capacity to alter a bill, resulting in it leaving Parliament substantially different in content than when it was introduced into Parliament?

The answer is that it does so only at the margins. The impact of Parliament on government bills, similar to its impact on the initiation of measures, is sporadic. The investment of considerable time and effort does not result in a significant viscosity. Government is normally assured of getting its measures passed. Moreover, it is normally assured not only of the principle of the bills being accepted but also the detail.

Rejecting measures

The most powerful weapon that Parliament has in the legislative process is the power to reject a bill. The pressures that we have identified (see Chapter 2) resulting in the growth of party and partisanship not only ensured that policy-making (initiation and formulation) was vested in the government but also that the same party government was supported by a parliamentary party willing to approve the measures it brought forward. MPs seek election on a party manifesto and, if their party is returned to power, expect to support their leaders in carrying out manifesto promises.

Consequently, the use of the power to reject a bill has been notable for its rarity. That is borne out by the figures already presented in Table 4.2. Government is in greater danger of losing bills because of the calling of a general election (no time to get all remaining bills through in time before Parliament is dissolved) than because of deliberate action by MPs or peers.

Given the pressures we have identified, one might anticipate that the loss of a government bill would be unknown. However, exceptional circumstances have produced the occasional loss. In terms of defeating a bill on second or third reading, however, it is very occasional.

On three occasions this century the House of Commons has defeated a government bill on second reading: on the Rent Restrictions Bill in 1924, the Reduction of Redundancy Rebates Bill in 1977, and the Shops Bill in 1986. On only one occasion has a bill been defeated on third reading: the Local Authority Works (Scotland) Bill in 1977. Only one of these defeats – that on the Shops Bill – took place at a time when the Government enjoyed an overall majority in the House.

However, to this list must be added a number of others which were withdrawn as a result of pressure from MPs and, on occasion, for fear of defeat if proceeded with. In 1969, the Labour Government decided not to introduce an Industrial Relations Bill after 55 Labour MPs had joined some Liberal MPs to vote against the white paper that presaged it. The same year, as we have seen (Chapter 2), the Parliament (No. 2) Bill, to reform the House of Lords, was not proceeded with after coming under sustained sniping from both sides of the House. In 1977, cross-voting by 22 Labour MPs resulted in a defeat of the guillotine motion for the Scotland and Wales Bill (Norton 1980: 239–40); fearing that the bill would fall prey to the same sort of prolonged sniping as the Parliament (No. 2) Bill, the government withdrew it, later introducing separate and modified bills for Scotland and for Wales.

In 1980, an Iran (Temporary Provisions) Bill was not brought before the House when it looked as if up to 100 Conservative MPs might have voted with Labour MPs against it. The following year, the provisions of a Local Government Finance Bill, providing for local referendums on supplementary rate levies, ran into opposition from government backbenchers and was withdrawn (Norton 1985: 29–31). In the 1984–85 session a Civil Aviation Bill also ran into opposition from Conservative MPs and was dropped; an Education (Corporal Punishment) Bill ran into trouble in both Houses, especially the Lords, and suffered a similar fate (Silk 1987: 113–14).

These defeats are significant when one considers what the contemporary British polity would look like had they been passed. However, the number and impact of these bills have to be contrasted with the number and impact of the bills that have been passed. Table 4.2 demonstrates the relative position. The hegemony of government in achieving passage of its bills is clear. Parliament's greatest influence exists rather in denying assent to bills introduced by its own members – private members' bills, which frequently fail to raise a majority to get through – than it does to measures emanating from Her Majesty's Government.

Amendments

The potential of Parliament is far greater in respect of amending measures. The committee and report stages provide specific opportunities to change the details of a bill. In practice, however, the potential far exceeds the practice.

The party majority that ensures the passing of bills on second and third reading is also deployed to ensure that government gets its way on the detail of bills. Even if government backbenchers were tempted to go against their own leaders, various constraints operate other than just the political. One is structural. The *ad hoc* nature of committees militate against the development of a body of expertise and a corporate, possibly bi-partisan, feeling. Another factor is time. Given the size of bills, there is often little time to consider the detail adequately. This is compounded by partisanship. The opposition will often keep debate going on the early contentious clauses, resulting in the government introducing an allocation of time (guillotine) motion. This then results in some clauses not actually being the subject of debate. Furthermore, committee members are limited in the information they have at their disposal. Standing committees are not empowered to receive evidence. That is, they cannot interview witnesses or receive formal submissions. Individual members may receive material from outside bodies, but the committee collectively may not do so. And individual members have limited resources with which to commission research on a particular provision.

As a result, standing committees are in a weak position and are characterized by the partisanship that exists in the chamber. For MPs, serving on a standing committee is often a frustration. Government backbenchers have traditionally been encouraged to remain silent in order not to delay proceedings; some have used the opportunity to read and reply to correspondence, only half-listening to committee proceedings. There is often little expectation by other members that their activities will have any tangible effect. As one submission to the Procedure Committee noted in 1984, 'If at the end of the day the *committee* has actually improved (made "more generally acceptable") the contents of the bill – as opposed to approving the amendments introduced by the minister in charge of the bill – it is in all probability an unusual and unexpected benefit' (Select Committee on Procedure 1984: 72).

The weakness is demonstrated by the limited number of occasions that non-government amendments are accepted by a committee. At least nine out of every ten amendments accepted are usually amendments introduced by the government itself. A study by J. A. G. Griffith (1974) of the three sessions of 1967–68, 1968–69 and 1970–71 found that, of 3,510 amendments moved in the

Commons by private members, only 171 were agreed to. The proportion of opposition amendments accepted was 4.3 per cent; for
those moved by government backbenchers it was 9.2 per cent.

The position is somewhat different in the House of Lords. More
time is given to bills – guillotines are not employed – and the
House has proved more willing than the Commons to amend bills
against the wishes of the government. As we saw in Chapter 2,
defeats were frequent during the period of Labour Government
from 1974 to 1979 and most defeats imposed by the Lords are on
amendments to bills. However, against this must be set the fact
that, as in the Commons, most amendments accepted by the House
are government amendments. The Upper House is as useful to
government for making last-minute revisions as it is to the institution of Parliament as a critical reviewing chamber. In the period
from 1970 to 1981, for example, more than eighty-five per cent of
the amendments made were moved by the government. Less than
fourteen per cent emanated from the opposition or from the government backbenches. (Though, unlike the Commons, more successful amendments came from the former rather than the latter.)[4]
Furthermore, an amendment made against the wishes of government may be reversed by the Commons; as we have seen, it is rare
for the Lords to insist on their amendments. Despite the number
of government defeats in the 1980s, a number of peers towards the
end of the decade were expressing to this writer their dissatisfaction at not being able to have a significant impact on the content of
legislation.

Some impact?

On the face of it, Parliament therefore seems to have little impact,
indeed almost none, on the content of bills placed before it. However, a number of caveats must be entered. Parliament is limited in
its impact, but not quite as limited as the foregoing would suggest.
It also has the potential to have greater impact in the future.
Firstly, though, the caveats.

1)   Firstly, the raw figures for the number of non-government
amendments accepted in committee are slightly misleading. Many
amendments are probing amendments, tabled to elicit information
(see Chapter 6). Others may not be accepted, either because they
are too widely drawn, are technically deficient or go beyond what

the government is willing to accept, but nonetheless prompt government to table amendments of its own to meet the points made. A minister may promise in committee to review a particular provision and then bring forward an amendment at report stage. At other times, the influence may be less observable, influencing ministers in how they treat subsequent amendments. Much depends upon the minister, but also on the other members. As Griffith (1974: 121) observed, 'it is . . . frequently very important, especially for the opposition, to press the minister in committee to the point where he gives an undertaking but not to press him so hard that he refuses to consider the matter'.

2.)   Secondly, the number of amendments carried by the Commons against the government increased significantly in the years following Griffith's analysis. Government lost twenty-four votes in standing committee in the 1970–74 Parliament and over 100 in the period from 1974 to 1979. In the same decade, government lost sixty-five votes on the floor of the House (see Chapter 2), most of them during committee or report stage of bills (Norton 1975; 1980). According to the analysis of John Schwarz (1980: 27–28) more than half of all government bills considered in the 1975–6 session were altered as a result of division lobby or standing committee defeats; in the remaining sessions, the proportion ranged from twenty-two per cent to forty-five per cent. Some of the defeats resulted in major amendments being made to bills, including the Scotland Bill and the Wales Bill: MPs insisted on amending both to require that forty per cent of eligible voters cast a 'yes' vote in the proposed referendums for the bill's provisions to be implemented.

The return of governments from 1979 onwards with clear overall majorities reduced the potential for defeat, though succeeding Parliaments were characterised by a somewhat greater willingness on the part of government to modify measures under pressure from backbenchers (Norton 1985: 28–36). They were also characterized by a more obvious linkage between MPs and outside groups, the latter providing substantial briefing and advice to members, the MPs then being in a stronger position than before to argue the case for a particular amendment. Studies of bills such as the 1986 Financial Services Bill have revealed the extent of these links and the willingness of MPs to listen to groups, resulting on occasion in amendments being carried against the government

(Norton 1990c). The extent of this group activity and the reasons for it constitute the focus of Chapter 10.

3.)   Thirdly, the impact of the Lords has not been given sufficient emphasis. The importance of the Upper House has been as much in the qualitative nature of amendments made as in the number. Several of the defeats in the 1980s affected the principal provisions of a number of bills, including the 1980 Education (No. 2) Bill in 1980, resulting in the Government abandoning a proposal to impose charges for school transport, and the Local Government (Interim Provisions) Bill in 1984, forcing the Government to revise the arrangements governing local government in London prior to the abolition of the Greater London Council (the GLC). The House has continued to demonstrate its independence under the Conservative Government of John Major. It amended several bills against government wishes in 1991 and 1992, including the 1992 Education (Schools) Bill, which changed the arrangements for the inspection of schools; the amendments made a material change to the nature of the bill but in order to get the bill through before the dissolution – it received royal assent on the last day Parliament sat – the government was forced to accept them.

The Lords has also sought to keep pace with the growth in the volume of public legislation by expanding the amount of time it gives to legislative scrutiny. In the 1970s, the House devoted between fifty and sixty per cent of its time to legislation. By the end of the 1980s, it had risen to almost sixty-five per cent (Shell, in Select Committee on the Committee Work of the House 1992: 255). This has allowed the House to maintain its practice of considering all amendments that are tabled.

4.)   Finally, the role of Parliament in defeating or amending measures emanating from private members has to be noted. Private members' bills will variously fail to muster a majority. If given a second reading, substantive amendments may be made in committee. This impact should not be ignored. Private members' legislation is often uncontentious and of a humdrum nature. Nonetheless, it can be of significance for particular groups in society. In Chapter 4 the social legislation of the 1960s was noted. More recent, if less spectacular, examples would include the 1984 Video Recording Act, regulating the sale of 'video nasties', the 1988 Motor Vehicles (Wearing of Rear Seat Belts by Children) Act, the 1990 Horses (Protective Headgear for Young Persons) Act, the 1992 Offshore

Safety (Protection against Victimization) Act, providing protection for 'whistle blowers', the 1992 Timeshare Act, providing some protection for property timeshare buyers, and the 1992 Sexual Offences (Amendment) Act, providing anonymity for victims reporting sexual offences.

These are hardly on the scale of major government bills. One or two may be claimed as surrogate government bills: the last one, for example, was drawn by its sponsor from the Home Office list. Nonetheless, the measures can probably claim to have saved lives – in various of the bills we have cited, human lives; many bills passed are animal welfare measures, and so have probably saved the lives, or improved the conditions, of many species of animals. They are measures that would not have become Acts of Parliament, or not have become Acts when they did, had it not been for the independent action of MPs and peers. It is also pertinent to record that many other measures of social significance would also now be law – measures limiting abortion, for example – were it not for the action taken by MPs and peers.

Parliament, then, does have *some* impact. The caveats we have entered, though, are not sufficient to counter the basic generalization we have made. Parliament devotes much time and effort to the legislative process, but to little effect. It is the area of parliamentary activity that is most time-consuming, yet in which Parliament is at its most inefficient.

Improving efficiency?

The deficiencies of Parliament in the legislative process have been variously recognised by parliamentarians themselves and by a number of parliamentary committees. The increasing amount of time devoted by the Lords to legislation has meant that it has had less time to spend on debating non-legislative issues. A 'significant minority' of peers surveyed by the Lords' Select Committee on the Committee Work of the House (1992: 20) wanted more bills to be considered in committee, rather than on the floor of the House, arguing that this would enable 'better consideration, particularly of drafting and technical amendments, by those with expert knowledge'. It would also reduce some of the pressure on the floor of the House. The committee itself recommended the greater use of committees, including special standing committees.

In the Commons, the Procedure Committee has variously argued the case both for the greater use of special standing committees – allowing for the taking of evidence – and for the regular timetabling of bills, thus permitting more balanced scrutiny of all the parts of a bill. In 1985, it recommended that any member – and not just a minister – should be able to move for a bill to be referred to an SSC. In 1986, the House approved the recommendation, but it has not resulted in any bill being referred to an SSC: the government majority has been used to prevent it. On the same occasion, in 1986, the House failed to approve the recommendation for the timetabling of bills. The Procedure committee has pressed the case. In 1992 the Select Committee on the Sittings of the House reported that, of MPs it had surveyed, fifty-three per cent favoured it; it itself recommended that all stages of government bills after second reading should be subject to a timetable. The Procedure Committee (1990: lxix) has also continued to press for the greater use of special standing committees.

These recommendations would go some way to facilitating a greater impact by MPs and peers on the provisions of legislation. Other steps can also be taken to achieve this goal, including increasing the resources available to individual parliamentarians and removing the *ad hoc* nature of standing committees. If the various constraints identified above can be overcome, the potential for Parliament to have a modest, even more than modest impact on legislation exists. Party will remain the biggest constraint, necessarily so, but relatively few measures passed by Parliament are exclusively partisan measures. Of eighty-seven government bills introduced in the 1970 and 1985 sessions, only twelve could be deemed 'controversial'.[5] There is thus considerable scope for influencing those bills – the majority – that are not at the heart of the partisan controversy.

Conclusion

Parliament is the principal actor in the deliberative stage of law-making in the United Kingdom. Its formal powers are considerable. It spends more time on legislation than on any other item of business. It has the potential to have a significant impact on the provisions of legislation.

However, as we have seen, the potential presently far exceeds the practice. Despite the considerable time devoted by both Houses to government legislation, Parliament has little impact on the content of that legislation. It has *some* impact, slightly more than before, and sufficient to make it a relevant target for pressure group attention, but it remains, at best, a proximate – at worst, a marginal – actor in determining the content of measures of public policy. In Blondel's terms, its viscosity is low.

Notes

1. This may take the form of a second reading committee or, for bills concerned wholly with Scotland or Wales, a committee comprising partly or wholly MPs drawn from Scottish or Welsh seats. The committees are appointed on an *ad hoc* basis. The second reading motion is normally taken formally in the House the following day. They are occasionally used: in the 1990–91 session, for example, four government bills were referred to second reading committees.
2. Although, as noted in Table 5.1, if a bill is taken in Committee of the Whole House and not amended, there is no report stage. The 1972 European Communities Bill is an example: no amendments were made during committee stage, taken on the floor, and so the bill proceeded from committee stage to third reading.
3. Like the Commons, the Lords has the power to refer a bill for select committee consideration. Between 1972 and 1988, seven bills were sent for such consideration, but only one (the 1975 Hare Coursing Bill) was a government bill; the rest were private members' bills.
4. In the 1970–71 session, for example, 115 amendments – 13.5 per cent of the total – were moved by peers who did not hold ministerial office. Of the 115, 71 came from Labour peers, 19 from government backbenchers, 7 from Liberal peers, 9 from no-party peers (law lords or bishops), 6 from peers with no declared party affiliation, and three from cross-bench peers (Baldwin 1985b). (Cross-benchers do not have a party affiliation but they do operate as an organized body within the House with their own leader. Non-party peers, such as law lords and those with no declared affiliation (in effect, 'unknowns') are not part of such an organized body.)
5. The remaining bills can be categorized as minor, significant reforming, and major reforming. The largest single number (34) were identified as minor. The research was undertaken by Edward C. Page and reported in Norton (1990c).

6

The Administration of Government

The final stage of the policy-making process is that of implementation. This chapter is concerned with Parliament's impact at this stage of the process, but its remit is wider. We are concerned here with executive actions. That encompasses decisions taken by government which do not require legislative sanction, as well as the conduct – the actual administration – of departments.

Parliament itself is not responsible for implementing public policy. Nor is it the principal initiator of such policy (see Chapter 4). It looks to government to propose policy, not just in the form of legislation, but also through powers already granted by statute or through prerogative powers. Unlike primary legislation, this policy does not usually require parliamentary sanction. Parliament, nonetheless, does have some impact on the actions – intended and actual – of government through subjecting them to public scrutiny.

By what means, then, does Parliament engage in such scrutiny and what impact does it have?

Means of scrutiny

The principal means of scrutiny available to both Houses have traditionally been those of debate and questions. Both suffer from various limitations. They are supplemented by the use of committees, both the departmental select committees and the long-established Public Accounts Committee. There is also a committee to scrutinize statutory instruments. MPs also have the power to refer cases of alleged maladministration to the Parliamentary Commissioner for Administration (the Ombudsman). They also have informal channels of scrutiny. In combination, these various means occupy considerable time both on and off the floor of the House.

Debates

Debates are the oldest method by which the two Houses subject the actions of the executive to critical scrutiny. There are several types of debate, other than those – covered in Chapter 5 – on the second and third readings of bills. In the Commons, there is the annual debate on the address – usually five days devoted to debates on the Queen's speech outlining the government's programme for the year. There are also debates in which the topics are selected by the opposition, by a committee of the House, and by private members, as well as by government itself.

There are twenty *opposition days* each session. These are days on which the subject for debate is chosen by opposition parties. The Leader of the Opposition chooses the topic on seventeen and the leader of the third largest party in the House selects the subject on the other three. Each day may be utilised for one or two debates and some debates will usually be conceded for topics chosen by other parties in the House. Subjects chosen during the 1990–91 session are listed in Table 6.1. If the opposition is dissatisfied with the conduct of government, it may also table a motion of no confidence in the government. Such motions are tabled very sparingly, but when tabled time is found to debate them as a matter of urgency. The last speech of Margaret Thatcher as Prime Minister was in a debate on a motion of no confidence.

There are also now three *estimates days* each session. Introduced in the 1982–83 session – the first debate was in March 1983 – these provide for debates on specific estimates selected by the Liaison Select Committee, a committee comprising the chairmen of select committees. Previously, estimates were not usually subject to debate. In practice, the committee has chosen estimates on which select committees have issued reports and the three days are, in effect, days for debate of particular committee reports. It is common for two reports to be debated each estimate day, though the 'day' itself may be held on more than one day's sitting: that is,

Table 6.1   Opposition days 1990–91

Date	Subject of debate
5 Dec 1990	Abolition of the poll tax
12 Dec 1990	Economy
16 Jan 1991	Hospital service Electricity privatization
30 Jan 1991	Recession in industry Famine in sub-Saharan Africa
6 Feb 1991	Training Science policy
14 Feb 1991	Agriculture[1] Fishing industry[1]
19 Feb 1991	Poll tax Manufacturing industry
21 Feb 1991	The Gulf[2]
13 Mar 1991	Abolition of the poll tax Family hardship
17 Apr 1991	Health Service and community care
14 May 1991	Health Service and community care Overseas aid
5 June 1991	Government of London Training and the unemployed
13 June 1991	Business
18 June 1991	Water industry
24 June 1991	Government of Liverpool[1]
2 July 1991	Crisis in housing Conduct of affairs in privatized electricity and gas industries
9 July 1991	Low income and quality of life
17 July 1991	Future structures of government in Wales[3]
24 July 1991	Government economic policy
16 Oct 1991	Decline in manufacturing industry

Notes: [1] Liberal Democrats' motion
[2] Scottish National Party motion
[3] Plaid Cymru motion

Source: House of Commons, *Sessional Information Digest 1990–91.*

one report may be debated in a 'half' debate one day and a second report in a 'half' debate on another day. Table 6.2 lists the estimate day topics in the 1990–91 session.

Table 6.2   Estimates days 1990–91

Date	Estimate	Principal subject
13 Dec 1990	Class IV, vote 2	Companies and financial services
11 Mar 1991	Class VII, vote 3	London Regional Transport
30 Apr 1991	Class VIII, vote 14 Class XV, vote 22 Class XVI, vote 11	Community charge
3 July 1991	Class II, vote 5 Class VI, votes 1 & 2	Iraqi refugees; Unemployment
4 July 1991	Class IV, vote 1 Class XV, vote 3 Class XIII, vote 1 Class XVI, vote 8	Steel industry; NHS waiting lists

Source: House of Commons, *Sessional Information Digest 1990–91.*

There are also the debates initiated by backbenchers through the medium of *private members' motions.* As we have seen, Friday sittings are usually divided between private members' bills and motions. Motions give members an opportunity to raise a particular topic for debate. Table 6.3 lists the topics selected by those MPs successful in the ballot for private members' motions in 1990–91. Backbenchers also have an opportunity to initiate short debates on the last day before a recess and following the formal completion of proceedings on the Consolidated Fund Bills: each of these sittings comprises a series of such short debates.

Private members also have the opportunity to raise a topic in the *half-hour adjournment debate* at the end of each day's sitting. Each such 'debate' is confined to half-an-hour (unless preceding business finishes early), with the member initiating the debate speaking for ten to fifteen minutes, perhaps allowing another member to intervene for a few minutes, and the remaining time occupied by the minister responding. No vote is taken. The occasion is most frequently used to raise specific constituency matters but may also be utilized to discuss more general issues of policy and administration such as, for example, problems of solvent abuse and water fluoridation.

The other main type of debate is that on *government motions.* These may take the form of substantive motions, inviting the

Table 6.3 Private members' motions 1990–91

Date	Sponsor	Subject of debate
30 Nov 1990	Sir M. Neubert (Con)	People and their local environment
7 Dec 1990	D. Amess (Con)	Political developments in the UK since 1979
4 Feb 1991	D. Martin (Con)	Family policy
8 Mar 1991	D. Fishburn (Con)	Leasehold reform
8 Mar 1991	Sir P. Emery (Con)	Boundary commission and parliamentary constituencies[1]
15 Mar 1991	T. Dalyell (Lab)	Ecology of the Gulf
15 Mar 1991	L. Stevens (Con)	Materials recycling[1]
22 Apr 1991	L. Cunliffe (Lab)	Funeral industry
17 May 1991	A. Kirkwood (Lib Dem)	Constitutional reform
14 June 1991	D. Fishburn (Con)	Taxation policies
21 June 1991	R. Knapman (Con)	Local government services
28 June 1991	M. Brandon-Bravo (Con)	Anti-social behaviour

[1] Debate of less than one hour's duration.

Source: House of Commons, *Sessional Information Digest 1990–91.*

House to approve or take note of some action or proposal. Or they may take the form of adjournment motions, allowing the House to discuss a particular topic but without having to reach a particular decision on it. These adjournment debates are clearly distinct from the half-hour adjournment debates we have just discussed, and are usually employed when the government itself has no fixed position and/or when it wishes to invite a wide-ranging discussion.

Most substantive motions tabled by the government will tend to be of a procedural or 'domestic' nature – proposing, for example, the creation of a new select committee, an amendment to existing pensions arrangements for members, or a vote of thanks to a retiring Speaker or clerk of the House. Some, however, will be on substantive items of policy. At the beginning of 1991, for example, the situation in the Gulf was debated twice by the House. The first occasion was on an adjournment motion on 15 January. Six days later, with troops in combat, a substantive motion supporting the action was moved. At the end of 1991, the government initiated

Table 6.4 Government substantive motions 1990–91

Date	Subject
11 Dec 1990	House of Commons Disqualification Act 1975: Amendment of Schedule
21 Jan 1991	The Gulf
22 Jan 1991	Procedure (European Standing Committees)
31 Jan 1991	Parliamentary pensions
13 Feb 1991	Autumn Statement
12 Mar 1991	War Crimes Bill (Procedure)
1 May 1991	Broadcasting
15 May 1991	Public expenditure
22 May 1991	Members (Resettlement Grant)
26 June 1991	Procedure (European Standing Committees)
9 July 1991	Sittings of the House (Select Committee)
18 July 1991	Procedure (Select Committees)
18 July 1991	Parliamentary pensions
14 Oct 1991	Defence Estimates 1991 (1st day)
15 Oct 1991	Defence Estimates 1991 (2nd day)
21 Oct 1991	National Health Service

Source: House of Commons, *Sessional Information Digest 1990–91.*

two two-day debates on the Maastricht summit, one before the summit and the other immediately after it. Government motions thus range from minor domestic issue to great issues of state. Table 6.4 lists the substantive motions tabled in the 1990–91 session.

In combination, then, these different types of debate provide the House with opportunities to discuss myriad aspects of executive actions. Tables 6.1 to 6.4 are noteworthy for the diversity of issues covered. They are also notable for the amount of time they occupy. About one-third of the time spent on the floor of the House is occupied by these various types of debate, including the annual debate on the address. In the 1990–91 session, the House sat for just over 1,373 hours: 440 of those were taken up by these various debates. If one excludes the daily half-hour adjournment debates, which are more appropriately discussed in a later chapter, they account for about a quarter of the time of the House.

In the House of Lords, the variety is not quite so great. In Chapter 5 it was mentioned that almost two-thirds of the time of the House is occupied now by legislation. Debates occupy just over twenty per cent of the time of the House. The principal debates are those held on a Wednesday (see Chapter 4), accounting for about fifteen per cent of the time of the House. About five per cent of the time of the House is taken up with 'unstarred' questions, which are dealt with under this heading because each question is debatable and results, in effect, in a mini-debate at the end of the day's sitting.

Questions ½ hour

On the first four days of the week, the Commons sits at 2.30 p.m. After prayers, any formal announcements by the Speaker (such as of the death of a member) and any private business (taken formally), question time commences. It lasts until 3.30 p.m. Departments answer questions on a rota basis, each one coming up every four weeks. All questions are tabled to the appropriate Secretary of State but all ministers in a department will be involved in appearing at the despatch box, dealing with those questions that fall within their particular remit. During questions to the Secretary of State for Education, for example, questions dealing specifically with universities will normally be answered by the junior minister with responsibility for higher education.

Small departments, and ministers without departmental portfolios, such as the Chancellor of the Duchy of Lancaster, are given slots towards the end of question time. The Prime Minister makes a twice weekly appearance, answering questions from 3.15 to 3.30 on Tuesdays and Thursdays.

Each member may table up to eight questions in ten sitting days and no more than two on any one day. Questions are tabled fourteen days in advance. Under rules introduced in 1990, members now have to hand in their questions in person (or on behalf of one other member) to the table office, rather than having it done for them by members of their staff. The questions are then randomly shuffled and the top twenty or thirty are then published. All questions tabled used to be printed, but new rules were agreed in 1990 limiting publication to those that stood some chance of actually being answered in question time.

Question time begins with the Speaker calling the member in whose name the first question stands. The member stands and says 'Number one, Madam' (all comments must be addressed to the Speaker, hence 'Madam' since the election of a female Speaker in 1992), and the relevant minister then rises and reads out a prepared answer. The member is then called again in order to ask a supplementary question and, at the discretion of Madam Speaker, one or two other members may also be called to ask supplementaries. If a member of the opposition front bench rises after the first supplementary, he or she enjoys precedence. The process is then repeated for subsequent questions on the order paper.

Questions must be confined to matters for which the answering minister has responsibility. This creates a problem at Prime Minister's questions as the Prime Minister has no department of his own. Consequently, questions are usually 'open' questions, asking the Prime Minister if he will pay an official visit to a particular place or – what is now the standard question – if he will list his official engagements for that day. The MPs lucky enough to have come high in the ballot then have an opportunity to put the questions they really wanted to ask in the form of supplementaries.

The number of questions tabled for oral answer – known as starred questions because each is printed with an asterisk beside it – has grown rapidly in recent years. In an average-length session between 1945 and 1985, the number tabled would not exceed 15,000 and sometimes would be closer to half that figure. Since then, the number tabled in an average session has exceeded 20,000 and is usually closer to 25,000 though since the 1990–91 session only about 4,000 a year are printed.

Members also have the option of tabling questions (unstarred questions) for written answer. These are printed, along with the minister's reply, in *Hansard*. Starred questions not reached in question time are also treated in the same way. Written questions allow members to get information in a form that may not be possible on the floor (in tabular form, for example) or to get answers to questions that may not be reached in question time. There is no limit on the number of written questions that may be tabled. It is perhaps not surprising, therefore, that its use is popular among MPs. In some recent sessions, the number tabled has exceeded 40,000. In the 1987–88 session, it was just over 47,000.

Successive governments have committed themselves to trying to ensure that written questions are normally answered within one working week. Members may designate a written question as a 'priority' question, stipulating the date on which they wish it to be answered, though a minimum of three working days' notice is required. Priority written questions are now as popular as those not marked as priority questions (Irwin *et al.*, 1993).

Questions are seen, not least by MPs themselves, as an important means for subjecting ministers and departments to critical scrutiny. One recent survey of some MPs on both sides of the House found that there was general agreement that questions were important for holding ministers to account (Franklin and Norton 1993, Chapter 4). Oral questions were seen as marginally more important than written questions in this context. Written questions were deemed more important than oral questions for obtaining information that would otherwise be difficult to acquire.

In the Lords, questions occupy less time on the floor of the House. As in the Commons, 'starred' questions are taken after certain formal items of business at the beginning of a day's sitting. However, unlike the Commons, proceedings are not subject to a precise time deadline but to a restriction of numbers: no more than four questions can be taken each day. Lords can ask supplementaries and each question tends to receive more time than a question in the Commons, the four questions being dealt with in about twenty to twenty-five minutes.

Peers may also table questions for written answer, though the number tabled each session – between one and two thousand – is small relative to the number in the Commons. Not altogether dissimilar to the Commons (though MPs use such questions for a range of other purposes as well), there is a tendency to use written questions to obtain information (Shell 1988: 173).

Departmental select committees

The establishment of departmental select committees in 1979 added a new and important dimension to the work of the Commons. There are now sixteen of them: see Table 6.5. The committees are multi-functional. Formally, they exist to consider the administration as well as the policy and expenditure of departments. Finding

Table 6.5   Departmental select committees (appointed July 1992)

Committee	Chairman
Agriculture	Jerry Wiggin (Con)
Defence	Sir Nicholas Bonsor (Con)
Education	Sir Malcolm Thornton (Con)
Employment	Ron Leighton (Lab)
Environment	Robert Jones (Con)
Foreign Affairs	David Howell (Con)
Health	Mrs Marion Roe (Con)
Home Affairs	Sir Ivan Lawrence (Con)
National Heritage[1]	Gerald Kaufman (Lab)
Science and Technology[1]	Sir Giles Shaw (Con)
Scottish Affairs[2]	William McKelvey (Lab)
Social Security	Frank Field (Lab)
Trade and Industry	Richard Caborn (Lab)
Transport	Robert Adley (Con)
Treasury and Civil Service	John Watts (Con)
Welsh Affairs	Gareth Wardell (Lab)

[1] New committees established in July 1992. At the same time, the energy committee was abolished.
[2] Re-appointed after being in abeyance in the 1987–92 parliament.

out what departments have done, why and with what effect, constitutes a central part of their activities.

The committees are responsible for determining their own agenda and they have significant advantages over the use of the floor of the House for subjecting departments to sustained scrutiny. Debates and questions can be deployed only for sporadic scrutiny of particular programmes and activities. Committees can pursue a particular issue at some length. They can do so by questioning not only the appropriate minister but also the relevant civil servants. They can also call witnesses from other bodies to offer their knowledge and advice and they frequently do so: the majority of witnesses are not drawn from government departments (Norton 1991a: 73). Oral evidence is supplemented by the submission of written evidence, both solicited and unsolicited. The committees are also empowered to appoint, and most do appoint, one or more specialist advisers – outside experts paid on a daily basis – to assist them throughout a Parliament or for particular enquiries, as well as specialist assistants – usually highly-qualified graduates in the field, employed on a fixed-term contract for two or three years.

Each committee normally meets each week while the House is sitting, with meetings lasting between sixty and ninety minutes. As noted in Chapter 4, they may undertake extensive, long-term enquiries or short, quick enquiries (see Judge 1990: 176–84; Drewry 1989). Some will have single sessions on a particular subject. The range of subjects on which the committees undertake enquiries, and subsequently issue reports, is diverse (Drewry 1989). Among the major enquiries undertaken by the Trade and Industry committee between 1983 and 1992 were the following:

* The growth in the trade imbalance in manufactured goods between the UK and existing and prospective EC members
* The British steel corporation
* Trade with China
* Tourism in the UK
* The tin crisis
* The UK motor component industry
* Westland plc (on which the Defence Committee also undertook a somewhat more publicized enquiry)
* Petrol retailing in the UK
* Information technology
* Trade with eastern Europe
* Financial services and the single European market
* The post office
* Company investigations
* The sale of the Rover Group to British Aerospace
* Takeovers and mergers
* The exporting of material to Iraq, the so-called 'supergun' enquiry, concerning the sale to Iraq of piping that could be used to manufacture a massive missile launcher.

Of these, the sale of the Rover Group and the 'supergun' enquiries attracted considerable, though not exhaustive, media attention (see Negrine 1992). Both concerned the role played by ministers and civil servants in what turned out to be controversial actions.

In the 1987–92 Parliament alone, the Trade and Industry committee – as it reported to the House – produced twenty-five reports
and took oral evidence on thirteen other subjects which were not
followed by reports (Select Committee on Trade and Industry
1992: v). This illustrates the prolific nature of the committees. In
the first Parliament of their existence (1979–83), they issued a total
of 193 substantive reports; in the 1983–87 Parliament, they issued
306; and in the longer, five-session Parliament of 1987–92, the total
was 403. In total, in twelve years, the committees have issued just
over 900 substantive reports.

Significantly, some committees have also taken to reviewing
previous reports to see what action was subsequently taken. The
Trade and Industry committee, for example, took written evidence, principally from the Department of Trade and Industry, on
developments following its reports in both the 1983–87 and 1987–
92 Parliaments, the evidence being published in special reports
from the committee (Select Committee on Trade and Industry
1988; 1992). The practice was one already established in the Lords
by the Science and Technology committee.

The committees have thus invested considerable time and
energy in reviewing government action in the different sectors of
public policy. By their questioning of ministers and civil servants,
they have required the occupants of government departments to
explain and justify particular policies and particular actions. They
have been able to do so by virtue of their special status. Though
the committees cannot force the attendance of ministers and civil
servants, there has usually been no problem in achieving the
attendance of the witnesses sought. Ministers do not wish to attract
the parliamentary opprobrium that would result from a refusal to
attend. Civil servants cannot make comments to the media.
Appearing before committees they can speak only in the name of
their ministers, but nonetheless by appearing they are in a position
to provide information and explanations that would likely not
otherwise be put in the public domain.

Committees are thus able to ensure that ministers and civil
servants are subjected to scrutiny in a public authoritative forum,
eking out explanations and data that otherwise may not be forthcoming. In so doing, they have ensured what, in Judge's terminology (1990: 167), is a greater transparency of departments, ensuring
that their actions are more visible to Parliament and to the public

Table 6.6   House of Lords Select Committee on Science and Technology
principal enquiries 1979–91

Session	Topic
1979–80	Electric vehicles
1979–80	Scientific aspects of forestry
1980–81	Hazardous waste disposal
1981–82	Science and government
1981–82	Electric vehicles: supplementary report
1982–83	Engineering research and development
1982–83	The water industry
1983–84	Remote sensing and digital mapping
1983–84	Occupational health and hygiene services
1983–84	Engineering research and development: supplementary report
1983–84	Agricultural and environmental research
1984–85	Education and training for new technologies
1984–85	Local Government Bill: scientific and technical services, interim report
1984–85	Hazardous waste disposal: review of the Control of Pollution (Special Waste) Regulations 1980
1985–86	Science and technology in local government
1985–86	Marine science and technology
1986–87	Civil research and development
1986–87	Innovation in surface transport
1987–88	United Kingdom space policy
1987–88	Priorities in medical research
1987–88	Agricultural and food research, interim report
1988–89	Agricultural and food research
1988–89	Research and development (R&D) in nuclear power
1988–89	Definitions of R&D
1988–89	Greenhouse effect
1989–90	Overseas aid
1989–90	Nature conservancy council
1990–91	Priorities in medical research: supplementary report
1990–91	International scientific programmes
1990–91	Science budget 1991–92
1990–91	Safety aspects of ship design and technology
1990–91	Systematic biology research

Source: House of Lords, Select Committee on the Committee Work of the House
1992: 67–68.

and outside groups. Through issuing reports and recommendations, they also serve to have some impact on departmental
thinking.

As already argued in Chapter 4, this impact does not usually
extend to initiating significant new policies, but it can affect the
implementation of existing policies and administrative practices.
The Treasury and Civil Service Committee, for example, has not
only subjected government economic policy to critical review but
has influenced how the Treasury presents the government's expenditure plans each year as well as the timing of the budget statement
(see generally Laugharne 1993). By taking evidence from interested bodies, the committees have the potential also to look at
policies from different perspectives and by so doing may influence
government to re-examine and re-appraise existing policy positions (Judge 1990: 198).

The House of Lords has no equivalent committee structure. The
one permanent select committee that it has for looking at a particular area of policy – on science and technology – has already
been mentioned in Chapter 4. Its enquiries have been wide-
ranging and numerous. In the twelve years from 1979 to 1991, it
undertook thirty-four principal enquiries (Table 6.6). In giving evidence to the Lords Select Committee on the Committee Work of
the House in 1991, the chairman of the committee – Lord Flowers,
a former professor of physics and expert on atomic energy –
identified no less than nineteen suggestions for further enquiries.
The committee draws on some well-qualified peers for its membership (and on some leading experts to serve as specialist advisers)
and it conducts extensive enquiries, not dissimilar in approach to
the Commons' committees. The status of its membership, though,
gives it a particular intellectual clout that some ministers find
daunting. Appearing before it, recalled one senior minister, was
like being grilled by dons in a university seminar.

Public Accounts Committee

In the Commons, the departmental select committees are reinforced by the more longstanding Public Accounts Committee
(PAC). First appointed in 1861, the PAC primarily undertakes
value-for-money audits of government programmes.

The audits themselves are undertaken by, and on the initiative of, the Comptroller and Auditor General, who heads the National Audit Office. The Comptroller and Auditor General presents his reports to the committee, reports that are often short but generally numerous: about thirty or forty per session. They focus on how money is spent and whether it is used most efficiently to achieve its intended purpose. Topics covered in the 1990–91 session included patient transport services, the European fighter aircraft, the sale of Herstmonceux Castle, the monitoring and control of charities in England and Wales, and the social fund.

Given the number of reports, the PAC cannot spend too much time on any one and tends to hold one hearing, rather than several, on a particular report. The Permanent Secretary of the relevant department will normally appear as the witness in the capacity of accounting officer. If not satisfied with the responses, the committee can issue a critical report. By virtue of the nature of the enquiry by the National Audit Office and the status of the PAC, such reports are treated seriously in Whitehall. Committee recommendations are considered by the Treasury in consultation with the relevant department and, if accepted, put into effect according to treasury instructions. If not accepted, a reasoned reply has to be given to the committee. The committee may then choose to return to the matter at a later stage.

The PAC was effectively strengthened in 1983 with the passage of the National Audit Act, a private member's bill that transformed the old Exchequer and Audit Department into a more substantial and more highly trained National Audit Office, put the expenses of the office under the control of Parliament instead of government, and affirmed the position of the Comptroller and Auditor General as an officer of Parliament (Norton 1986: 85–86). The National Audit Office now has a staff of approximately 800, including trained accountants.

PAC reports and enquiries contribute substantially to the scrutiny of the administration undertaken by the house, forcing departments to justify their actions in spending monies in the way that they do. A committee hearing ensures that a Permanent Secretary devotes considerable time and effort to being able to provide such an explanation (see Wilson 1977: 183). The committee is chaired by an opposition MP, usually one who has had some experience as a treasury minister, and it enjoys a considerable reputation in both Whitehall and Westminster for its work.

The Select Committee on Statutory Instruments

We have considered Parliament's role in the passage of primary legislation. That legislation may provide for the later promulgation of regulations – delegated legislation – which may be subject to parliamentary approval. Under the affirmative resolution procedure, parliamentary approval is required. Under the negative resolution procedure, the regulations take effect unless Parliament votes otherwise. Some regulations are not subject to parliamentary attention at all.

Usually more than a thousand regulations – known as statutory instruments – are laid before Parliament each year. Most – more than three-quarters – are subject to the negative resolution procedure. Motions (known as prayers) to annul such orders are not often debated in the Commons because of constraints on time and rarely in the Lords because very few are tabled. Some are occasionally referred for debate by standing committees; as with bills, they are appointed *ad hoc*, but only have one-and-a-half hours to debate the instrument.

The most consistent and structured consideration given to statutory instruments is by the Select Committee on Statutory Instruments. If instruments are subject to approval by both Houses, it forms part of a joint committee with the Lords; if subject only to Commons approval, it meets as a Commons' committee. All instruments are sent to the committee. The committee is very much concerned with administration in that its remit covers the form rather than the merits of instruments. It considers whether instruments are properly drawn, that is, within the powers granted and not subject to drafting deficiencies. It is then up to government to decide what to do. The committee has no formal powers and it is possible that an instrument may be approved before the committee has even reported. However, adverse reports from the committee may result in an instrument being withdrawn. Such occasions, though, are extremely rare.

The Parliamentary Commissioner for Administration

Question time and debates in Parliament do not lend themselves to detailed investigation of particular administrative actions. In order to allow for some detailed enquiry, a report in 1961 – the Whyatt report – recommended the appointment of an ombudsman, similar to the one already in existence in Sweden, to investigate cases of alleged administrative injustice. The result was the passage in 1967 of the Parliamentary Commissioner Act, creating the position of a Parliamentary Commissioner for Administration (Stacey 1971).

The Parliamentary Commissioner, or Ombudsman, was given power to investigate complaints of maladministration brought to his attention by MPs acting on behalf of members of the public. Maladministration was confined to administrative actions: the remit did not encompass policy decisions nor matters affecting contracts, personnel, the armed services, or relations with other countries. The type of 'maladministration' involved would encompass, for example, unnecessary delay in processing a particular claim, misinterpreting rules or ignoring material information when taking some particular action.

The Commissioner was given powers of access to departmental papers, though not Cabinet papers. He has no powers of enforcement but makes quarterly reports to the Select Committee on the Parliamentary Commissioner for Administration. The committee is responsible for considering reports and pursuing them as appropriate with departments. Where maladministration is found, a department will usually act to provide compensation or remedy the fault in procedure. Where it fails to act, the select committee may pursue the issue. In 1977, the Commissioner told the Procedure Committee that he regarded the select committee as 'an effective sanction in the rare cases where the departments have not been prepared to implement a remedy I recommend' (Select Committee on Procedure 1978: lviii).

The number of cases referred to the Commissioner each year by MPs is relatively small. He and his staff of just under 100 deal with under 1,000 cases a year, most of which come in as a result of the PCA also being the ombudsman for the National Health Service, in which capacity he receives complaints directly from members of the public. The remit and the activity in respect of departments are thus limited but the presence of the Commissioner may have a useful deterrent effect, constituting in the words of one observer 'a worthwhile check on bureaucratic bungling' (Silk 1987: 33).

Informal methods

The formal means available to MPs and peers are supplemented by informal means. One means, already discussed, is the back bench committees. On the government side, ministers will variously address the appropriate committee and be subject to questioning. Ministers will also regularly meet with committee officers, allowing an opportunity to review and comment on developments within the department.

2.)   Another means is through the correspondence that takes place between members and ministers. This is usually in pursuit of constituency casework (see Chapter 9) but it is also a device for obtaining information from ministers and ensuring that they are aware of particular issues that are concerning members and their constituents. As such, it can be seen as supplementary to parliamentary questions, requiring ministers to respond to particular points, but to do so less publicly and usually at greater length.

This means may be supplemented by personal contact. A member may supplement the official means such as debates and questions with private meetings with ministers to pursue particular points about the conduct of their departments. Such contact may be through a scheduled meeting, at the department or in the minister's room in the Palace of Westminster, or through a chance – or, indeed, planned – meeting in the division lobby or corridor. Such contact is a regular feature of activity in the division lobbies, being popular with members for the reason already noted in Chapter 3: it is difficult for a minister to give a negative response when face to face with a member making a particular request.

The important point about these informal means is that they do tend to supplement the formal means available. In combination – and it is the combination that is important – these various devices result in both Houses of Parliament, and the Commons in particular, devoting considerable time and attention – both on and off the floor – to the actions and administration of government.

Impact?

But what impact does all the time and energy devoted to the conduct of government actually have?

There are obvious problems in attempting such an evaluation. For one thing, there is the problem of disentangling the scrutiny of administration from the other tasks fulfilled by Parliament. The scrutiny itself, as we have seen, takes different forms and embodies a range of consequences. For another, there is the problem of generating criteria for measuring Parliament's impact (Nixon 1986; Judge 1990). Even if the contours were clear, generating measurable objectives offers a virtually insurmountable obstacle.

However, we can identify some of the obstacles that militate against Parliament being able to undertake a *continuous* and *comprehensive* review of the conduct of government. It is also possible to identify some of the *apparent* impact of the scrutiny that is undertaken. We can also speculate as to what appears to be its most important, but least observable, impact.

Limitations

The limitations are considerable. Both debates and questions offer only sporadic opportunities to review particular departments. Debates are a misnomer in that there is rarely a 'debate', members delivering set-piece orations, often – after the front bench speeches – to an almost empty chamber. This applies in both Houses, peers actually submitting their names in advance to speak, with lists of speakers then being prepared and circulated, formalizing to some extent the procedure adopted in the Commons, where members let the Speaker know in advance they would like to speak and the Speaker maintaining an informal list, often intimating to members privately when they might expect to be called. Speeches and the outcomes of debates are usually predictable.

At question time, there is limited opportunity to question the whole range of departmental activities. There is a substantial list of topics on which ministers will not answer questions, such as arms sales and budgetary forecasts (see Sedgemore 1980: 184–87) and now the new 'next steps' agencies established within departments. Ministers are well armed with information to deflect probing questions and question time is becoming used more and more for partisan point scoring, with interventions from the opposition front bench now a common occurrence. In the Commons, there is also a conflict between breadth and depth, between trying to get through as many questions as possible against allowing one particular and important question to be pursued at some length (see Franklin and Norton 1993: Chapter 8), with the pressure to get through as many as possible helping rather than hindering ministers.

Indeed, the limitations are particularly marked in the Commons. The randomness of question selection militates against pursuing an issue in a structured form. Recent years have seen a growth in the practice of 'syndication', a practice originating with minister's parliamentary private secretaries in which several members are encouraged to table similar or identical questions in order to increase the chances of that question coming high in the daily 'shuffle'. The practice spread to the opposition side. Despite changes in the rules governing the submission of questions in 1990, the practice remains a common one (Irwin et al., 1993).

Select committees offer the opportunity for more sustained scrutiny of departments. Even so, a committee meeting once a week for just over an hour has to be highly selective in what it chooses to investigate. Furthermore, 'witnesses do not always make it easy for committees to do their work' (Negrine 1992: 406). Though committees normally get the witnesses they want, they do not always get the answers they want, civil servants being prohibited from giving information on internal discussions, interdepartmental negotiations, or anything that is commercially sensitive. Ministers and their officials can prove tight-lipped, offering nothing of substance.

The committees themselves are advisory bodies. Their reports are made formally to the House, but – other than the three estimates days each session – there is little formal linkage between committee activity and the floor of the House. Committee members themselves are under increasing pressures from their other parliamentary responsibilities and cannot always give the time necessary to prepare for committee meetings. Attempts to strengthen members' resources have fallen foul of the complacency of the procedure committee (Select Committee on Procedure, 1990).

The Public Accounts Committee continues to play an important role in auditing public spending but is limited by the amount of time it has available relative to the number of reports made by the Comptroller and Auditor General. The limitations of the Select Committee on Statutory Instruments are apparent from our review of the committee. It has no formal powers and can be, and variously is, ignored by government keen to see a regulation in place.

The Parliamentary Commissioner for Administration suffers from very limited powers, unable to delve into cabinet papers and unable to require action by a department. He relies usually on legal advice offered by departments and cannot consider the merits of decisions taken by departments in the exercise of their discretionary powers. He could also be considered to be limited by a reluctance on the part of many members to refer cases to him, preferring to deal with the complaints themselves, and by limited public interest in his activities; few cases excite media attention (Norton 1981: 125).

The result is that Parliament cannot claim to subject the conduct of government to continuous and comprehensive scrutiny. Much of what government does avoids parliamentary attention. When it is the subject of such attention, the attention is frequently sporadic and fleeting, affected by partisan considerations, pressures of time and lack of knowledge. Ministers are variously able to deflect probing by members and to ignore recommendations for a change in practice or policy.

Strengths

Parliament's capacity to review government actions and administration is, then, clearly limited. However, it is not so limited as to be of no consequence. Indeed, it can be argued that Parliament, limitations notwithstanding, has a considerable impact.

Questions, debates and committees have the effect of ensuring that ministers present themselves in order to explain and justify their actions and their stewardship of their departments. A failure to attend would be politically damaging. When ministers have variously failed to make statements about a major decision or have tried to announce that decision through an answer to a written question instead of on the floor of the House, a flurry of points of order on the floor often has the desired effect. When they appear at the despatch box or before a committee, ministers know that any failure on their part to justify their actions will be seized on. Though party ensures that the government can usually win a vote, the party *system* ensures that it is subject to critical scrutiny. Ministers may win the vote: they may not necessarily win the argument. An inadequate answer or response to a debate can harm both a minister and consequently the government.

Television has proved a powerful reinforcement to Parliament's capacity to ensure ministers explain their actions (see Barnett and

Gaber 1992: 418). A minister unable to answer a question or squirming before difficult questions posed by committee members makes good television. To avoid it, ministers need to be well briefed. Hence, even before a minister appears in the chamber or in the committee room, Parliament has had an impact: ensuring not only his or her physical presence but also that the minister is well acquainted with the issue that concerns members.

MPs and peers, through the devices available to them, thus have an opportunity to set the agenda in terms of scrutinizing the conduct of government. Government back-benchers may table friendly questions, but they are subject to the luck of the draw. Opposition members can raise issues that ministers may not wish to have raised. They can pursue them in a way not available to the ordinary citizen or even to journalists. (Journalists, if necessary, can be avoided.) Ministers may rely on partisanship to protect them in difficult circumstances, but if they put up a palpably inadequate case they may be left languishing in a sea of silence or even jeering on the government side of the House.

In extreme cases, if ministers' conduct of affairs loses the confidence of their own side as well as that of the opposition, they may feel constrained to resign, as happened – as we have noted in Chapter 3 – with Scottish law officer Nicholas Fairbairn over his handling in the Commons of a particular prosecution in 1982; with Foreign Secretary Lord Carrington and two other Foreign Office ministers over Foreign Office policy on the Falklands, also in 1982; with Trade and Industry Secretary Leon Brittan over his conduct of the Westland affair in 1986; and Edwina Currie over the salmonella in eggs affair in 1988.[1] Such occasions are rare, but a salutary reminder to other ministers. Less overtly, parliamentary criticism may lead to a minister being moved to a less demanding or sensitive post or even dropped from government altogether.

Partisanship, then, does not guarantee protection. It may also not be a relevant concept in certain areas of parliamentary activity. Select committees tend to avoid highly contentious partisan issues, focusing instead on how government is conducted – on means rather than ends – and on issues of concern to outside interests. Those issues may not be at the heart of partisan conflict, but they can be controversial, as with the Defence Committee inquiry into the Westland affair in 1986 and the inquiry by the Trade and Industry Committee in 1990 into the sale of the Rover Group.

They may also focus on otherwise neglected topics, thus bringing them on to the agenda, or tackle major issues not tackled by departments. The Lords' Science and Technology Committee, as previously observed, has been especially important in reviewing government activity in the field of civil research and development.

By these various activities, Parliament serves to open up the conduct of government for wider scrutiny, putting a range of otherwise unavailable material into the public domain. When material has not been forthcoming, committees have pushed harder to get it or subjected the Government to embarrassing criticism. In the case of the Trade and Industry Committee, for example, when information has not been disclosed, 'the committee has been quick to publicise the intransigence of government and to point out the constitutional implications of such action' (Judge 1990: 196).

Critical questioning may also influence ministerial actions. Questions may result in attention being given to an issue previously neglected by the minister and some consequent modification of departmental policy. That modification may occur in advance of the minister appearing at the despatch box. Recommendations from committees may result in government action. The Public Accounts Committee is especially influential but other committees have some impact in the administration of government. Committees have little impact in initiating policy (see Chapter 4), but have more success in influencing the means by which policy is pursued as well as influencing some middle-level nonpartisan policy (see Drewry 1989; Judge 1990: 196–7; Select Committee on Trade and Industry 1992). Most of the 150 recommendations accepted by government in 1985–86 (see above, Chapter 4) fell basically into the category of administration rather than policy.

Parliament, then, has some tangible impact on ministers and civil servants. At a minimum, it obliges them to prepare for and appear before parliamentary bodies. It has some impact upon ministerial actions and departmental operations. However, what is probably its most important impact is neither observable nor quantifiable. Parliament acts as a deterrent.

Ministers and their officials are aware of the various devices available to both Houses to subject government actions and the administration of departments to public scrutiny. They may be asked questions on the floor of the House. They may be subjected to more sustained questioning in committee. Sometimes they know they will be subject to scrutiny. Treasury officials know, for example, that the advisers to the Treasury and Civil Service Committee will run their economic forecasts through different economic models (see Laugharne 1993). Such knowledge keeps ministers and their officials alert to the scrutiny to which they *may* be subjected. It is likely to influence their actions. They may refrain from a particular course of action if they feel they cannot justify it to MPs and peers. They may ensure that policy is implemented efficiently and fairly, knowing the potential repercussions if they fail to do so. The impact of Parliament in this respect is basically pervasive. Ministers and officials may be dismissive of its influence and grasp of issues, but they dare not ignore it.

Conclusion

Parliament devotes a substantial amount of time to questioning the actions of government, including the implementation of policy goals (a decision to commit troops abroad, for example) and more mundane administration of public programmes (payment of benefits, for instance). It has a range of devices at its disposal. Each suffers from certain limitations that prevents these devices from collectively enabling Parliament to subject the conduct of government to continuous and comprehensive scrutiny.

Those devices, nonetheless, have considerable consequences for government. They provoke responses in the form of information, explanation and justification. They absorb the time and intellectual energy of ministers and senior civil servants. They create a critical environment for the discussion of particular programmes and actions. They ensure greater openness on the part of government. For government, there is no equivalent to the legal right of silence. Use of these parliamentary tools may influence a change of policy or minister or, more frequently, some change in administrative techniques and departmental practices. And their very existence, and the observable impact they sometimes have on policies and careers, have a pervasive deterrent effect throughout the corridors of power.

Parliament has some, but not a great deal of, impact in terms of initiating policy and affecting the content of legislation; it has far greater consequences for the government's general conduct of affairs. It does not have the impact that it might – that is clear from our review of the different devices at its disposal – but what impact it has is nonetheless considerable.

Note

1. In Chapter 3, we also noted the resignation as a consequence of back bench pressure of National Heritage Secretary David Mellor in 1992. His departure was over conduct not related directly to his ministerial duties: indeed, there was a general recognition in Parliament – and the arts world – that he was good at his particular ministerial job.

7

The European Community

The United Kingdom became a member of the European Community on 1 January 1973. Membership created a new dimension to the British constitution. It resulted in policy-making competence in a number of sectors passing from the United Kingdom to the supra-national institutions of the Community. The policy-making strength of the EC was increased by the Single European Act (the SEA), which took effect in 1987. In the process of Community policy-making, Parliament has a peripheral role, both formally and in practice.

EC institutions

The 'European Community' formally comprises three communities – the European Coal and Steel Community (ECSC), the European Atomic Energy Community (Euratom), and the European Economic Community (EEC) (see Clinton-Davis 1991). However, the institutions of all three were merged in 1967 and it is now common to refer to them collectively as the European Community or simply the Community.

Within the Community, the principal institutions are the Commission, the Council of Ministers, the European Parliament, the Committee of Permanent Representatives and the Court of Justice. The Commission constitutes the permanent bureaucracy of the Community, headed by a college of seventeen Commissioners. It is divided into divisions (Directorates-General) and has responsibility for the initiation and formulation of proposals to be placed before the Council of Ministers (Freestone and Davidson 1988:

114

93–94). It has responsibility also for ensuring the enforcement of community law and has certain limited powers of decision making, independent of the Council.

The stage of deliberation and assent is dominated by the Council. This council comprises ministers from the member states and takes decisions on proposals laid before it by the Commission. It seeks to proceed by unanimity, but certain issues can be resolved by a process of weighted majority voting. Provision for the use of weighted majority voting was extended by the Single European Act in 1987, encompassing measures necessary to achieve a single market.

Prior to 1987, the European Parliament was an advisory body in respect of EC legislation. It had power to reject the budget and dismiss *en bloc* the college of Commissioners, but no power to amend the measures proposed by the Commission and accepted by the Council of Ministers. Measures were sent to the Parliament for its comments and these were sent, with the proposal, to the Council. Until 1979, it was also an appointed body, members being drawn from the national Parliaments.

In 1979, it became a directly-elected body and in 1987 its powers were effectively extended by the Single European Act. Under the provisions of the Act, measures for achieving a single market are now subject to what is called the co-operation procedure, which allows the Parliament to force the Commission to re-examine proposals. The Parliament can propose amendments and reject measures. The Council can reinstate a proposal rejected by the Parliament, but can do so only by unanimity (see Jacobs and Corbett 1990: 169–71). The SEA also changed the name of the Parliament. Until 1987, it was formally titled the European Assembly: the Act gave it the name – the European Parliament – by which it had called itself for some time.

The Committee of Permanent Representatives (known as COREPER) comprises officials from the member states who do the preparatory work of the Council of Ministers. The Court of Justice is responsible for the legal interpretation of the treaties. Its judgements are binding on the member states and enforceable through the national courts.

This substantial infrastructure is supplemented by the regular meetings of heads of government of the member states. Formally titled the European Council, but often referred to as the European

Summit, it was given formal treaty status by the Single European
Act. It meets on a regular basis twice a year and at other times as
deemed necessary. It has no formal powers of its own, action to
implement its decisions having to be taken by the Council of Ministers. However, what it decides can determine the future shape of
the community.

EC competence

The responsibilities of the EC are substantial. It administers major
structural funds: the social fund, the regional development fund,
and the agricultural guidance and guarantee fund. The guarantee
part of the agriculture fund supports the common agricultural policy (the CAP). It administers other funds, including through the
European investment bank.

It has responsibility for removing trade barriers and ensuring
the free movement of persons, services and capital within the
Community (the single market) and with generating policies on
external trade, overseas aid, energy and consumer affairs. In
order to achieve a single market, it has power to adjust national
legal rules, through what is called harmonization procedures –
that is, to ensure that rules are standardized throughout the
community.

Further responsibilities can be added through the amendment
of the existing treaties or the promulgation of new ones. It was in
order to speed up the process for achieving the single market that
the Single European Act was agreed by member states. The
Maastricht treaty negotiated in December 1991 constituted an attempt to move towards economic and monetary union. For such
changes – known as primary legislation – the agreement of all
member states is required.

Acting within the Community's sphere of competence, the
institutions can promulgate a range of measures – regulations,
directives, decisions, recommendations and opinions. Recommendations and opinions have no binding force. Decisions are binding
on those to whom they are directed. Most EC law, though, takes the
form of regulations and directives. Regulations are binding and directly applicable in all the member states. Directives are binding in
terms of their ends, but it is left to the member states affected to
choose the most appropriate means to achieve those ends.

The role of Parliament

In EC law making, the UK Parliament has a marginal role. The position was well summarized by the Select Committee on Procedure in 1989. EC legislation, it noted, was initiated almost exclusively by the Commission

> with which the United Kingdom Parliament has no formal relationship and over which it has no direct control. More importantly, the United Kingdom has, as a condition of of its community membership, bound itself to accept the collective authority of a legislative body (the Council of Ministers) only one of whose twelve members is accountable to the House of Commons. These facts may be unwelcome in some quarters, but they spring unavoidably from the United Kingdom's treaty obligations. (Select Committee on Procedure 1989: ix)

The treaties accord no formal role to national Parliaments. When Parliament in Britain passed the European Communities Act in 1972 it gave the force of the law in the UK to existing community law and to all future EC law. In other words, the assent of Parliament was not required for each future measure of EC law: it was given already under the provisions of the Act.

In so far as Parliament retains any formal powers in relation to EC law, it is responsible for approving legislation that may be introduced to give effect in the UK to EC directives. More importantly in constitutional terms, its assent is required for amendments to the community treaties. Such treaty changes (primary legislation) require the assent of all member states. Constitutional practice for giving approval varies from state to state. A minority employ referendums. In most, parliamentary assent is necessary and sufficient. The Single European Act constituted primary legislation and was approved by Parliament under the provisions of the 1986 European Communities (Amendment) Act. In 1992, the government introduced another European Communities (Amendment) Bill to give effect to the Maastricht treaty.

However, the principal role of Parliament is to seek to have some influence on the regular law-making process within the Community. The principal means for achieving this are European committees in both Houses, supplemented by debates. These mechanisms are employed primarily to influence the government.

Some attempts have also been made by both Houses to develop links with community institutions.

The Commons

In the Commons, there is the Select Committee on European Legislation and, since the beginning of 1991, two special standing committees on EC documents. There is also provision to debate documents on the floor of the House and for two debates each year prior to meetings of the European Council. The departmental select committees also have the power to consider the EC dimension of departmental activities.

The Select Committee on European Legislation

The committee has sixteen members and is chaired by an opposition MP. It was established in 1974 to consider draft proposals by the Commission, and other documents published by it, which were to be submitted to the Council.[1] The Commission proposals are sent to Parliament by the relevant government department, which also submits an explanatory memorandum on each one.

All the commission documents are considered by the committee and sifted into one of four categories:

* those of sufficient legal or political importance to justify debate;
* those of legal or political importance but not warranting debate;
* those of no legal or political importance; and
* those of legal or political importance in respect of which the committee is not yet in a position to decide whether debate would be justified.

The committee has a substantial workload. It considers between six hundred and nine hundred documents each year. Most are usually technical and routine and raise no important political or legal questions. The committee will usually recommend between nine and fifteen per cent – roughly eighty to one hundred documents – for further consideration. In 1983, it recommended 107 – sixteen per cent of the total – for further consideration.

Following a resolution of the House in 1980, ministers are expected to withhold agreement to any proposal in the Council of Ministers which the committee has recommended should be debated but which has not yet been considered by the House, unless the committee has indicated that agreement need not be withheld or the minister concerned considers that 'for special reasons' agreement should not be withheld. Such special reasons have been taken by government to include the need to avoid a legal vacuum and the desirability of getting a measure of benefit to the UK into force as soon as possible.

In practice, a number of proposals are accepted each year by the Council prior to debate in the Commons, even though recommended by the committee for further consideration. The number is usually a small one. Between 1983 and 1987, for example, between two and nine per cent of documents recommended for Commons' consideration were adopted before any debate took place. As the Procedure Committee observed (1989: x): 'Whilst these figures are not negligible, they do not suggest that the scrutiny safeguards are being by-passed on any substantial scale'.

European standing committees

Documents recommended for further consideration can be referred for debate by a standing committee. Before 1991, such committees were appointed on an *ad hoc* basis. Each committee considered a document on a motion moved by a minister, to which amendments could be moved, and sat for two-and-a-half hours. It then reported to the House. Various documents, especially those that were technical in nature, were deemed appropriate for such scrutiny and in the latter half of the 1980s an average of just over twenty documents were referred each session, giving rise – as more than one document could be considered at any one time – to about ten committee deliberations.

Such committees suffered often from a poor attendance and were of only limited use in saving time on the floor of the House. Most documents recommended for consideration were taken on the floor of the House. To try to improve scrutiny, and reduce some of the burden on the chamber, the procedure committee in 1989 recommended the appointment of five special standing committees to consider EC documents in particular sectors, each committee having a membership nominated each session. This it was felt would allow for greater specialization and greater commitment by members. The Government accepted the committee's argument but recommended only three such committees. Following problems with recruiting members, the House approved the creation of two such committees, each with thirteen members, early in 1991.

EC documents recommended for debate are now referred (unless the House votes otherwise) to these committees. One committee deals with documents concerning agriculture, transport, environment and the Forestry Commission; the other deals with all remaining documents. Chairmen are appointed for consideration of individual documents. As with the previous *ad hoc* committees, any MP who is not a committee member can attend and seek to speak, though not vote. However, they differ from the previous committees in that, prior to the usual debate on the documents, they can question the relevant minister for up to one hour.

The effect of the creation of the committees has been, in the words of one MP, a 'modified success' (Sir Peter Emery, speaking to a Lords committee): 'They have taken a lot of work which was done late into the night off the floor of the House of Commons and allow it to be considered at a reasonable time by people in a much more detailed manner' (Select Committee on the Committee Work of the House 1992, Vol. 2: 94). The committees, though, absorb the energies of their members but have rarely attracted the attendance of other members.

Floor of the House

Before the creation of the European standing committees in 1991, most documents were debated on the floor of the House. In the latter half of the 1980s, an average of sixty-five documents a session were considered in twenty-one debates. The debates were taken after 10.00 p.m. and subject to a one-and-a-half hour time limit. They were generally poorly attended and those who did attend were often members with stronger views on the issue of European union than on the merits of the particular documents (Select Committee on Procedure 1989: xviii). Scheduling debates at an earlier hour would create pressures on existing business and so the Procedure Committee recommended the use of special standing committees. The government was also keen that discussion of documents should be taken off the floor of the House as much as possible. The new committees now absorb some of the business previously taken on the floor, though at the end of the first full session of their existence (1991–92, cut short by the dissolution in March) it was not clear that they had saved that much time. On the floor, discussion of EC documents occupied two-and-a-half per cent of the time, not much less than the percentage in preceding sessions.

In addition to the new committees, the government also agreed with the recommendation of the procedure committee that two days each session, currently used to debate half-yearly reports from the Foreign Secretary on developments in the Community, should be used for forward-looking debates prior to the six-monthly meetings of the European Council. As the government noted in its response to the committee, such debates could combine debate on issues likely to come up at the council meeting with the half-yearly report. Such debates are now held.

Select committees

Select committees can examine European issues that impinge on departmental responsibilities. In 1989, the Procedure Committee advised against the creation of a single committee to consider EC policy issues, preferring to leave the task with the existing departmental committees. However, the demands made on the time of committees is such that very little time is devoted to EC matters. Some committees, such as agriculture and environment (and, until its demise in 1992, energy) have given more time to EC issues than other committees, but no committee undertakes systematic scrutiny of EC legislation. As the Procedure Committee (1989: xxix) put it, 'the total amount of time and resources devoted to this subject does not appear to be very great'. Conflicting priorities are likely to ensure that this remains the case.

Links with EC institutions

Attempts to go beyond influencing government and having some direct input into EC institutions have not been notably successful. The House has tended to be jealous of its privileges and has declined to accord any special status, for example, to Members of the European Parliament (MEPs). The Procedure Committee in 1989 recommended the development of more informal contacts, with select committees making greater use of MEPs as witnesses and through greater contact through party groupings. Both parliamentary parties permit their MEPs to attend meetings of their various backbench committees. However, the timing of meetings make it difficult for MEPs to spend much time in London and they are rarely seen at such gatherings.

The House of Lords

Like the Commons, the Lords has a committee for the scrutiny of draft EC legislation. However, its work is more extensive than its Commons' equivalent. It encompasses, in effect, the work done in the Commons by the EC Legislation Committee *and* the European standing committees. As in the Commons, debates may also take place on the floor of the House.

The European Communities Committee

Created in 1974, the Lords' committee is titled the European Communities Committee (see Grantham and Moore Hodgson 1985). It has wider terms of reference than its Commons' equivalent. It is appointed to consider documents and to make reports to the House on those which it considers raises matters of principle and policy and also on other questions to which the Committee believes the attention of the House should be drawn. As such, it can comment on the merits of proposals. Also, unlike its Commons' equivalent, it draws heavily on the work of sub-committees.

The committee has twenty-four members, and meets fortnightly. It operates principally through its five sub-committees (from 1986 until December 1992, there were six).[2] Each is known by a letter of the alphabet (sub-committee A etc.) and has responsibility for considering documents in a number of sectors. One sub-committee, for example, covers law and institutions. Each comprises two or more members of the committee and usually between five and twelve co-opted members. As a result, about seventy peers are actively involved in committee work.

Other peers may attend sub-committee meetings, thus allowing the sub-committees to benefit from peers' expertise in particular areas.

On the committee and sub-committees, a rotation rule operates. Each member serves for five years and sub-committee chairmen for three years. Committee activities are notable for their lack of partisanship. The main committee is chosen to reflect the broad political balance within the House, but interests and experience largely determine which peers are co-opted to the sub-committees and which become chairmen. The chairman of the law sub-committee is always a law lord.

EC documents and explanatory memoranda are submitted to both Houses. The chairman of the Lords' committee – presently Lady Serota – undertakes a weekly 'sift', sorting out the more important documents, requiring further consideration (sift A), from the less important documents (sift B). In this, she is assisted by a legal adviser as well as by the clerk of the committee. Documents from sift A are then sent to the relevant sub-committees. It is then open to the sub-committees either to clear the proposals without subjecting them to further scrutiny or to undertake enquiries.

If a sub-committee decides to undertake an enquiry, it can be a short one, with some evidence taken, and followed by a letter to the appropriate minister, or it can be a substantial enquiry, with oral and written evidence taken and a report made to the House. When undertaking full-scale inquiries, a specialist adviser will normally be appointed and bodies such as the EC Commission, professional and trade organizations, and other organized interests – including pressure groups – invited to submit evidence. Evidence from the government will be invited as a matter of course. Sub-committees have also variously invited Members of the European Parliament (MEPs) to give evidence. Some will also undertake occasional visits in order to obtain evidence: Sub-committee D, for example, visited an irradiation plant in Holland in 1989 when enquiring into irradiation of food.

When a sub-committee has completed an enquiry, a draft report is submitted to the main committee for approval. The committee decides whether the report should be sent to the House for information or for debate. The reports themselves are often substantial documents and, though addressed to the House, copies are sent to the EC Commission, Parliament and the UK representative in Brussels.

In addition to sub-committee enquiries, the committee itself may establish *ad hoc* enquiries that span the interests of sub-committees. For example, in the latter half of the 1980s it created a group drawn from members of the relevant sub-committees to enquire into the subject of fraud against the EC budget. However, because of the pressure on time and resources such *ad hoc* enquiries are relatively rare: a total of thirteen in the period between 1978 and 1990.

The remit of the committee is such that its enquiries will often range more widely than those of its Commons' counterpart. It has reported on such subjects as car exhaust emissions, nitrates in water, mutual recognition of higher education diplomas, the liberalization of capital movements, economic and monetary union, and border controls. It will scrutinize EC documents to get some idea of the direction in which the community appears to be moving in particular sectors and may then undertake, through the appropriate sub-committee, what amounts to a forward-looking enquiry.

The floor of the House

The committee will usually make between twenty and thirty reports a year to the House, with the majority of these recommended for debate. Reports are longer than they used to be but are fewer in number. When a report is recommended for debate, then it is debated. The problem tends to be one of when rather than if. Pressure on time means that some reports are squeezed into inconvenient times. They are now more likely to be debated immediately after questions – prime time in parliamentary terms – but difficulties can arise in the period before the summer recess when the House is heavily burdened with bills sent from the Commons. Such debates occupy a relatively small part of the House's time: usually less than five per cent each session (Group on the Working of the House 1987: 30). When a report is debated, then the issue gets a more public airing and a minister replies for the government. Some are not short debates. The report on economic and monetary union and political union was debated in November 1990 for almost eight hours. Most, though, last less than four hours.

Given the need to move quickly to influence some Community decisions, the practice of undertaking short enquiries followed by letters to the relevant ministers is now more frequently employed. It has proved especially valuable for sub-committee E, dealing with legal issues.

Links with EC institutions

The Lords has gone further than the Commons in developing links with EC institutions. The sub-committees have variously taken evidence from commission officials and from *rapporteurs* of European Parliament committees. The committee clerks attend regularly the plenary sessions of the European Parliament and liaise with parliamentary and commission officials. The chairmen of the main and sub-committees visit Brussels every two or three years to meet the President of the Parliament and officers of relevant committees to discuss matters of common interest. Some contact also takes place through correspondence. Such links, though not necessarily substantial, are reasonably regular and have been developed over the years since the committee was appointed.

Impact

The impact of Parliament on the European Community is relatively slight. As we have seen, it is constitutionally constrained. The treaties accord no formal role to national Parliaments. The potential for influence has been limited by the passage of the Single European Act. Even if a national Parliament influences government to take a particular stance in the Council of Ministers, that government can be outvoted by the other members.

Within Parliament, the opportunities to influence government are notably restricted in the Commons. The European Legislation Committee has a limited remit. An attempt to widen it in 1986 was rebuffed by the government (Griffith and Ryle 1989: 438). Debates on the floor or in European standing committees attract relatively little interest and what interest it does attract is usually from members with a particular view on the wider issue of European union. There is little if any evidence of the Commons exerting significant influence on government, or the institutions of the Community, in the deliberative stage of law making.

The Lords, as we have seen, has adopted a more extensive and wide-ranging procedure, employing sub-committees and extensive evidence-taking. It has also developed closer links with MEPs and commission officials. Its reports are often substantial and widely acknowledged as thorough and authoritative (Grantham and Moore Hodgson 1985; Norton 1992b; Select Committee on the Committee Work of the House 1992: 24–25). It enjoys a substantial reputation not just in Whitehall but in Brussels (Bates 1983: 34). Its reputation encouraged the government in 1991 to obtain from heads of government at the Maastricht summit a declaration encouraging 'greater involvement of national Parliaments in the activities of the European Union' and calling for contacts between national Parliaments and the European Parliament to be stepped up.

In practice, the reputation of the committee probably exceeds its impact. 'Government responses to the reports have been varied: most are complimentary; but some are opaque, either for fear of giving away the government's negotiating position, or because the government disagrees with the report' (Wheeler-Booth, in Griffith and Ryle 1989: 492). This is borne out by the committee's own analysis of the government's responses to its reports in the 1989–90 session (Select Committee on the Committee Work of the House 1992: 49–57). Of twenty-eight reports considered, there are none that appear to have influenced the government to take a stand in the Council of Ministers that it otherwise would not have taken.

This is not to say that reports do not on occasion influence the government's thinking, and help move it in a particular direction; the committee's report on the future of rural society (Select Committee on European Communities 1990) appears to have been particularly important in shaping the government's stance. The committee's reports have also served on occasion to influence the Commission and the European Parliament, most notably on internal practices but also on some substantive policies, such as on nitrates in water. More importantly, in terms of regular impact, the committee plays an important role in contributing to debate within Whitehall and Brussels. It fulfils a significant informing function, a point of relevance to our later discussion.

Indeed, it could be argued that the Lords has gone almost as far as is possible in developing a well-informed mechanism for the scrutiny of EC documents. 'With the possible exception of Denmark, the United Kingdom Parliament has perhaps developed the most systematic scrutiny system' (Bates 1983: 34). EC commissioners have described the reports of the Lords' committee as unique: 'no other Parliament (not even the European Parliament) attempted to undertake comparable analysis of material, let alone assemble and make available such extensive evidence' (Select Committee on the Committee Work of the House 1992: 69). However, the information is often more useful than the recommendations.

Conclusion

Parliament has a marginal role in the different stages of policy making in the European Community. It is constrained constitutionally and, in the case especially of the Commons, politically and procedurally.

Neither House enjoys any formal sanctions that it can employ in relation to the Community. Each can seek to influence the UK Government and also the thinking within the Commission and the European Parliament. However, the UK Government can be, and on occasion is, outvoted in the Council of Ministers. The Commission and the European Parliament are subject to a mass of demands from a wide range of bodies. The directly-elected Parliament is now more significant in the process than before. The Lords has developed a mechanism for extensive scrutiny and comment on community documents, but operates within the same constraints as all national Parliaments.

Ironically, the occasions when Parliament has the potential to have a major impact are on the big issues: those involving treaty amendments. These are subject to parliamentary approval. In 1992, the European Communities (Amendment) Bill, to ratify the Maastricht treaty, was delayed by the government, because of the uncertainty following the rejection of the treaty by Denmark. The delay was also influenced by uncertainty as to whether the Government could ensure a majority for the bill because of opposition from some of its own backbenchers.

Such occasions are, by their nature, exceptional. In terms of having any regular influence on policy within the European Community, the role of the UK Parliament is the same as that of other national Parliaments: sporadic and operating largely at the margins.

Note

1. As such, it has no responsibility for considering legislation made directly by the Commission, either under powers granted by the treaties or through implementing powers delegated in council legislation.
2. The number was reduced by the House at the end of 1992 following a recommendation from the Liaison Committee of the House. It was agreed to review the situation at the end of the 1992/93 session.

Part II
Parliament and Citizen

8

Giving the Seal of Approval

Governments which make some claim to popular legitimacy rely upon the existence of legislatures. Legislatures foster support for the moral right to rule. Through their existence and activities, they confer legitimacy on government and the measures it puts forward.

The function of legitimation, as Packenham (1970) noted, can be both manifest and latent. By manifest, he meant 'putting the legislative stamp of approval on initiatives taken elsewhere' – in other words, the formal and public approval of measures of public policy. This is the core defining function of legislatures (see Chapter 1). Latent legitimation derives from engaging in activities which serve to raise popular and elite acceptance of the right to govern, even though those activities are not geared explicitly to conferring approval and are not always clearly understood by legislators themselves as conferring legitimacy. As Packenham noted of the Brazilian congress, 'Simply by meeting regularly and uninterruptedly, the legislature produced, among the relevant populace and elites, a wider and deeper sense of the government's moral right to rule than would otherwise have obtained'. Given the longevity of Parliament, one might infer that this function of latent legitimation has particular significance in the United Kingdom.

Manifest legitimation

The task of giving approval was the earliest function of the House of Commons: knights and burgesses were summoned to the king's court to give assent to the king's request for additional taxation (see Chapter 2). The task remains fundamental to the institution.

The formal giving of assent takes two forms. One, common to all legislatures, is giving assent – the formal seal of approval – to measures of public policy which are to be binding on citizens. Only the Queen-in-Parliament can pass Acts of Parliament. As we have seen, the assent of the monarch is governed by convention. The various stages through which a measure has to pass in each House before being sent to the monarch for her signature have been discussed already in Chapter 5: the two most important stages in each House are those of second and third reading. The manifest legitimation takes place not during debate but when the House approves the motion that the bill be read a second, or third, time.

The other form of legitimation is that conferred on the government itself. The government rests on the confidence of the House of Commons. By convention, a government which loses the confidence of the House must either resign office or request a dissolution (Norton 1978b). In practice, a government which enjoys an overall party majority in the House is not going to lose the confidence of the House. A minority government may not be so fortunate. The House confers formal legitimacy through passing a vote of confidence. Some authorities contend that votes on important issues may also be deemed 'confidence' issues, and the government itself may declare a particular motion to be one of confidence. The second reading of the European Communities Bill in 1972, for example, was made a vote of confidence by the government.

Most parliamentary systems share this characteristic – indeed, it is normally offered as one of the defining characteristics of such systems. This distinguishes it from presidential systems, where the executive – the President – is elected separately and derives legitimacy from that direct election. Neither the legislature nor the executive in a presidential system depend upon the other for continuance in office.

Formally, then, Parliament is a powerful body because its assent is required for a bill to become law. Within Parliament, the House of Commons is a powerful body because its assent is required to maintain the government in office. But is Parliament as powerful as the formal position suggests?

On the one hand, there is clearly a case for saying no. Many critics argue that the strength of party has meant that the giving of assent is a foregone conclusion. Any government secure in an overall majority in the House of Commons will get its measures passed and will have no fears of losing the confidence of the House. The task of legitimation is thus seen as essentially symbolic – as 'rubber stamping' measures drawn up by government. Members of Parliament are expected to spend time, often late at night, trooping through the division lobbies in order to give the seal of approval to measures which every parliamentarian knows are not going to be defeated. To some MPs, and to many observers, the exercise seems a pointless one.

However, symbolism should not be confused with pointlessness. Even if the actions of its members are predictable, Parliament remains a vital body for compelling popular compliance with measures of public policy. Why do people obey the law? One reason is practical and immediate: the fear that one may be arrested, imprisoned and, for some, suffer public shame. Another reason is moral and abstract: the very fact that it is 'the law'. For some, compliance is essentially an unthinking exercise, the product of being socialized into accepting the law of the land. For those who reflect on it, the justification is usually that some binding measures of public policy are necessary for public safety and for regulating relations between citizens.

What gives 'law' its legitimacy? The approval of the Queen-in-Parliament. The authority of the Queen and the House of Lords is essentially traditional, resting on established historical practice. The authority of the House of Commons is rational, deriving from the fact that it is the elected chamber and hence in a position to confer approval on behalf of the citizenry. As we have seen, within the triumvirate of the Queen-in-Parliament, the elected chamber is now the pre-eminent body.

It is the claim of the Commons to be a representative assembly that, above all, bolsters the popular legitimacy of Parliament. Pitkin (1967) identified four separate usages of the term 'representation': acting on behalf of some individual or group; being freely elected; replicating the typical characteristics of a group or class; and acting as a symbol ('standing for' something). The Commons can claim to be a representative assembly under the first two usages of the term (Norton 1991d: 293–94) and the Queen-in-Parliament under the fourth, symbolising the unity of the estates of the realm. Citizens abide by measures that have been approved by the body that they themselves have chosen to act on their behalf.

The power of Parliament derives from the fact that it is seen as the authoritative – the legitimate – body for conferring legitimacy on measures of public policy. Not all measures passed by Parliament are popular measures, but they are nonetheless obeyed. The community charge, or poll tax, introduced in England and Wales in 1990 (and in Scotland in 1989) proved extraordinarily unpopular. In many respects, it tested the legitimacy of Parliament, with widespread demonstrations and some riots; London witnessed its worst riot in recent decades. A substantial minority refused to pay the tax. The reaction to the tax was a contributory cause of Margaret Thatcher losing the leadership of the Conservative Party (Norton 1992c). Yet reaction to the tax also demonstrated the deep attachment to the principle of Parliament as the authoritative law-giver. The Labour Party refused to countenance resistance to the tax through non-payment. It did so not because it approved the tax – it had strenuously opposed it in Parliament – but because it constituted the law of the land. Parliament had approved the tax – it was embodied in law as the Local Government Finance Act – and as such it must be paid.

The example of the poll tax reveals, then, the strengths but also the limits of the legitimacy of Parliament. The willingness of many citizens to abide by the law was stretched to the limit; in some cases, it disappeared. Citizen compliance cannot be taken for granted. Parliament has to work to maintain its legitimacy. What has been remarkable has been the extent to which it has managed to do so.

The power of Parliament in this context has been recognised more by radical than by pluralist writers. Pluralists focus on issues of dispute and how they are resolved. Elitists focus more on those who are in a position to set the agenda of political debate than on the issues that reach the agenda. More radical writers have drawn attention to the structures within which agenda-setting and issue-resolving take place. (These three approaches correspond to the three faces of power identified by Lukes (1974).) Parliament is recognised as a powerful body because it can confer legitimacy. Within Parliament, MPs may exert little influence but that fact is not central to recognizing Parliament's real power in society. As Ralph Miliband (1984: 20) has noted, the elected nature of the House of Commons now renders illegitimate any radical alternative, 'for it

suggests that what is required above all else to bring about fundamental change is a majority in the House of Commons'.

  Reinforcing the power of Parliament is the doctrine of parliamentary sovereignty. The doctrine was confirmed by the Glorious
Revolution of 1688 and asserts that Acts of Parliament can be
changed or set aside by no body other than Parliament itself (see
Norton 1989). In other words, the courts cannot strike down acts as
being contrary to the provisions of the British constitution. Hence
the outputs of Parliament are binding, thus establishing control of
Parliament as the sole focus for those wishing to achieve change in
society. Those refusing to recognise the legitimacy of this route for
achieving change are very much at the margins: the IRA in Northern Ireland, for instance, though even it has a political wing, Sinn
Fein, which has contested parliamentary seats.

Latent legitimation

If Parliament engaged solely in manifest approval of measures,
meeting occasionally to approve whatever was laid before it, then
– despite the fact of popular election of the House of Commons –
it would be in danger of jeopardising popular legitimacy, both for
itself and the government. What bolsters popular and elite acceptance of its legitimacy as an assent-giving body and of the
government are the activities it engages in which engender latent
legitimation.

  Packenham, as we have seen, has called attention to the regular
and uninterrupted meeting of the legislature as a significant con-
tributor to popular acceptance of the government's moral right to
rule. Parliament has the advantage in this context both of its
longevity – having met on a fairly regular basis for several centuries – and of continuing to meet each year for longer than virtually any other legislature. Though the number of days the House
of Commons sits each year is not exceptional, it is – as was noted in
Chapter 2 – a world leader in the total number of hours that it
spends in session.

  The importance of Parliament in this context is best demonstrated by the experience of when it is not sitting. If the government takes an important decision during the summer recess, or if
some crisis occurs, there are frequently calls for Parliament to be

recalled. During the 1992 summer recess, for example, various Labour MPs asked for Parliament to be recalled to discuss Britain's policy towards the conflict in the former Yugoslavia. When there was a sterling crisis in September, the Labour Party demanded – successfully – that it be recalled to discuss the situation. (Parliament was recalled for two days, discussing the economic crisis on the first, and foreign policy on the second.) Though the outcome of any parliamentary deliberation is usually predictable, it is the meeting and the airing of views that is important. For government to take any fundamental decision without some parliamentary debate, even when no parliamentary sanction is formally required, is to convey the impression of acting improperly.

The legitimacy of government and of Parliament itself also derives from the substantive activities that occur on and off the floor of the two Houses. Previous chapters, especially Chapter 6, have considered the extent to which Parliament seeks to hold government accountable for its actions. By questioning, by probing – not least now through committee – the actions of ministers, and by doing so in public, Parliament may be seen to be acting on behalf of the citizenry.

Likewise with what Packenham identified as the 'safety valve' role fulfilled by legislators. Various of their activities, he noted, had no effect on the allocation of values but nonetheless had consequences for the political system 'in so far as they reduced tension, provided reassurance, and generally enhanced satisfaction with or acquiescence in the policies and programmes of the ruling government'. The legislature can thus prove an important mechanism for letting off steam. In the context of Parliament, the safety valves are various and are covered in the succeeding chapters. Chapter 9, in particular, considers the importance of Parliament for acting as an outlet for the views of constituents. However, all the consequences identified in the remaining chapters contribute to the latent legitimation of Parliament and hence of government.

By meeting regularly, by debating, by requiring ministers to justify their actions, by allowing Members to express conflicting views, by allowing Members to make representations to ministers on behalf of constituents and different groups in society and by operating usually in public session – observable to the visitor and, now, to the television cameras – Parliament provides an outlet for tensions, grievances and demands which otherwise might find no outlet and by so doing – and by being seen to be so doing – enhances its own legitimacy in the eyes of the citizenry and also of the body drawn from it: the government. By engaging in such activity, it is not making policy. It is, though, serving to bolster mass support for the political system of which it is a core institution.

Problems

The task of legitimation is fundamental to Parliament's very existence. It has profound implications for the health of the political system. However, fulfilling the task is far from problem free.

Influencing government

Though most of the functions of Parliament are analytically separable, they are not empirically separable. There is a tremendous overlap. The basic relationship between government and Parliament discussed in the first section cannot be divorced empirically from the relationship under discussion here between Parliament and citizen. If Parliament was seen to be going solely through the motions in debating measures and rubber stamping bills without exerting any influence on government, then popular support for the legitimacy of Parliament as an assent-giving body would likely be dented.

Legitimacy is enhanced if members of Parliament are seen to be engaging in activity that has *some* effect. The stranglehold of party could thus potentially serve to strangle the life out of the political system. Conversely, the absence of party would almost certainly result in incoherence in decision making and offer an even greater threat to the health of the political system. The experience of the *vs. U.S.* United States, where weak parties allied with divided government has facilitated a collapse in trust in government (see Norton 1990a: 401), is instructive. There has been no comparable collapse in the UK. For Parliament, therefore, maintaining popular legitimacy entails having some effect independent of party but without jeopardising the coherence offered by the party system. Electors vote for a party to be in government, and expect it to be able to govern, yet at the same time look to MPs to be more than sheep in the division lobbies.

The balance is a difficult one to maintain. There are grounds for suggesting that it is somewhat better maintained now than before. For one thing, the behavioural changes identified in Chapter 2 have resulted in MPs – and peers – having somewhat greater effect on policy, especially the detail of policy, than in preceding decades. The structural changes, especially the creation of departmental select committees, have also rendered the institution more relevant to many groups in society. We shall explore the consequences in more detail in subsequent chapters. The effects, though, are limited. As we have seen, the outcome of votes in the Commons are usually predictable. Select committees have no sanctions.

Furthermore, the perception of Parliament as a body capable of taking any action independent of government wishes was significantly reduced in the 1980s, especially in the Parliaments of 1983–87 and 1987–92, when the government enjoyed three-figure majorities in the House of Commons. Even though the reality did not match the perception, it was the perception that was important in determining popular attitudes toward the institution. The experience of the poll tax, the failure of MPs to reflect popular opinion by rejecting it or achieving significant amendments to it, bolstered the perception of an institution unwilling or unable to stand up to a determined Prime Minister.

Legitimacy is also affected by three other aspects of Parliament. As we have seen, the pre-eminence of the House of Commons derives from the fact that it is the elected chamber. That underpins its legitimacy as the principal assent-giving body. However, the *method* by which it is elected can affect perceptions of its legitimacy. So too can *who* is elected and the political configuration of the *areas* from which they are drawn.

Method of election

There are 651 Members of Parliament. Each is elected to represent a single constituency. The method of election is popularly termed that of first-past-the-post, the candidate receiving the largest single number of votes being declared elected. No absolute majority is necessary. Single-member constituencies and the first-past-the-post method of election have been the norm since the 1880s, though some two-member constituencies survived until 1950, as did a system of proportional representation in university seats (see Norton 1982a: 228).

The nineteenth century, as we have seen, witnessed pressure for an enlargement of the franchise and for a more equitable drawing of constituency boundaries. By the end of the century, there was a mass male franchise. The second and third decades of the twentieth century saw the franchise enlarged to encompass women. With the abolition of the university seats in 1950 (seats that had allowed graduates to vote for their university MP as well as for their constituency MP), the principle of 'one person, one vote' was achieved. The extension of the franchise bolstered the legitimacy of the House of Commons as the body for acting on behalf of the citizenry and established its primacy within the triumvirate of the Queen-in-Parliament (see Chapter 2).

However, a number of critics have argued that the representativeness of the institution – under Pitkin's second definition – is undermined by the fact that 'one person, one vote' is not the same as saying that each vote is equal. Such critics argue for 'one person, one vote, one value'. The first-past-the-post system, it is pointed out, can produce 'wasted' votes (votes cast for losing candidates have no effect) and, given that it is difficult to ensure constituency electorates of precisely equal size, a vote in a constituency with a small electorate will count for more than one cast in a large constituency. Furthermore, the system is non-proportional, in that it can – and usually does – result in a party winning an absolute majority of seats on the basis of less than fifty per cent of the votes cast. In the 1992 general election, for example, the Conservative government was returned to office with 336 seats – almost 52 per cent of the total – with just under 42 per cent of the votes cast nationally. In 1983, the disparity had been even greater, the Government achieving 61 per cent of the seats on just over 42 per cent of the votes cast.

Critics of this situation argue the case for a new electoral system, claiming that a more proportional system of election – the percentage of seats equalling the percentage of votes cast – would be a fairer system and hence more legitimate, serving to bolster support for the political system (Norton 1982a: 231–2). They also claim that a consequence would be greater continuity in public policy and hence a more stable system (see especially Finer 1975). Supporters of the existing arrangements counter that a system of proportional representation would likely result in no overall majority for any one party, necessitating either coalition or minority government and thus jeopardising the coherence of the existing system. Electors, it is argued, know what they are voting for in a general election. Under a system of proportional representation, the fear is one of post-election bargaining between parties, resulting in a coalition which has not been endorsed by electors at the polls (see Norton 1992d). That, it is argued, would constitute a greater threat to the legitimacy of the political system than any flaws in the existing arrangements.

The legitimacy of the existing system is thus contested. In this, there is nothing particularly startling. The electoral system has frequently been the subject of political dispute (Norton 1982a: 227). Nor is the United Kingdom exceptional in this regard. When a political system is under pressure, there are often demands for a change in the electoral system. Recent years have seen pressure for change in Italy and Israel, both with list systems of election, and more recently in Ireland, where the principal opposition party (Fine Gael) has argued for the existing single transferable vote (STV) system to be replaced by the alternative vote (AV), a non- proportional system. The essential point, though, for our purposes is that the legitimacy of the existing system in the UK does not go unchallenged and the critical voices are louder now than in post-war decades.

As previously noted, it is election that gives the Commons primacy over the Upper House. The unelected nature of the House of Lords renders it both subordinate and a continuing target for reform. There is pressure for a wholly or partly elected second chamber or for a more functional chamber (see Norton 1982a: 116–33). Those advocating change contend that Parliament would enjoy greater popular legitimacy if both Houses were elected. Supporters of the existing system argue that two elected Houses would offer the potential for conflict, with the possibility of stalemate reducing, rather than increasing, popular confidence in the institution.

The members

We know how many MPs are elected and we have considered already some of the things they do. However, MPs are not some disembodied and abstract entities. Who is elected to the House of Commons has important consequences, not only for what they do and how they do it, but also for how the House is seen by different groups in society.

Both Houses of Parliament are predominantly white, male and middle class preserves. There is no formal requirement that either House be socially typical (Pitkin's third definition of representation) and, indeed, it would be near-impossible to achieve such typicality. The job of a Member of Parliament is essentially a middle class one. Some members on the Labour side of the House, especially in pre-war years, were drawn from manual backgrounds and a proportion on the Conservative side drawn from upper-class backgrounds. In post-war years the House has become more middle class (see Chapter 2). The House of Lords is aristocratic in social terms and overwhelmingly middle and upper class in economic terms. In terms of occupational background, it is notably professional, with a preponderance of lawyers, former civil servants, and teachers of one form or another (Baldwin 1985a: 105).

Though an MP of whatever background may claim to speak for different interests – not least those of sixty or seventy thousand constituents who have only geographic proximity in common – there are various groups in society who may feel alienated if at least one of their number does not serve in Parliament. Most such groups are minorities. The exception is women. They form a majority of the population but less than ten per cent of Members of Parliament are female. Among the minorities, ethnic groups have been prone to feel alienated by the absence, for most of the century, of any of their number in Parliament.

If groups feel excluded, perceiving Parliament as essentially the *Threat to legitimacy* preserve, and hence the voice, of the dominant white middle class, then there is the real danger of the institution not being accepted as a legitimate – a 'representative' – body for the consideration of the interests of those outside that dominant grouping. The election of MPs from different groups in society may thus have more than symbolic consequences, serving to buttress the legitimacy of Parliament in the eyes of previously disaffected groups.

Again, as with influencing government, there are some grounds for suggesting that the situation has improved in recent years, though – again, as with influencing government – the changes are not great. They are, though, far from insignificant.

In the 1970s and 1980s, it was the unelected House that provided a platform for members drawn from non-white backgrounds.

In 1975, Dr David Pitt, a West Indian, was elevated to the peerage. Two years later he was joined by Pratap Chitnis, an Indian. They have since been joined by other non-white members. The House also boasted more female members – both in absolute terms and expressed as a proportion of the membership – than the Commons, with a growing number of life peeresses. In 1970, there were forty-two peeresses. Twenty years later, there were eighty, constituting just under seven per cent of the membership. Only in 1992 did the elected House pass the unelected House in the proportion of its membership drawn from blacks and women. In the general election of 1992, the proportion of women and non-white MPs reached an all-time high.

The first woman elected to the House of Commons was Baroness Markiewicz in 1918. However, she was a Sinn Fein candidate and refused to take her seat. Nancy (Lady) Astor became the first woman to sit in the House after she was elected as Conservative MP for Plymouth in 1919 (in succession to her husband, who had been raised to the peerage); she sat until 1945. The number of women MPs increased only gradually. In the 1983 general election, only twenty-three were elected. In 1987, the number increased to an all-time high with the return of forty-one, just over six per cent of the total. In 1992, the figure increased to sixty, just over nine per cent of MPs. Though a historical high, and proportionally greater than the number of women in the Upper House, it was still well under the figure sought by the 300 Group, an organisation that campaigns for the return of at least 300 women to the House.

The first non-white MP was elected in 1892: Dadabhai Naoroji, an Indian, was returned as Liberal member for Finsbury Central with a majority of five. (As some electors found it difficult to pronounce his name, he was dubbed 'Mr Narrow Majority'. See Gifford 1992: 33.) Mancherjee Bhownagree became the second Indian to sit in Parliament when he was elected as Conservative MP for Bethnal Green in 1895; he was knighted two years later. A third – Shapurji Saklatvala – was elected as member for Battersea North in 1922, sitting initially as a Labour member; after the 1924 election, he sat as a Communist (Gifford 1992: 40). He lost his seat in 1929.

There was then a gap of fifty-eight years before the return of another non-white member. In 1987, four black MPs were elected (Diane Abbott, Paul Boateng, Bernie Grant, and Keith Vaz), all representing Labour. Though the number was small – less than one per cent of the House – it constituted the largest number of black MPs ever to sit in the House of Commons. They were briefly joined by a fifth from 1991 to 1992 (a by-election victor who lost his seat in the 1992 election) and then by two more in 1992, one of whom was a Conservative, Nirj Deva. Again, the figure is small but a historical high.

Other members from different groups have also been returned. The House has had MPs with various disabilities, including a wheelchair-bound member (the Lords has several such members), a deaf member and more than one blind member. Both Houses have members drawn from a variety of religions. Though several MPs are known to have been gay, the current Labour member for Islington South and Finsbury (Dr Chris Smith) constitutes the only openly gay MP.

Though such members will normally seek to avoid being single-issue members – not confining themselves to women's issues, black issues and so on – their presence provides the basis for some reson-ance with members of society with similar characteristics. By being seen to be in Parliament, and in a position to serve some safety valve function, they can serve to enhance the legitimacy of Parliament among groups that otherwise may feel alienated from it.

That resonance may also be enhanced as such members achieve leadership positions within Parliament. Margaret Thatcher be-came the leader of the Conservative Party in 1975 and Britain's first female Prime Minister in 1979. Betty Boothroyd became the first woman Speaker in 1992 and Margaret Beckett was elected deputy leader of the Labour Party in the same year. Several peeresses have held leadership positions in the Upper House, including that of government Chief Whip (Baroness Llewellyn-Davies, from 1974 to 1979). David Blunkett (who is blind), Paul Boateng and Chris Smith have all been appointed as opposition spokesmen; in 1992, both David Blunkett and Chris Smith were elected to Labour's Shadow Cabinet.

Regional balance

Legislatures have the potential to act as agents of integration, not just of different and often diverse groups in society but also of the different regions that make up the state. By ensuring equitable or even generous representation for different regions, such regions may feel that they have an adequate input in national deliberations. In federal countries, such as Germany and the United States, this is usually achieved by giving the different regions or states representation in the upper chamber.

In the unitary state of the United Kingdom, there is no equivalent. Instead, Scotland and Wales, lacking elected assemblies of their own, have been given more seats in the House of Commons than their populations would strictly justify. Northern Ireland, which had its own elected Parliament at Stormont from 1922 to 1972, had – until the 1979 election – fewer seats than its population would justify. In 1978, the House of Commons (Redistribution of Seats) Act was passed, increasing the number of seats in the province from twelve to 'not greater than eighteen and not less than sixteen'. (Seventeen were created.) The change was made in recognition of the fact that the province had lost its devolved assembly, with decisions being taken centrally.

On the face of it, England is treated less equitably than the other components that form the United Kingdom. However, problems have arisen as a result of the political distribution of support in the other parts of the UK. Migration has tended to result in more geographically concentrated support (see Norton 1990a: 110–12). At general elections, Conservatives tend to win a majority of seats in England. Given the population of England, that – despite the inequity in terms of the electoral quota – has proved sufficient in most recent elections to produce an overall Conservative majority in the House of Commons. Since 1959, Labour support in Scotland has increased to a point where it now wins an absolute majority of seats. In 1987, for example, it won fifty of the seventy-two Scottish seats. The Conservatives won ten. Likewise in Wales, where Labour won twenty-four of the thirty-eight seats. In 1992, the Conservatives improved their position marginally in Scotland – wining eleven seats to Labour's forty-nine – but did less well in Wales, where the number of Labour seats increased to twenty-seven. In Northern Ireland, none of the seventeen MPs represents either of the two mainstream British parties. Until 1972, the Ulster Unionists were allied with the Conservative party, but broke away in protest at the imposition of direct rule in the province.

The contemporary position is that there is a Conservative Government in the UK but with Labour being the dominant party in

Scotland and Wales. This is seen as generating a crisis of legitimacy for Parliament in respect of those two countries. Does Parliament have the moral right to legislate for countries which do not want to be governed by a Conservative administration? Critics of the existing arrangements argue that the best or only way to bolster legitimacy is to devolve power to elected assemblies in Scotland and Wales. An attempt to achieve this in the 1970s floundered. Critics argue that the need for such a change is now greater than before, contending that – without such a change – pressure for Scottish independence (the goal of the Scottish National Party) will grow even further. Supporters of the existing system retort that any devolution would necessitate a major reduction in the number of Scottish and Welsh seats in the House of Commons, thus reducing Scottish and Welsh influence on UK issues. It is also argued that, under the present arrangements, Parliament is a vehicle through which a redistribution of national resources is achieved, to the benefit of Scotland and Wales (as well as Northern Ireland), with public spending per capita being greater there than in England.

The slight, and unexpected, improvement in the Conservative performance in Scotland in the 1992 election did not stem the pressure for change in the country. There was some indication during the election campaign that the government recognised that some political initiative may be necessary to address the problem. In the new Parliament, the Select Committee on Scottish Affairs was resuscitated, though critics argued that much more was needed if the legitimacy of Parliament was to be maintained.

In Northern Ireland, there was some attempt to achieve a greater degree of integration with the mainland with the formation of Conservative Party constituency associations; Conservative candidates contested, albeit unsuccessfully, eleven of the seats in the province in the 1992 election. Following the 1992 election, a campaign was also begun in the Labour Party – led by Labour MPs Kate Hoey and Nick Raynsford – to establish a Labour presence in the province.

Conclusion

As the body accepted by both mass and elites for legitimating measures of public policy, Parliament is a powerful body. It stands at the heart of the political process. For competing ideological forces, keen to achieve change in – or preserve – society, the goal is to achieve a majority in the House of Commons.

The popular legitimacy of Parliament as the body for giving authoritative assent is affected by factors of structure and composition as well as by the actions of its members. There are problems associated with how members are chosen, with the backgrounds from which they are drawn and with the regional distribution of political support. The last of these problems appears to be becoming more pronounced, the first two marginally less so.

So far, these problems do not appear to have been sufficient to undermine popular confidence in Parliament. A MORI poll for the Rowntree Trust in 1991 found that almost sixty per cent of respondents felt that Parliament was doing a good job, a higher proportion for example than favoured a change in the electoral system (MORI, British Public Opinion, May 1991). A Gallup poll in 1991 found that less than ten per cent of respondents had no trust at all in Parliament, compared with eighteen per cent giving a similar response in 1989 (Gallup Political Index, 368, April 1991). In the 1991 poll, forty-seven per cent said they had a great deal or quite a lot of trust in Parliament; the proportion in 1989 had been thirty-eight per cent. What, then, may help explain this maintenance and, if anything, increase in confidence in Parliament? The answer, as we have seen, is not to be found in the structural, compositional and political problems we have identified. The most plausible explanation would appear to lie in the activities of Members of Parliament. It is the nature of, and increase in, these activities – at the heart of the link between Parliament and citizen – that forms the focus of subsequent chapters.

9

The Voice of the Constituents

There are 651 constituencies in the United Kingdom. Each elects one member to serve in the House of Commons. The relationship of members and constituents is fundamental to the British political system. Over the years, demands made of members by constituents have increased dramatically and members have sought to meet those demands in various ways. The ways in which they have responded have significant implications both for the workings and the popular support of Parliament.

Growth of constituency demands

The phenomenon of constituents making demands of Members of Parliament is not a recent one. In the nineteenth century and before, members were the target especially of job hunters, those seeking the intervention of the MP to achieve some particular appointment (Rush 1979: 119). At the beginning of this century, it was not unknown for members to raise personal constituency cases with ministers (see Chester and Bowring 1962: 104–5). Requests for action by constituents with problems – war disabilities, unemployment and tax problems, for example – increased as the century progressed. This was reflected in a notable increase in the number of letters that flowed between MPs and ministers. In 1938, for example, the Financial Secretary to the Treasury wrote 610 letters to members. In 1954, the number was 3,349 (Couzens 1956). There

147

was also a marked increase in the number concerning the Post Office (Phillips 1949).

However, pursuing cases with departments and other public bodies on behalf of constituents was not extensive. Peter Richards (1959) estimated that a typical MP received between twelve and twenty letters a week; in other words, about two or three a day. Nor was dealing with such correspondence, limited in volume though it was, something that members necessarily wanted to do. 'One of the chief torments of a member's life', wrote one Labour MP who sat in the 1920s, 'is the answering of letters, most of which should not have been written' (quoted in Rush 1979: 119). This attitude was still to be found among MPs in the 1940s and 1950s. One MP in the 1990s recalled his father-in-law, an MP who sat from 1950 to 1961, telling him that members should not reply to letters from constituents: 'it only encourages them', he said, 'and it's not fair on those who don't write'. The attitude lingered even beyond that. 'In 1970 there were still several of the old school around who firmly believed that any letter unanswered for six weeks answered itself' (Cormack 1992: 4).

The detached relationship between members and their constituents was reflected in the number of MPs who did not live in or near their constituencies. There is no residency requirement in the UK. (A statute of 1413 did require members to be resident in the county or borough they represented, but this was largely ignored and the statute was repealed in 1774. See Rush 1979: 88.) In the 1940s and 1950s, the overwhelming majority of members had homes some distance from their constituencies. In the 1959–64 Parliament, for example, less than one-third of members listed addresses that were within their constituencies (Norton and Wood 1993). One Conservative MP who sat for a Lancashire seat had addresses in London, Yorkshire and Iraq. Another had an address in Norway and two Labour MPs (the Noel-Baker brothers) lived in London and Greece.

It was not uncommon for some MPs to visit their constituencies on an extremely infrequent basis. 'A Labour newcomer in 1945 told of his visit to the constituency after the election. A top-hatted station master met him to ask whether he would be following the previous member in paying his annual visit at that time of year' (Mitchell 1982: 183). As late as the 1960s, one senior Conservative member is reputed to have confined his visits to his London constituency to his party's annual dinner. Others were more frequent, but still irregular, visitors to the constituencies which they served in Parliament.

The 1950s and, more especially, the decade of the 1960s witnessed a move towards a more constituency-active member. Since the 1950s, there has been a clear and growing trend towards greater demands made of members by constituents and of members adopting, and more willingly adopting, a 'welfare officer' role in pursuing cases on behalf of constituents.

Since the 1960s, the number of letters written by constituents to their MPs has increased several times over. By 1970, the typical member received between twenty-five and seventy-four letters a week (Barker and Rush 1970). In 1972–73, Tony Benn, the Labour MP for Bristol South-East, received an average of forty-one letters a week from or about constituents (Morrell 1977). A survey of members by the Letter Writing Bureau in 1986 found that the figure for the average member had increased to between twenty and fifty letters *a day*, with more than half coming from constituents (Griffith and Ryle 1989: 72). Members sitting for seats in the South-West tended to receive the largest postbag, members returned for seats in Northern Ireland receiving the smallest. Housing, health and social security benefits tended to be the subjects about which constituents most often contacted members (Marsh 1985: 72; Griffith and Ryle 1989: 72).

A typical example of the scale of the correspondence now faced by members is that of a Conservative MP sitting for an extremely safe Midlands seat. Following the 1992 summer recess, he recorded returning to his office to find three large cardboard boxes of letters – 'over 500 in all' (Cormack 1992: 5).

Members have responded to these demands in a number of complementary ways. At Westminster, the most popular form of action has been to write to the appropriate minister (Gregory and Alexander 1973; Marsh 1985: 84). The member will normally pass on a constituent's letter, accompanied by a printed card requesting a response. Letters from MPs have priority within a department and must be replied to by a minister. (Letters from members of the public are normally answered by civil servants.) Once the minister's reply is received, the MP normally sends a copy to the constituent. If the member or the constituent is not satisfied with the reply, the member may pursue the matter through further correspondence, a

meeting with the minister, tabling a parliamentary question, refer-
ring the matter to the Parliamentary Commissioner (the Ombudsman) or seeking a half-hour adjournment debate at the end of a
day's sitting.

The volume of member-to-minister correspondence grew enormously in the 1970s (Norton 1982b) and even more so in the 1980s,
with a fifty per cent increase in the number of letters written (Norton and Wood 1993: Chapter 3). Edwina Currie recalled her experience as a junior minister in the Department of Health and Social
Security:

> If you wanted a reply signed by me, you had to write to your own
> MP. Lots did. In a typical week, when Parliament was sitting, when
> I'd made a speech, when the Department of Health was in the news,
> I would expect to sign over 300 such letters. . . . In a normal year I
> must have signed 10,000.
>
> (Currie 1989: 231–2)

A survey in 1990 found that ministers answered 250,000 letters a
year, mostly from MPs (Elms and Terry 1990).

MPs now spend about three hours a day working on constituency correspondence. They have also responded to the increased
demands of constituents by spending more time in their constituencies. In the 1950s and 1960s, there was a growth in the number of
'surgeries', publicly-advertised meetings at which constituents
could come along to discuss a problem privately with the MP. The
proportion of members holding such surgeries increased in the
1960s from somewhat over sixty per cent to over ninety per cent
(Dowse 1963; Barker and Rush 1970). During the 1970s and 1980s,
members also began spending more time in the constituencies,
attending events and just being seen. A survey in the mid-1980s
found that most members spent at least eight days a month in the
constituency when the House was sitting; one in five claimed a
figure of thirteen or more days. Furthermore, the number living in
their constituencies has shown a marked increase. Of MPs returned in the 1987 general election, most of those first elected at
earlier elections did not give an address in the constituency; a
majority of those newly returned in that election did give such an
address (Norton and Wood 1993).

Time spent in the constituency is also variously supplemented
by other forms of contact with constituents. Members are keen to
exploit opportunities afforded by local media, newer members in

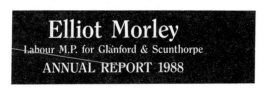

Elliot Morley
Labour M.P. for Glanford & Scunthorpe
ANNUAL REPORT 1988

Dear Constituent,

I will shortly be completing my first full year as your member of parliament for this constituency. As a strong believer in local accountability it is my intention to send every elector an annual report of some of my activities over the year. This is the first of that series.

I promised when I was elected that I would work tirelessly for the benefit of this constituency, for all its residents whatever their personal political views, not in a parochial and divisive way, but by recognising and using all the various agencies of government; local, regional and national and encouraging co-operation and collective support. If you have any questions on this report please get in touch. Can I also take this opportunity to wish you and your family a Merry Christmas and a Happy New Year.

PARLIAMENTARY WORK

For a new MP I have been very fortunate in the number of times I have spoken in the House of Commons. I have taken part in debates on: **the steel industry, alternative energy, education, housing, social security, health, the environment, poll tax, the economy, agriculture, the ozone layer, public transport, the disabled.** I served on many committees including the Education Reform Bill Standing Committee, committees on pesticide levels in food, farm forestry, the Norfolk Broads Bill. On these committees I was successful in getting the government to accept a number of amendments. I managed to strengthen the provision for children with special educational needs in the Education Act and amend some of the proposals for testing in the National Curriculum. I moved a Private Members' Bill on Credit and Debt control. Although the government defeated it, they subsequently adopted, as policy, parts from it; including written warnings on credit agreements when someone's house may be at risk, and a duty for credit companies to give a better explanation of what the annual percentage rate (APR) means in cash terms. I was appointed to the Parliamentary Select Committee on Agriculture and elected vice-chairman of the PLP Education Committee. I received delegations in London from local people on; nurses pay, the education bill, mental health matters, agriculture and the pig industry. School and college parties as well as individuals were arranged tours of the House of Commons by me.

CONSTITUENCY ORGANISATION

Since becoming M.P. I have devoted considerable time to setting up an efficient organisation to assist local people with advice and support. I have opened an office in Scunthorpe in the Kinsley Labour Club, Cole Street. This is in addition to the office attached to my home in Winterton. To enable me to reach as wide an area as possible a mobile office/surgery is now in use. Many of you have seen this at shows and functions in the towns and villages. I have appointed two efficient and enthusiastic staff members. Both are local people. They are based in my Scunthorpe office which is open Monday to Friday 9am to 5pm. This service located in the constituency, rather than remotely at Westminster, is something that has never existed here before.

Setting up the constituency office was a multi-thousand pound investment in the local economy. All the equipment has been and will continue to be bought from local firms. Because of the success of this office it has become a little cramped for its role. For that reason I am hoping to move into newer, larger accommodation over the course of the next year.

FOR SURGERY APPOINTMENTS AND ASSISTANCE TEL: SCUNTHORPE 842000

Surgeries are held at the Citizen's Advice Bureau, Oswald Road, Scunthorpe on alternate Saturdays. People in the North Glanford villages can be seen at the Winterton Office by appointment. Home visits can be arranged for the elderly and the disabled.

Elliot Morley's personal numbers   Home: Scunthorpe 734510
London Office: 01-219-3569

Figure 9.1 A constituency newsletter

particular recognising the value of relatively recent innovations such as local radio and 'freesheets' (free newspapers). A number of members also distribute regular newsletters to constituents, detailing their activities and their availability. Figure 9.1 shows one such newsletter.

The typical Member of Parliament in the 1990s, and especially the newly-returned Member of Parliament, is a constituency-active member with a home in the constituency, with a far greater proportion of time given over each week to correspondence and constituency engagements than was ever the case with his or her predecessor. For many MPs, constituency work is becoming the predominant part of their parliamentary work (see Norton and Wood 1993). Not all members are typical. Some, because of the nature of their constituencies and their own predispositions and experience, resemble the MP of the 1950s, devoting little time and attention to their constituencies. However, where they were once the norm, they are now the exception.

Explanations of change

There is no single explanation for the emergence of the constituency-active MP. The change would most plausibly appear to be the consequence of several, complementary developments.

Constituents' demands

The increased demands made of members by constituents would appear to be the consequence of the growth in the size of the electorate and, more especially, in the public sector. The number of electors has grown enormously over the course of the century. In the 1992 general election, the electorate was more than six times that of the electorate in the general election of 1900 (43.1 million to 6.7 million). The century has also witnessed a massive growth in the size of the public sector, with greater provision of public benefits and services.

The latter half of the 1940s saw the establishment of the Welfare State. Government has acquired an extensive role both in the provision of public services and also in economic management. Its actions touch more directly than before the lives of individual citizens. There is thus a far greater likelihood than in pre-war years of citizens encountering some problem with public bodies. When such a problem is encountered – be it with a body for which central government has responsibility or even one for which it has no direct responsibility – the preferred action by a constituent is to write to the local MP (see Marsh 1985; Norton 1990d: 25). The greater the public provision, the greater the potential for citizens to get in touch with their MPs.

There has also been a growth in educational provision and a citizenry characterised by greater awareness of political issues and opportunities (what has been termed, rather inelegantly, cognitive mobilization; see Inglehart 1977; Dalton 1988). Citizens are more likely to be aware of opportunities for expressing their demands and indeed, as we shall see in Chapter 10, for getting organized to pursue shared concerns. They are thus more aware of the option of contacting the MP to pursue some action, and in a better position than their predecessors to exploit that option.

These developments in combination would appear to explain the increase in constituents' demands and they may have been reinforced by greater activity encouraging greater demands. As MPs have been seen to be pursuing constituents' demands, so other constituents with grievances have turned to the MP to ask for help as well. 'The longer you go on', as one long-serving MP put it, 'the more constituents know you are approachable' (Sir Bernard Braine MP to author, 1990).

MPs' responsiveness

There also appear to be a number of independent variables that explain why MPs have responded to constituents' demands in the way that they have. Though some members have not proved over-ly keen to assume the 'welfare officer' role on behalf of those who elected them, most have done so and with varying degrees of enthusiasm. The explanation for the relatively high degree of re-sponsiveness would appear to lie in changes in electoral behaviour and in the ambitions of members themselves.

The change in electoral behaviour has been towards greater volatility in voting intentions. Since the 1960s, the link between class and voting has weakened (Franklin 1985). Parties have not been able to rely on the support they previously enjoyed. This has been reflected in rapid shifts in voting intentions, manifested in by-election results and opinion polls. What are deemed very safe seats are now frequently lost by the incumbent party in by-elections. The Conservative Party, when in office, has been prone to lose seats to the Liberals and their successor party; in 1990, it lost the 'safe' seat of Mid Staffordshire to Labour, giving Labour its best by-election performance since the 1930s. Following one particularly bad by-election result for the Conservatives in the 1980s, the BBC commentator, Peter Snow, pointed out that if the result was repeated at a general election, there would only be one Conservative seat in the country; then turning to the Cabinet minister present to discuss the result he observed, 'and it wouldn't be yours'.

Though the Conservative Party was returned to office for a fourth consecutive time in 1992, that outcome was by no means apparent a few weeks, or even a few days, before the result. It was certainly not obvious two years before. In the spring of 1990, the Party trailed Labour by more than twenty points in the opinion polls. Such volatility in voting intentions had an effect on the Conservative Party, contributing towards Margaret Thatcher's loss of the party leadership later that year (see Norton 1992c). It also contributed towards members' perceptions of their own vulnerability.

Though the number of safe seats is actually increasing – the product of the changing geographical distribution of political support (see Chapter 8) – the perception of members themselves is of less rather than greater security. Consequently, to bolster their position in the constituency, they are keen to be seen to be working on behalf of constituents. The reputation of being a good constituency member may help to temper a swing to the other party. Some constituency-active members have held on to marginal seats against the national tide. One analysis of the results in the 1987 general election found that there appeared to be some electoral reward for incumbency. The most notable finding was that first-term incumbents – those MPs first elected in 1983 – achieved better results than all other candidates (Norton and Wood 1990; Wood and Norton 1992). The most plausible explanation for this finding was that new MPs were far more constituency active than longer-serving members and consequently reaped some electoral reward for their activities. This finding appeared to gain reinforcement from the results of the 1992 general election, when a dozen constituency-active Conservative MPs held on to their marginal seats against both the regional and national tide (Norton 1992e).

This electoral incentive is also linked to the stance of local parties. In the 1950s, constituency parties – especially Conservative Parties – appeared more concerned that 'their' local members should make names for themselves at Westminster. As voting intentions became less predictable, the need for members to be seen to be more active in the constituency was taken on board by many party activists. Constituency inactivity gave the party a bad image locally. There was an increasing tendency to elicit from new candidates a promise that, if elected, they would live in the constituency.

Following the adoption of the policy of compulsory re-selection by the Labour party in 1981, requiring all sitting Labour members to go through a full re-selection process during the life of each Parliament, Labour members became even more conscious of the importance of constituency activity. Attempts to de-select members were usually politically motivated – left-wing party activists seeking to unseat a right-wing member, for example – but were usually doomed to failure if the member was protected by a reputation as a 'good constituency member'.

It has been in the interest of parties for MPs to be responsive to constituency demands. However, there is another powerful motivation. Members are now much keener than ever before to stay in the House of Commons. Post-war decades have seen a growth in the number of career politicians entering Parliament. In the first half of the century, amateur politicians – those who may have been keen for office but who did not regard political life as necessarily a life-long commitment – were more prevalent. Recent decades have seen members who see parliamentary life as a full-time and long-term career (King 1981; Rush 1979: 94–96). Whereas amateurs may be willing to turn to some other career if they find constituency work or parliamentary life unrewarding, the career politician cannot afford to – indeed, by definition, does not – take such an approach. Attention to the constituency must thus be combined with Westminster activities designed to achieve advancement (see Chapter 3). Achieving re-election is a necessary but not sufficient condition for career advancement.

These variables, then, would appear to have coincided, producing the remarkable increase that we have charted of constituency activity by MPs. But what have been the consequences?

Consequences

The consequences for the political system have been several. They have served to strengthen the link between Parliament and the citizen and bolster support for the political system. There are, though, limitations to members' constituency work which render the link less strong than otherwise it might be and which threaten the capacity of members to devote time to scrutinizing and influencing legislation and the activities of government.

Strengths

The constituency work of MPs serves as a powerful form of latent legitimation and as a safety valve. Constituents, as we noted in Chapter 1, expect their Member of Parliament to give priority to the needs of the constituency (Marsh 1985: 77; Cain et al., 1979: 7–8; Crewe 1975: 320–21), serving – as one observer put it – as 'a County Councillor at Westminster' (Jeger 1978). One public opinion survey in 1990 found that two-thirds of respondents thought that MPs ought to be 'working on behalf of individual constituents' (Select Committee on Televising of Proceedings of the House 1990: 85). For citizens, the most appropriate – the most legitimate – means of personal action to take to achieve a redress of grievance, or to express themselves on an unjust measure being considered by Parliament, is to contact the Member of Parliament (Jowell and Witherspoon 1985; Jowell, Witherspoon and Brook 1987). As an increasing number of constituents have made use of their local MP, so the actions of the MP have served to meet popular expectations.

There is no doubt that the demands made of MPs have increased. In the 1986 social attitudes survey, eleven per cent of respondents claimed to have contacted their Member of Parliament. This is one to three per cent higher than earlier estimates and, if an accurate sample, suggests that more than four million people have been in touch with an MP. Given a ripple effect – relatives and friends of those who have made contact being aware of the contact – the number of citizens having some knowledge or experience of contacting the local MP is thus substantial.

The extent to which the actions of the MP meets expectations is reflected in a 1978 survey which found that, of those who contacted their MP, seventy-five per cent reported a 'good' or 'very good' response (Cain *et al.*, 1979: 6–7). An earlier Granada survey also found that the closer the contact, the greater the belief that the MP was doing a good job. 'Familiarity appears to breed content' (Crewe 1975: 322). Members' responsiveness may also have facilitated 'a widespread and growing self-confidence on the part of the electorate', identified by the social attitudes survey in the 1980s, 'to try to bring influence to bear on Parliament' (Jowell, Witherspoon and Brook 1987).

The way in which MPs meet constituents' demands is not so much through achieving changed decisions but rather through serving as a safety valve. Some decisions may be – and are – changed as a result of an MP's intervention, especially in such areas as welfare payments and immigration where ministers or officials have some discretion to vary decisions (see Rawlings 1990: 168), though they constitute a minority of cases (Norton 1982b). In most cases, ministers are fettered by statute and have no power of discretion. In many instances, constituents are not seeking a changed decision, but rather an authoritative explanation of why some decision has been taken or, quite simply, just a reply that demonstrates the matter has at least been considered. Of the responses to MPs' enquiries in just over 700 cases studied by Rawlings (1990: 42), 314 (44%) involved the provision of further information and 127 (18%) confirmation that the matter was in hand.

By providing that information, the MP may be doing a service that no one else has been able to provide. One Liberal MP observed:

> Sometimes what we get for the constituent, and what he is really pleased to get, is a reply. That may sound rather odd, but one of the things you may find your constituents have struggled in vain for months to do is elicit any reply whatsoever from a body they have written to.
>
> (Beith 1976: 8)

By their actions, MPs can force responses that otherwise may not be forthcoming. By eliciting some authoritative response from a minister, they can also have an important psychological effect. A Labour MP put it specifically in terms of a safety valve. 'The main satisfaction is to the constituent who feels he has gone as far as he can in getting his grievance aired' (Norton 1982b: 65).

The contact between constituent and MP also has a number of other consequences as well. Two affect the MP. Firstly, the contact adds to the member's body of knowledge, sensitizing the member, as one put it, to 'the concerns that are pressing on at least a portion of our fellow citizens' (Brandreth 1992: 24). Secondly, it appears to contribute to the member's job satisfaction. Barker and Rush (1970: 194) found that most members they interviewed welcomed the constituency 'welfare officer' role and forty per cent considered it the most valuable part of their work. Such satisfaction continues to be expressed. One MP about to retire from Parliament in 1992 made a point of recording that 'I enjoy my constituency mail, and have always taken great trouble over it. . . . I shall genuinely miss both my surgeries and my heavy correspondence, which I never expected' (Rhodes James 1991: 10). As another put it, the value lies in the realisation that one has helped people: that the member 'is doing something for somebody'. A survey of new MPs carried out by the Study of Parliament Group in 1992 found that helping constituents was seen as the most important part of the member's job.

Another consequence is for government. Letters written by members on behalf of constituents help alert departments to particular problems and can act as something of a barometer, indicating issues that are arousing parliamentary concern (Norton 1982b: 65, 70). If many letters are received suggesting a problem with a particular programme, it may result in the programme being modified or even replaced. Constituents' letters in 1990 helped contribute to the pressure on Conservative MPs to press for a reform or abolition of the poll tax.

Contact between constituents and MPs is extensive and clearly has major consequences. However, there are variables that limit the relationship, preventing it from having a more positive effect.

Limitations

There are a number of variables that limit MPs from achieving as much as constituents may wish. There is also a significant consequence of their growing constituency work that could undermine their other tasks.

The limitations are those of resources and time. Members have only a limited amount of time in which to attend to the growing constituency casework. Constituency work has to compete for attention with a range of parliamentary activities. Members themselves have limited resources with which to cope with the increasing work-load, usually relying on a single secretary and sometimes a part-time researcher. With limited support, mail builds up. Even during summer recesses, there is no escape. Secretaries, members and researchers may take holidays: letter-writers do not. There is, as one member put it, the constant 'drip, drip' effect of mail (Norton 1992a: 151), the cumulative effect stretching the member's capacity to cope. Members themselves are not specialists in all sectors of public policy and hence may have difficulty tackling government departments on complex issues on behalf of constituents (Norton 1982b: 66). Lacking adequate research support, they remain amateurs in pursuing casework.

There is a further limitation caused not by constituents who write, but rather by those who do not. MPs are essentially, though not totally, reactive, waiting for constituents to contact them. Those constituents who make contact tend to be the more literate and persistent. Others may have problems but can be reluctant to contact the MP or may simply not know how to (Norton 1982b: 67). The survey evidence that reveals that most citizens would contact their MP if they wanted to influence the government suggests that the problem is not a profound one in terms of latent legitimation. It may, though, affect perceptions of a minority unable or unwilling to utilise – or contemplate utilising – the services of the Member of Parliament.

The most significant consequence, though, is the effect on MPs' capacity to devote time to other concerns. There is the danger that the growing burden of constituency casework may result, as Rhodes James (1991: 10) warned, in 'the MP becoming too constituency oriented, and too parochial'. The more time the member devotes to constituency work, the less time there is to focus on Westminster activities, not least those involved in scrutinizing legislation and the activities of government. Members may not be able to attend debates, party committee meetings and standing or select committees; quite often, they do not have the time to read all the paperwork necessary for meetings or simply to think about the various issues coming before the House (see Norton 1992a). There is therefore a real danger of MPs suffering from an overload of business, with increased constituency demands reducing their capacity to attend to parliamentary duties. Without increased resources, overload may become a reality.

There is also a potential threat to the effectiveness of government. Ministers not only have to respond to MPs pursuing constituency casework but as constituency members themselves also have to devote considerable time to constituency duties (Norton and Wood 1993: Chapter 3). 'Ministers who have constituencies to look after don't stop and can't hand over the work to someone else: it just has to be fitted in somehow' (Currie 1989: 233). Time has to be found to meet with the constituency secretary and some ministers utilize car journeys to dictate letters hastily into pocket dictaphones. Having ministers who are in the House of Lords helps share the ministerial load; they do not have constituents to deal with. But there remains the problem of ministers becoming over-burdened with ministerial, parliamentary, party and constituency duties. One minister in his memoirs outlined a fairly typical week when his 'weekend' did not begin until four o'clock on Sunday. The process, he thought, 'had become dangerously all-devouring. It pushed out everything else' (Fowler 1991: 322).

Conclusion

The constituency work of the Member of Parliament has increased dramatically in recent years. Members have responded by devoting considerable time and attention to constituency demands. Evidence suggests that their activities have proved successful in meeting constituents' expectations. Surveys indicate that constituents rate members as doing a good job, and satisfaction with MPs increases following contact with them. The constituency work of the MP would appear to contribute enormously to popular perceptions of parliament's legitimacy and hence to the function of latent legitimation.

There are limits to what the MP can do on behalf of constituents and the more constituency work that the MP undertakes the greater the danger of reducing the capacity of the MP – backbencher and minister alike – to engage in other tasks. However, with increased secretarial and research resources it is possible, though not certain, that the MP may be able to cope with the pressures. For the moment, the work done for constituents is a powerful tool for maintaining popular support.

10

The Voice of Organized Interests

Members of Parliament are elected for defined constituencies. As we saw in Chapter 9, constituents expect them to give priority to local interests and an increasing amount of time is devoted by members to constituency casework. However, members also devote considerable time to listening to, and expressing the demands of, different groups in society.[1] Some groups may be composed of a member's constituents: a local charity or the local chamber of commerce, for example. Others may have no direct constituency connection but believe they have a case that will engage the member's attention.

Like constituency casework, the task of pursuing the demands of different groups is a growing one. However, unlike constituency work, it is not confined to the House of Commons. Peers are also important targets for, and voices of, groups seeking to have some influence on the content of public policy. By expressing the views of different groups in society, members of both Houses fulfil a number of functions. They act as a safety valve and ensure that various interests are articulated, variously resulting in some changes in policy. The most significance consequence is one of latent legitimation of the political system.

The role of party

For more than a century, the most important organized interest has been that of party (see Chapter 2). MPs are elected on the basis of their party label. Parties serve to aggregate interests. Candidates stand on the basis of their party's manifesto and are expected, if elected, to support the party in implementing the promises made to the electorate. Hence, as we have seen, the growth in party cohesion in Parliament. Within Parliament, and especially the House of Commons, parties dominate not only voting but most other aspects of parliamentary behaviour. Debate is frequently, though not always, partisan and members are called to speak on the presumption that it is (hence called from alternate sides of the chamber). Question time is seen increasingly as representing a partisan tussle between government and opposition front benches, and especially on Tuesdays and Thursdays a gladiatorial contest between the Prime Minister and the Leader of the Opposition (see Franklin and Norton 1993). Standing committees, as we have seen, are essentially the chamber in miniature, with proceedings dominated by the party clash and the operation of the whips.

As was argued in Chapter 8, this domination by party has advantages for the political system. It ensures some degree of coherence. Electors know what they are voting for. The names of individual candidates may not mean much to them. They understand the party label. Parties compete essentially for the all-or-nothing gains of electoral victory. Once returned with a majority of seats, a party can implement a particular programme of public policy and is then answerable to the electorate at the next general election. Under the existing electoral system, election day – to quote Sir Karl Popper (1988) – is 'judgement day'. Electors are offered a choice. They can turn a government out.

A number of problems with this system have been identified. Some critics have queried whether there is much to choose between the parties. The more they resemble 'catch-all' parties (Kirchheimer 1966) the less differentiated choice they offer. Other critics have contended that during the 1980s the choice was far too stark, with little point of contact between the Conservative Party of Margaret Thatcher and the Labour Party of Michael Foot (leader from 1980 to 1983). Some critics of the political system have also challenged the basic legitimacy of an electoral system that can produce an absolute majority of seats on the basis of less than fifty per cent of the votes cast (see Chapter 8). There is also an important question of legitimacy stemming from popular perceptions of party domination.

The stance of electors towards Parliament and its members

offers a conundrum. On the one hand, voters elect MPs on the basis of the party label. On the other, they expect the MP to do far more than merely support the party in Parliament. Greater emphasis is given to a local than to a national role. For MPs, there is thus an important balance to be maintained, loyally supporting the party on whose label they were elected, while on the other carving out a role independent of party, not least in order to pursue constituency demands. At times, the roles may conflict, as when local interests are threatened by government policy and the the local MP is a member of the governing party.

In post-war decades, the balance appears to have been tipped predominantly, if not overwhelmingly, in favour of party. Party cohesiveness reached its peak in the 1950s. Independent activity by members was extremely limited. The stranglehold of party rendered Parliament essentially a closed institution, with no means of independent access (Norton 1991b). Though party was essential for ensuring a coherent system, its hegemony conveyed the appearance of MPs as 'lobby fodder' and the institution as a body for little more than rubber stamping decisions taken elsewhere. The consequence was frustration for MPs wanting to have some effect in the political system and a tendency for voters to ignore or dismiss the institution. There were few opportunities for members of the public to follow what was going on and little point in making the effort (Norton 1991b: 223–24).

The situation was to change in the 1970s and subsequent decades. As shown in Chapter 2, the stranglehold of party was relaxed. The change was relative, but significant. The demands made of MPs by constituents increased. So too did the demands made by organized interests. Increasingly, MPs – and peers – found themselves being the target of representations, better known as lobbying, from a vast range of organized interests. The most important organized interest, still largely determining their parliamentary behaviour, was that of party. But it was no longer the exclusive interest determining their actions. Parliament became a more open institution.

The impact of groups

The 1970s, and most especially the years since, saw a massive increase in the lobbying of members of both Houses by organized

Table 10.1   Group contact with Members of Parliament – a survey of 253 organized interests conducted in 1986

Q: *Do you or does your organization have regular or frequent contact with one or more Members of Parliament?*		
Response	*n*	*%*
Yes	189	74.7
No	64	25.3
Total	253	100.0

Source: Rush (1990: 280)

interests. Such interests included large companies, professional bodies, charities, unions, consumer groups and a vast array of pressure groups seeking a change in public policy.

Lobbying by such interests is not new. There are a great many antecedents and the presence of pressure group representatives in the corridors of Westminster was noted in the 1950s and 1960s (Finer 1958; Walkland 1968). What has changed is the extent and the visibility of such lobbying. Organized interests now impinge massively on the time and consciousness of members of both Houses. One survey in 1986 of more than 250 organizations – encompassing the range just noted (companies, charities, consumer groups and the like) – found that three-quarters maintained 'regular or frequent contact with one or more Members of Parliament' (Table 10.1).

That contact is sometimes in person, not least during the committee stage of bills. The representatives of groups with a particular interest in a bill will normally be present during sittings and committee members will sometimes be seen leaving the room for a quick discussion in the corridor with a lobbyist for a group on whose behalf the member is speaking. Such lobbyists are frequently in evidence in the public gallery during the report stage of bills and on occasion fill the public seating during select committee hearings.

Even more frequently, the contact is by correspondence. The increase in constituency mail has been supplemented by an even greater increase in mail from pressure groups of one type or another. A survey of Tony Benn's correspondence as MP for Bristol South-East in 1972–73 focused on constituency correspondence, with issue-based correspondence from groups apparently being of such limited volume that it did not figure in the tabulations (Morrell 1977). The 1986 survey of organizations found that thirty-four per cent of them sent information or briefings regularly or often to MPs and almost sixty-per cent did so occasionally. Only six per cent of them did not send such material (Rush 1990: 280). A survey in 1991 of a new MP's correspondence found that most of it was from pressure groups.[2] Such is the extent of correspondence from such groups that at least one MP uses a black plastic binliner in place of a wastepaper basket to accommodate the unwanted material (see also Shaw 1990: 108).

The burden is not just in the number of letters written to members. There has been a qualitative change as well. Correspondence, in the words of one long-serving member, has become more complex and more technically demanding (Robin Maxwell-Hyslop MP to author, 1990). Groups interested in a particular clause of a bill will write to explain why it needs amending. During the committee stage of the Financial Services Bill in 1986, for example, committee members were inundated with a mass of briefing material from financial and other bodies on the intricacies of particular provisions (see Norton 1990c: 186–88). Grasping the precise point being made was frequently a demanding exercise.

For members, then, the burden lies in more than simply being the recipients of straightforward information. The material is often detailed and complex and will often involve the member being invited to take some action. Of the 189 organizations found in the 1986 survey to maintain contact with MPs, eighty-three per cent had asked an MP to table a parliamentary question. Most had also asked an MP to arrange a meeting at the Commons (seventy-eight per cent), to table an amendment to a bill (sixty-two per cent) and to table a motion (fifty-one per cent). Approximately half of the groups had also asked MPs to arrange meetings with ministers. More than a third had asked a member to sponsor a private member's bill (Rush 1990: 281).

Lobbying becomes intense during the passage of a bill, especially at committee stage. Members of the standing committee will often be swamped with letters and briefings from interested bodies. During the committee stage of the 1986 Financial Services Bill, one committee member estimated that the amount of material received was 'a couple of feet thick and may have amounted to a couple of hundred letters and documents' (Norton 1990c: 186). During the committee's proceedings, there were at least eighty references to group representations made to members; for example, 'I am no

expert in such matters, but it is an important point, which G. Warburg and Co. Ltd. has raised with me' (Tim Smith MP, quoted in
Norton 1990c: 187). Such intense lobbying is not confined to government bills. Private members' bills can be the subject of even more
intense pressures. Bills on abortion and animal welfare, for example,
elicit extensive lobbying by pressure groups and their supporters. At
the beginning of 1991, for example, some members revealed that they
had received more letters on the subject of the Pig Husbandry Bill, a
private member's bill sponsored by a leading animal welfare suppor-
ter (Sir Richard Body), than they had on the subject of the Gulf war.

Nor is such lobbying confined to MPs. Peers are also subject to
the same pressures.

> Given the legislative role of the House of Lords, its procedural
> practices, the relatively low level of party cohesion, and the pres-
> ence of a large number of cross-benchers, it would be surprising if it
> were not a focus for pressure politics. The very composition of the
> House of Lords and its mode of operation specifically encourage
> such activity.
>
> (Baldwin 1990: 155)

Seventy per cent of groups surveyed in 1986 had used the Lords to
try to influence public policy. Of the groups that had attempted to
influence legislation, almost eighty per cent had contacted one or
more members of the House of Lords; indeed this was the most
popular form of action (Rush 1990: 289, 284). A separate survey of
active peers found that almost all of them had asked written questions on behalf of pressure groups. Over sixty per cent had tabled
starred questions and a similar proportion had raised a point in
debate (Baldwin 1990: 162–63).

Members of both Houses are thus subject to extensive lobbying
by organized groups. The groups take many forms (companies,
charities and the like) as does the form of lobbying and the requests made. Such lobbying has grown enormously in recent years,
and especially since the 1970s. Lobbying of parliamentarians is not
new, but it has reached an unprecedented level of intensity.

Explanations of change

As with the growth of constituency demands, there is no single
explanation for the remarkable increase in parliamentary lobbying

by organized interests. There are several independent developments which appear to have coincided, producing this phenomenon (Norton 1991a: 65–69). Changes in the nature of groups, of
government, and of Parliament have contributed to the change.

Pressure groups

The most significant change in organized groups in recent years
has been the increase in their numbers. As we saw in Chapter 2,
interests began to organize more extensively than before during
the nineteenth century. That trend has continued in the twentieth
century and has been pronounced in the period since 1960. Of 628
groups listed in one 1979 Directory of Pressure Groups and Representative Organizations, more than forty per cent had come into
existence in the years between 1960 and 1979 (Shipley 1979). With
increased education and political awareness (the cognitive mobilization mentioned in Chapter 9), so more and more people have
been willing to join together to seek some change in public policy.

Growth in the number of groups has led to an increase in demands made of members of both Houses of Parliament. However,
there has also been a change in the resources available to groups to
engage in parliamentary lobbying. One has taken the form of improved technology, providing the facility for more rapid communication. Much, probably most, of the material received by MPs and
peers is now the product of word processors and desk top publishing facilities. The other change has been in the professional bodies
available to undertake such lobbying activities. Some organizations have in-house lobbyists. Others now employ lobbying firms,
known formally as political consultancies.

Before the 1970s, there were very few firms of political consultants. Since 1979, their number has grown significantly. By the end
of the 1980s, there were more than thirty such firms, with the
number of freelance lobbyists running into three-figures (see
Grantham 1989; Grantham and Seymour-Ure 1990). Such firms,
often composed of former civil servants, parliamentary officials,
party officials and Members of Parliament and, in some cases,
serving members, offer a range of services, including monitoring
activities in Westminster – and Whitehall – for clients, advising on
how to lobby effectively, and lobbying politicians and civil servants
on behalf of clients. A number of consultants have written guides

on how to lobby (see, for example, Greer 1985; Dubs 1988; Miller 1989).

One 1985 survey of 180 sizeable companies found that more than forty per cent of them used political consultants (*Financial Times*, 23 December 1985). The range of bodies using their services is now extensive (see Grantham and Seymour-Ure 1990: 50–56). Not only do such consultancy firms facilitate lobbying, it is also in their commercial interests to encourage it. The more they engage in such activity, and especially if it appears to have some effect, the more it encourages other organizations to use their services.

Government

In the 1950s, when Britain enjoyed relative economic prosperity, it was possible for government to engage in distributive policies: groups competed for a share in an expanding economic pie. As economic conditions worsened, government had to switch to redistributive policies. Groups thus had to compete for the same share of the economic cake. If their demands were not met by government, they thus looked for allies elsewhere, including in Parliament.

This tendency to look to Parliament has been reinforced since . 1979. The era of Thatcher Government witnessed a new relationship between government and organized groups, particularly the larger economic groups. Government sought greater autonomy in policy making (see Gamble 1988), resulting in more distant relationships with organized interests. Bodies such as the Trades Union Congress were virtually frozen out of policy discussions. The more groups perceived that they lacked the access they previously enjoyed to government, the more they turned to Parliament as a means of achieving some input into the deliberations on public policy.

Parliament

Groups thus variously turned to Parliament. At the same time, there were developments internal to the institution that increased its attractiveness. The greater behavioural independence of members (see Chapter 2) meant that changes to public policy, and especially to the detail of bills, might be achievable as a result of backbench pressure. The introduction of the departmental select committees also provided groups with a very clear focus for their activities.

Previously, groups seeking to have some input in parliamentary deliberations had usually to adopt a blunderbuss approach, sending material to a wide range of members in an attempt to find those who might have an interest in their cause. The select committees now provide them with a clear target audience, and one, furthermore, that can determine its own agenda.

Groups can thus lobby committee members to try to persuade them to undertake an enquiry on an issue of concern to the group. There are various examples of such lobbying having the desired effect. One study of the Transport Committee in the first Parliament of its existence, for example, found that some of its inquiries were the product of suggestions from pressure groups (Ganz 1989: 255). More controversially, in 1991 the principal gay rights lobbying group pressed the Home Affairs Committee to hold an enquiry into the age of consent for homosexual relationships. Had it not been for a change in chairmanship in 1992, it would probably have been successful.

Once enquiries are under way, groups can then submit evidence to the committees. Such submissions ensure that the groups get their views on the public record. As one Labour member of the Trade and Industry Committee observed, 'trade unions are delighted with the committee . . . the main benefit is to put into the 'public domain' information that otherwise might not be available' (Judge 1990: 192). They may also serve to influence the recommendations of the committee and hence be considered by the department, which has to respond to the committee's report. Once one group has submitted evidence, the more likely it is that other interested groups will want to have their voices heard. The degree of committee attractiveness to groups is reflected not so much in the oral evidence provided by the representatives of groups – they attend by invitation of the committee – but in the volume of written evidence submitted. Many pressure groups have ensured that they are on committees' mailing lists (see Rush 1990: 143), and once an enquiry in their area of interest is announced they prepare and submit written evidence. Committees are often inundated with memoranda. In the 1986–87 session, for example, the Transport

Committee received 365 memoranda from interested organizations (Norton 1991a: 74; see also Marsh 1986: 166).

Parliament may also have increased its attractiveness to organized groups as a result of the televising of proceedings. Since the
cameras entered the two Houses, the activities of the two chambers, especially the Commons, have been far more publicly prominent. Parliamentary items now enjoy greater priority in news
programmes and, it would seem fair to hypothesize, have raised
the visibility of Parliament among pressure groups and encouraged
lobbying of Parliament in the hope that the cameras may be present if the issue is raised on the floor or in committee proceedings.

These various developments have coalesced to produce the increase in parliamentary lobbying. The volume of such lobbying
shows no sign of receding. But what effect has it had?

Consequences

As with the increase in constituency casework, the burgeoning of
lobbying by pressure groups has had several consequences for the
political system. Such lobbying has served to strengthen members
of both Houses in carrying out various tasks; it has also served to
enhance the legitimacy of Parliament among organized groups. In
addition, it appears to have contributed towards some changes in
public policy. Against that must be set the fact that there are
problems as a result of perceived inequities in group influence and,
as with constituency casework, problems for the capacity of parliamentarians to cope with all the demands made of them.

Strengths

Much of the material that is sent to MPs and peers is of little use to
most of the recipients. Some is outside the members' areas of
interest. Some is so badly prepared and argued, and sometimes too
late, to have any effect. One member estimated that in 1986 he
threw away without a glance about two-thirds of the material he
received. 'On that basis each MP receives a pile of unread lobbying
mail per annum ten feet high' (Fred Silvester MP, quoted in Shaw
1990: 108). There is thus much wasted paper. However, what is
more important is the fact that not all the material sent is wasted.

The material supplied by organizations outside Parliament ensures that members, and committees, of both Houses have a source of information independent of government and party. That material adds to the members' store of knowledge and provides the basis for questioning the detail of provisions laid before them. The survey of active peers conducted by Nicholas Baldwin in the early 1980s found that all of those questioned felt that contact with groups in their areas of interest was useful (Baldwin 1990: 162). One MP on the standing committee considering the Financial Services Bill described the material received by committee members as 'pretty good and certainly very influential in pointing us to issues that ought to be raised' (Norton 1990c: 197). Such is the value of the material supplied by interested organizations that members will sometimes actively solicit it (Norton 1990c: 197). Within the context of their particular enquiries, departmental select committees do so, of course, on a regular basis.

Given their own limited resources, MPs and peers use outside groups almost as substitutes for research assistants, their own areas of interest and political predispositions serving as a filter for the material that they are sent. Information likely to be of use is read and retained; the rest is discarded. For members who may be critical of a particular measure, or may have been unaware of inherent problems with it, the information supplied by groups can be invaluable. As a result, it adds to their critical capacity and ensures that Parliament is a more effective body of scrutiny than otherwise it would be.

A combination of better information and the relatively greater behavioural independence of Members appears to have combined to influence the content of public policy. Well-briefed members of standing committees have pressed amendments, on occasion being willing to carry them against the wishes of government and on occasion finding that the case they put is accepted by ministers (see Norton 1990c: 190–91). The capacity for Members to have any significant impact in the legislative process remains very limited indeed (see Chapter 5). The link with outside groups ensures that at least it is not quite so limited as it once was.

Similarly, well-informed select committees have variously had some impact on public policy, or rather, as was noted in Chapter 6, the detail of policy. Outside organizations have ensured that the committees have material that supplements or challenges that

Table 10.2 Group influence on legislation

Q: *Speaking generally, how would you rate your efforts in seeking to influence legislation before Parliament?*

Response[1]	n	%
Very successful	15	7.2
Quite successful	100	48.3
Not very successful	80	38.6
Unsuccessful	12	5.8
Total	207	99.9

[1] There were four non-respondents.

Source: Rush (1990: 285)

provided by ministers and officials. Knowing that committees may obtain information from other sources may have an effect on departmental thinking and intentions. Again, the impact of departmental select committees may be limited, but their existence – and their extensive use of evidence from organizations independent of government – has provided a new dimension to parliamentary scrutiny.

The pursuit of group demands by members of both Houses, and the effect it sometimes has, has also helped enhance the legitimacy of Parliament among such groups. The perception of groups is generally a positive one. The 1986 survey found that, of those groups that had sought to have some influence on legislation, more than half claimed to have been successful (Table 10.2). Lobbying is often inefficient (see Norton 1990c: 193–96) but nonetheless the perception of groups involved in the exercise is that it has some effect. As can be seen from Table 10.2, less than six per cent of the groups questioned deemed their efforts to have been unsuccessful.

Select committees have elicited particularly positive assessments (Marsh 1986: 167–76). For many groups, getting their views on the record in an authoritative forum is an end in itself; they have had an opportunity to express themselves. Parliament thus serves as an important safety valve for groups as well as for individuals. The possibility of actually influencing some change in public policy is an added attraction, enhancing the legitimacy of the institution.

The legitimacy of the institution is also enhanced by the fact that it serves as an important transmission belt between groups and government. As we have seen, this role has acquired greater significance since 1979. Parliament offers not only an opportunity to give a public airing to group demands, it can also help channel those demands to government, both publicly and privately. As we have seen, half the groups questioned in the 1986 survey had asked MPs to arrange meetings with a minister (Rush 1990: 281). Through arranging such meetings, through tabling questions, and through tabling amendments to bills, members in both Houses can ensure that group demands are considered by government.

The significance of these activities should not be exaggerated. Public policy is determined by government (see Chapter 4). For the purpose of groups, ministers and senior civil servants remain the principal targets of their lobbying activities. Despite the arms length relationship of government to many economic groups since 1979, the contact between departmental ministers and organized interests remains extensive and continuous. Parliament remains a supplementary rather than a primary point of contact. Though half the groups questioned in 1986 may have asked MPs to arrange meetings with ministers, the other side of the coin is that the other half did not.

Nonetheless, Parliament occupies the time and attention of organized interests on a more extensive basis than before. Though persuading government remains the essential and normally sufficient task for most groups seeking some change in policy, Parliament fulfils an important role in providing groups with a safety valve and another opportunity to fight a battle that may have been lost in Whitehall. Their activity also adds to the store of members' knowledge, thus providing them with the means to adopt a more critical stance and, in so doing, reinforce the legitimacy of the institution in the eyes of citizens.

Limitations

Though the increased activity of groups may have helped bolster perceptions of Parliament's legitimacy among such groups, there are problems of legitimacy arising from the access that such groups enjoy. There are perceived inequalities of access between groups, and also between groups and the individual citizen.

Larger and more powerful groups can afford the services of professional consultants. There is a perception on the part of less powerful groups that they are squeezed out. As the representative of one voluntary organization put it, 'those like us with little money, staff and resources can't mount such a good show and tend to be overlooked' (Grantham and Seymour-Ure 1990: 76). Wealthy groups are believed to buy influence. The position is further complicated by the fact that a significant proportion of parliamentarians are themselves consultants or retained by consultancy firms. In 1989, 180 MPs – 137 of them Conservatives – were retained by outside groups as parliamentary consultants or advisers (Grantham and Seymour-Ure 1990: 67). Nor are consultants confined to the Lower House. Several peers are to be found in the lobbying field. This adds to the perception of influence-buying by groups, and creates the potential for a conflict of interest between commitment to a group paying a salary or fee and commitment to the constituents that elected the member.

The problem of professional lobbying is sometimes exaggerated. MPs recognize easily attempts at influence and, thanks to the protective cloak of party, can resist it if not persuaded of the arguments advanced. The problem may not so much be one of democratic accountability (the lobbyist–Parliament link) but one of consumer accountability (the lobbyist–client link); for those wishing to lobby Parliament, there may be a problem in choosing a good lobbying body to undertake the task (Norton and Grantham 1986: 4–8). Furthermore, some of the most effective lobbying is undertaken not by wealthy firms (some lobbying by City bodies on the Financial Services Bill, for example, was inept) but by consumer organizations such as the Consumers' Association (Norton 1990c: 198). Nonetheless, so long as there is a popular perception of influence-buying, then it serves to undermine Parliament's legitimacy.

Various attempts have been made to allay some of the fears about the role of lobbyists and of politicians who serve as consultants. The House of Commons – though not the House of Lords – maintains an annual register of members' interests, though members who act as consultants are not required to identify their clients. Journalists and those who work for MPs have also now to register outside interests, though the register (unlike that on members' interests) is not a public one. In 1991, the Select Committee on Members' Interests recommended the creation also of a register of professional lobbyists; the following year, it recommended various changes to the rules governing members' declarations of financial interests (Select Committee on Members' Interests 1991: xxiii; 1992: xxiv-xxv). The changes were not as radical as some witnesses had advocated and would not affect the capacity of members to act as consultants.

The other negative consequence is the impact on members' workloads. The more they are lobbied, the less time they have to devote to other activities. Sifting the unsolicited material into useful and useless material is itself a time-consuming exercise. Secretaries can carry some but not all of the burden. The qualitative as well as the quantitative change adds to the burden.

The fact that members' have limited research resources means that they often rely on the material they are sent by outside groups. However, those limited resources also mean that the member has difficulty evaluating its significance. The quote already given from a member of the standing committee on the Financial Services Bill – 'I am no expert in such matters, but . . .' – illustrates the problem. Without the information, the member would not have known that the issue was one that should have been raised, but without research support of his own may not be certain of its significance.

Lobbying by outside groups adds considerably to the burden of parliamentarians, forcing them to establish priorities in terms of their parliamentary activities and the demands made of them. Some activities may be abandoned as a consequence. Lobbying contributes significantly to the potential of parliamentary overload. Without significantly increased resources, there is the danger of Members of Parliament not being able to cope with all the demands made of them.

Conclusion

Members of both Houses of Parliament help articulate the views and demands of organized interests. The principal organized interest that dominates both Houses is party. Recent decades have witnessed a massive increase in the representations made to members by other organized interests and an increased facility on the part of members to pursue the demands of these interests.

The effect of this increased activity has been to increase the legitimacy of Parliament in the eyes of many groups, though not necessarily in the eyes of all. It has provided members of both Houses with information that has proved useful in subjecting government and legislative measures to more critical scrutiny. Members themselves have served as an important safety valve for various groups in society. They have helped articulate group demands and make sure they are considered by government.

Such activity is now extensive and, as such, threatens the capacity of Members of Parliament to cope with all the demands made of them. Limited resources mean that they are in danger of being overloaded with work. So long as they manage to cope with the representations made to them by outside groups, they help to bolster the standing of the institution of which they are members. So long as they continue to do so without increased resources, they threaten their own capacity to cope.

Notes

1. Throughout this chapter, the terms groups, organizations and organized interests are employed as synonyms for all organized bodies and not just groups set up for the exclusive purpose of promoting a particular issue or cause.
2. During the month of July 1991, the Liberal Democrat MP for Ribble Valley, Michael Carr, received 186 letters or other form of communication (newsletters and annual reports for example) from organizations and 99 letters from or about constituents (Eddleston 1992). These figures are important for their relationship to one another rather than their combined total. Relative to many members, the total volume is not excessive.

11

Other Voices, Other Interests

In his work on comparative legislatures, Michael Mezey distinguished between particularized and generalized demands. 'Generalized demands are those that require government actions that can affect the nation as a whole. Particularized demands are couched in narrow terms relevant to a more specific group' (Mezey 1979: 146). Most of the demands that we have considered already (see Chapters 9 and 10) are essentially, though not exclusively, particularized demands that emanate from individuals or groups. But what of more generalized demands and those particularized demands that are the product of unorganized sections of society?

Many people in society lack an organized voice. On some issues, it may be a majority. An issue may suddenly arise on which the parties have no opinion, or no united opinion, and for which no other groups exist to express citizens' views. There is at least one majority – women – that lacks any clear, unified organization to speak for it.

More frequently, the unorganized voice will be that of a minority. The form and size that each minority takes will vary enormously. It may be a particular body of citizens that is definable by location, ethnic background, physical condition, or simply a shared ideology or instincts. For example, local residents may be aggrieved about a decision to site a remand hostel in the locality. Blacks may feel they are being unfairly singled out for attention by the police. People who are left-handed – about twelve per cent of the population – may feel that not enough is being done to cater to their needs. Pacifists may feel that government is pursuing policies at odds with their fundamental beliefs.

Taking cognizance of the views and needs of unorganized sections of society is a significant task for Parliament. One study of three other countries found that acting as a 'tribune of the people' – the member telling the government what people in the constituency thought about an issue – constituted, in the opinion of citizens, a 'very important' role for the MP (Mezey 1979: 165). We have already seen that in Britain citizens give particular emphasis to an MP's local role. Expressing the views of one's constituents as a whole is a separate task to that of pursuing the particular needs and grievances of individual constituents.

Recognizing and considering the views of unorganized groups that are not just within but also extend beyond constituency boundaries has important implications for the maintenance of parliamentary legitimacy and hence popular support for the political system. Being seen to consider the interests of such groups is likely to enhance Parliament's standing in the eyes of those comprising such groups. A failure to consider their needs is likely to undermine confidence in the institution. It may undermine it especially if it fails to express the generalized demands of the majority, but also if it ignores the particularized needs of unorganized minorities.

How, then, are the views of the unorganized in society heard and acted upon by Parliament? Given that they are, by definition, not organized, how can they compete with the interests that are organized?

The past century

For much of the past century, <u>Parliament has been a relatively</u>
 <u>closed institution to those who lacked an organized voice.</u> Indeed, unorganized opinion has suffered from the same difficulty as opinion that has been marshalled through established organized groups. Party has provided a cocoon (see Chapter 10). Party has acted as a means of aggregating and channelling opinions, but what of those interests and opinions not catered for by party programmes? For most of the twentieth century, the party stranglehold has resulted largely in such views finding little or no outlet through parliamentary means.

The dominance of party has ensured that there has been little time for consideration of issues outside the context of partisan debate. It has also ensured, for most of the past century, members' commitment to Westminster. As was noted in Chapter 9, the first half of this century witnessed little direct contact between members and their constituents. Members were motivated by partisan considerations and their time was occupied by activities at Westminster and by outside business and more leisurely pursuits. Even as late as the Macmillan Government (1957–63), one member is reputed to have accepted government office only on condition that he would still have time to go hunting twice a week.

There was thus little point of contact between parliamentarians and unorganized interests. By definition, the interests lacked organization and hence a clear means of channelling their views to Parliament. Parliamentarians were essentially reactive rather than proactive in dealing with problems affecting citizens. They did not go out and solicit the views of constituents.

There were exceptions. Some members did voice the concerns of particular and not well-organized interests and did so independent of party. But if the problems of particular sections of society were recognised and voiced, it was usually through the medium of party. Party could thus be useful, indeed – if the governing party – invaluable. But it could also be, and was, a major obstacle to allowing an outlet for other groups in society.

A good illustration is to be found in the case of the disabled. Despite post-war decades seeing some bodies being formed to make demands on behalf of disabled people

> the disabled were still an under-represented and ill-organized sector of society, and their problems were only dimly perceived by the public and by politicians.
>   Before . . . 1964 disablement had simply not figured on the parliamentary agenda at all. There had been no mention of the problems of the disabled in either of the major party manifestos, and there had been no debate on disablement in the whole of the parliamentary term from 1959 to 1964.
>
> (Topliss and Gould 1981: 4)

For such people in society, Parliament thus appeared to offer little. MPs represented parties and were seen during election campaigns but infrequently – if at all – between them.

A growing voice

Recent years have witnessed a number of changes that have affected Parliament's capacity to heed the views and needs of those who have traditionally lacked an organized voice. The changes are disparate and have largely been chronicled in preceding chapters. They can be grouped under four headings: greater organization and – on the part of Parliamentarians – greater knowledge, greater willingness, and greater opportunities.

Greater organization

Possibly the most important development in recent years affecting those who are unorganized is the fact – already chronicled in the preceding chapter – that many have ceased to be unorganized. As we have seen, there has been a remarkable growth in the number of organized groups formed in recent years, especially since 1960. In the field of disablement, for example, the period since the 1960s has witnessed a burgeoning of groups such as the Disablement Income Group, the Central Council for the Disabled, the National Campaign for the Young Chronic Sick, the Disabled Living Foundation and a range of other voluntary organizations geared to particular needs (see Topliss and Gould 1981: 4–5). The poverty lobby gained a powerful voice through the Child Poverty Action Group (Field 1982: 42–44). The range as well as the volume is extensive.

The reasons for this change have been discussed already in Chapter 10. A more educated and politically confident population has become more organized in order to make demands of the political system. As groups have been formed, others with opposed interests and views have found it expedient to organize in order to counteract their influence. Consequently, the extent of the unorganized groupings in society has diminished as the organized sector has increased.

Greater knowledge

The growth of mass communications and investigative journalism has extended public and parliamentary awareness of previously neglected groups in society. The more extensive use of opinion surveys has provided a more frequent gauge of public opinion on a range of issues. Politicians know what are the principal concerns and to some extent what people would like done about them. The growth of regional television and local media has also served to extend awareness of more localized problems. An increase in road accidents, opposition to a new airport in the area or concern over drug use are all newsworthy items. A number of constituents may write to local MPs about them. Coverage by the local media, especially where the reaction of MPs may be sought, ensure that members know about them.

Greater willingness

There is a greater willingness on the part of MPs to act on behalf of constituents (see Chapter 9). The same applies to more general constituency views and those of wider interests. The reasons are those we have previously identified. MPs are more career oriented. They want to stay in Parliament. They are less willing to call it a day and go off and pursue other interests. At the same time, as we have seen, there is a greater sense of insecurity on the part of MPs. The old class-based support cannot be taken for granted in the way that it once was. To maintain support, parties have to work harder. To maintain support locally, MPs see a need to work harder. Hence an increased responsiveness to local demands, not just those coming from individuals but also those channelled through the local media. And, to some extent, arising also as a result of the member actually seeking out local problems. Bruce Cain and his colleagues (1987) found that over a quarter of members adopted a proactive stance, going out to discover constituents' problems rather than waiting for the problems to be brought to them.

The problems of constituents will not necessarily be constituency specific. The different unorganized groups mentioned in the opening paragraph are not confined to a particular town or city. They may group more extensively in some areas, in which case their potential impact may be even greater: they form a more substantial part of the local electorate than would be the case if they were spread evenly throughout the country. In some marginal constituencies they may have the potential to affect the outcome.

This greater willingness, though, does not appear confined to the elected House. The changes in the House of Lords which have taken place in recent decades (see Chapter 2) have resulted in a different and more active House than existed in the 1940s and 1950s. Peers come from a range of backgrounds, in some cases professional backgrounds – such as the medical and caring professions – that provide them with knowledge and experience of the problems faced by some sectors of society. The extent of this knowledge should not be exaggerated – in 1981, for example, only nineteen peers had a medical background (Baldwin 1985: 105) – but the willingness of those with current expertise in particular sectors to contribute has been a significant feature of the House in recent decades.

Whereas electoral pressures may increase MPs' willingness to acknowledge the existence and needs of particular groups, the absence of electoral pressures may have the effect of allowing peers to consider the interests of minorities that may be unpopular and for which, consequently, MPs are reluctant to speak. One example, already touched upon in Chapter 4, is that of some conscience issues. In the 1960s, peers could discuss homosexuality without having to face the sort of pressures faced by supporters of homosexual law reform in the Commons (see Berkeley 1972: 128–9). Given the relative lack of partisanship on the part of peers, there is arguably a greater willingness on their part – compared with their counterparts in the Commons – to take up issues outside the context of party.

Greater opportunities

Even if parliamentarians are more willing to pursue such wider interests, do the opportunities to do so exist? To a limited extent, they do and on a slightly greater scale than before.

The traditional opportunities we have discussed in Part 1: questions, debates, and private members' legislation are the most prominent. They are variously used to raise the needs and concerns of unorganized groups in society. Various illustrations appear in earlier chapters. Tables 4.3 and 6.3, for example, show examples of private members' bills and motions in the 1990–91 session that were motivated by members' concerns to protect certain unorganized individuals and groups: Conal Gregory's smoke detectors bill, designed especially to assist the elderly, and Dudley Fishburn's motion on leasehold reform, designed to help people who lived in leasehold property and had no right to purchase the freehold. Another example, already discussed, was Austin Mitchell's House Buyers' Bill designed to help reduce costs for purchasers.

In the Lords, the opportunity has existed not only through questions but through 'unstarred' questions and through the monthly balloted motions, allowing backbench peers to raise what have proved to be a tremendous range of issues. Among topics raised through unstarred questions in the 1985–86 session, for example, were welfare provisions for the multi-handicapped, after-care provisions for prisoners, and pay deductions for the territorial army. The same session also saw debates on community education and employment, preventing crime in London, disability prevention, criminal legal aid, care of the mentally ill, and protecting the public from violent crime.

The opportunities in the Commons have been extended through the creation of the departmental select committees. They have on occasion investigated topics affecting unorganized or largely ill-organized groups. In the 1991–92 session, for example, the Employment Committee issued a report on employment in prisons and for ex-offenders, the Social Security Committee held a highly publicized investigation into the operation of pension funds, and the Welsh Affairs Committee issued reports on community care for the elderly and on the provision of cardiac services.

In undertaking such enquiries, the committees have called evidence from officials and from some bodies with particular responsibilities for providing the services under consideration. On occasion, a committee has not just called witnesses to give evidence at Westminster but has actually gone out and held hearings where the problem exists. One notable example was in 1980. Following riots in the St. Paul's district of Bristol, the Home Affairs Committee went to Bristol to listen to some of the residents and those involved in the troubles. Meeting away from Westminster is also a feature of the Welsh and Scottish Affairs Committees. Some of the other committees – Health, for example, and Energy (until its demise in 1992) – also go on fact-finding visits to different parts of the UK. In the Lords, the *ad hoc* committee appointed in the 1988–89 session to consider the offence of murder and life imprisonment actually spent a considerable period of time visiting HM prisons.

There is also the possibility that reports may be the subject of debate on estimates days. Thus, during the 1987–92 Parliament, subjects discussed on estimates days included sea defence and flood damage, gipsy sites, storm damage and Iraqi refugees, all in different way concerned with people who have no organized voice to promote their interests.

The opportunities thus exist for members of both Houses to raise and discuss the views and needs of people who are not organized or not particularly well organized and, as we have seen, the willingness to do so is greater than before.

Limitations

Despite these developments, there are a number of variables that continue to militate against the interests of those who are unorganized being heard and pursued in Parliament. Though many previously disorganized interests have now come together and achieved a structured means of expressing themselves, many still remain disorganized. Others – such as the elderly, the unemployed and the young – have seen some attempt at organization but still remain largely unorganized or poorly organized.

Unorganized groups still often go unnoticed or the full extent of their problems go unrecognized. There are various explanations for this, many not particular to the United Kingdom. Some groupings may have a culture that militates against seeking to express themselves politically. Some may not feel that their needs are such as to require a remedy through the political process (left-handers, for example). Some may be formed of individuals who are so geographically disparate that there are few means of getting organized, sometimes little knowledge of the existence or location of others with the same characteristics (individuals with extraordinarily rare medical conditions, for example). Some may not know how to get organized and may not feel that there is much point in getting organized for political purposes. Gangs of inner-city youngsters may have some form of organization but not one geared to making demands of elected representatives. When the then Environment Secretary, Michael Heseltine, visited Liverpool in the wake of the riots there in 1981, he asked some disaffected youngsters whether they had contacted their local councillors. The response was: 'What's a councillor?' (Norton 1982a: 27).

There also remains the problem of competition. Even if parliamentarians are aware of the views of such groupings – be it a particular minority body or more widespread public opinion – there is still the dominant influence of party. Party still dominates in terms of the political agenda. If a party takes up an issue on behalf of an unorganized sector of society, then that sector will find its concerns on the agenda. Without that, it has to rely on one or more parliamentarians exploiting the still limited opportunities. Furthermore, the competition is arguably now greater than ever before, with organized interests competing energetically for attention. We have already noted the disparity of resources between organized interests. Even if MPs and peers are keen to ensure a fair hearing for all interests, organized or not, there is still the danger of smaller or unorganized groups believing that they can never achieve the same attention and action as that achieved by the better-resourced groups. The observation of the representative of one small group cited in the preceding chapter – 'those like us with little money, staff and resources can't mount such a good show and tend to be overlooked' – illustrates a perception that is likely to be even stronger among those who lack any organization to express their interests.

There is also a wider economic consideration. Chapter 10 recorded the problems associated with a lack of economic growth, that is, groups having to compete for the same slice of the non-expanding, even on occasion, contracting pie. With economic downturn, there is less to go round. It thus becomes less possible to satisfy all the demands made. Those who lose out as a consequence of this may find their plight is given voice by a political party but nonetheless feel alienated from the political system. Those who lose out, such as the unemployed, are often the unorganized.

Conclusion

Members of both Houses of Parliament have proved more willing and able in recent years to elicit and express the grievances and needs of unorganized sectors of society. In so doing, they have served as an important safety valve, interest articulator and legitimizer. Those previously ignored have acquired, to some degree, an authoritative outlet for their views. Parliament can ensure that the interests of different 'publics' are articulated and heard by decision makers. The more parliamentarians engage in such activities, the more they legitimize Parliament in the eyes of those who may previously have felt alienated from the political system.

By their activities, members may also have enhanced the capacity of Parliament to fulfil a limited function of conflict resolution.

Packenham (1970) defined the task of resolving conflict in terms of being a power broker. In his study of the Brazilian congress, he found that the congress had little decision-making power, so it made 'little sense for interest-group representatives to present their demands to congressmen and to try to have political conflicts resolved in congress'. Parliament, as with the Brazilian congress, is not a decision-making body. Nonetheless, by providing a forum in which the views of different groups, often with competing demands, can be heard, Parliament not only enables the demands of such groups to be heard by the decision-makers – which otherwise might not occur (in essence, Packenham's interest articulation function) – but also allows the groups to hear the demands of the other competing groups. Parliament may thus be able to facilitate a dialogue between groups in a way that government departments cannot.

Furthermore, by listening to the different groups, Parliament may enhance its own legitimacy as an arbiter between them. Ian Marsh's study of pressure groups involved in giving evidence to select committees in the 1981–82 session found that seventy per cent regarded the select committee process as fairer than departmental procedures, and more than forty per cent regarded MPs as' more legitimate arbitrators of an issue than departmental officers (Marsh 1986: 173–74). This study was of organized interests but it is suggestive of what Parliament may be able to achieve beyond those groups. The more that previously alienated sectors of society are brought into this process, the greater the capacity for Parliament to help lessen and possibly even resolve conflict.

Parliament has thus gone further than before in being able to identify and raise the views and needs of unorganized groups. By voicing their concerns and demands, members of both Houses have been able to ensure some government response. Nonetheless, major problems remain. In terms of the linkage between Parliament and citizen so far considered, this remains the weakest. Party remains a conduit for expressing the demands of different sectors, but unorganized interests that are not accommodated by party remain at a disadvantage in seeking to have some input in the political process. They also remain at a disadvantage compared with those who are organized and are able to express their demands directly, frequently and extensively in both Houses. The disparity may now be less than before, but it still remains great.

12

Educating and Mobilizing Citizens

Individual citizens and a vast array of groups in society, both organized and unorganized, make demands of Members of Parliament. MPs raise the concerns of constituents, groups and different publics in Parliament and can ensure the Government takes note. The flow of communication in this relationship is essentially from those outside Parliament to those inside. But what about the communication from Parliament to those outside?

One of the functions ascribed to Parliament by Walter Bagehot was that of 'teaching' – 'to teach the nation what it does not know' (see Chapter 1). More recently, Samuel Beer has identified the potential of legislators to mobilize popular support for policies. He had in mind policies that had been approved by Parliament and which imposed often complex requirements on the citizen. Such policies, he contended, were numerous and a consequence of having a welfare state and a managed economy.

> A great deal is expected of the citizen in the form of new necessities that oblige him to conform his behaviour to the complex requirements of economic and social policy. . . . To win both the mind and the heart of the citizen to an acceptance of these coercions is a major necessity, but a severe problem.
>
> (Beer 1966)

If the policies were explained to citizens, then support would more likely be forthcoming, thus facilitating the desired effect. However,

Beer argued, the potential was not one that had been fulfilled by the British Parliament.

To what extent, then, does Parliament today educate and raise support for measures to which it has given its approval? Are citizens better informed and more supportive of policies as a result of the activities of parliamentarians?

Lack of contact

The developments of the nineteenth century have resulted in party domination of Parliament and an increase in both the volume and the complexity of legislation. As was shown in Chapter 2, Parliament failed to keep pace with these developments. Successive governments were prepared to use their party majorities to prevent detailed and critical scrutiny by Parliament. They were prepared to rely on the mandate of a general election victory and the resulting party majority as sufficient to legitimize their measures.

The consequence was a Parliament that was able and prepared to debate policy on a partisan basis but denied the resources, and largely lacking the political will, to subject that policy to informed and detailed scrutiny. Lacking information about the detail and the case for particular provisions of the bills they were approving, Members of Parliament were in no position to mobilize popular support for those provisions.

The position was exacerbated in post-war decades, with the realization of the 'closed' institution outlined in Chapter 10. Legislation became more specific and reached more than ever before into the economic and social lives of the citizenry. Far from being in a position to inform and mobilize support among citizens, parliamentarians appeared increasingly to have little scope for action independent of assenting to what government placed before them. MPs and peers were generalists having to cope with a mass of highly detailed legislation. They had no mechanism for specialized enquiry. Their inability to engage in independent action appeared to lessen interest in their activities and hence their capacity to influence those affected by the measures they were approving.

During the 1950s and 1960s, there was little opportunity for individuals to find out what Parliament was doing. Continuous daily reporting of Parliament was confined to the serious press.

Television and radio coverage was limited. The BBC actually had a self-imposed rule prohibiting the broadcast of any statement or discussion on matters to be debated in Parliament within a period of fourteen days. The 'fourteen-day rule' was only removed in 1957. For those interested in knowing what was said throughout an entire debate, it was a case either of sitting in the public gallery or consulting *Hansard*, the official report of proceedings. Sales of both Commons and Lords *Hansard* were small.

For individuals, there was little incentive to find out what was said in debate. For pressure groups and all bodies affected by legislation, there was some reason to follow what was going on, but attempts to do so do not appear to have been extensive. Occasions when either House debated matters of interest to a particular group would, in any event, be few and far between.

Individuals and groups were thus faced by an institution that was essentially enveloped by party and which appeared to offer little of relevance to them (see Chapters 10 and 11). Parliamentarians had limited contact with constituents (see Chapter 9) and what they said in the chamber had a very small audience. The communication from members of the two Houses to the outside world could thus be described as extremely muted, making little contribution to understanding on the part of individuals and organizations.

This was the position recognized and sketched by Samuel Beer in 1966. It was to change soon after his words were published.

Developing links

In his analysis of Parliament, Beer contended that there were two obstacles that clearly stood in the way of Parliament being able to mobilize support in the period between general elections. One was secrecy, both in government and in Parliament itself. The other was the lack of specialized committees for investigating what government was doing.

> If the public is to be given a greater sense of participation, not only must secrecy be reduced, but MPs must be given better instruments for understanding, explaining, and – inevitably – criticizing what the government is doing.
>
> (Beer 1966)

Both obstacles have been tackled. If not totally removed, they have at least been substantially eroded. They have been supplemented by another change that undermines a third obstacle implicit in Beer's analysis: the hegemony of party. Greater independence on the part of members enhances their capacity to mobilize support.

More openness

Parliament itself has moved toward greater openness in its proceedings. Both Houses retain absolute power to determine whether proceedings should be open or closed to the public. The public are granted access to watch the proceedings in each chamber unless the House votes to go into secret session, as occasionally happened during the Second World War. In the Commons, select committees often sat in public in the nineteenth and early twentieth centuries. However, private sittings became the norm after the Second World War. This only changed in the latter half of the 1960s. Today, public sessions for evidence taking are the norm among the departmental select committees.

Exceptionally, a departmental select committee will go into closed session, the most obvious example being the Defence Committee when hearing sensitive details affecting national security.[1] (The published proceedings appear with the sensitive information 'sidelined', that is, omitted.) Some of the 'domestic' committees, such as the Privileges Committee, continue to hold closed meetings. Others – such as the Procedure Committee – hold public sessions and they were joined in June 1988 by the Select Committee on Members' Interests. Meetings of standing committees are open to the public, unless the committee votes otherwise. Consequently, the position now is one where closed committee hearings are rare.

However, meeting in public session is necessary but not sufficient for ensuring that parliamentary activities are widely known about. Media coverage has, as we have seen, been limited. This changed dramatically in the 1980s, with the admission of the television cameras to the chamber and the committee rooms of both Houses.

An early attempt by the BBC in the 1920s to be allowed to broadcast special occasions in Parliament came to nothing (Griffith and Ryle 1989: 81). Little then happened until 1966, when a select committee in the Commons recommended a closed-circuit experiment, on the basis of which the House could then decide whether limited public broadcasting should be permitted. The recommendation was defeated by 131 votes to 130. The House of Lords was less reticent and passed a motion declaring that it 'would welcome the televising of some of its proceedings for an experimental period as an additional means of demonstrating its usefulness in giving a lead to public opinion'. The reason given reveals a sensitivity to Bagehot's teaching function. The experiment duly took place, in 1968, but was not pursued, partly for technical reasons, partly because of the expense, and partly because the Lords did not wish to be out of line with the practice of the Commons (Wheeler-Booth 1989: 511–12).

In 1975, the Commons approved an experiment in sound broadcasting and, following the experiment, both Houses approved the principle of proceedings being broadcast on radio. The decision on principle was taken in 1976 and sound broadcasting began in both Houses in April 1978.

Pressure for proceedings to be televised continued. In 1983, the Lords voted to endorse its earlier decision of 1966 and to take steps to implement it. An experiment began in 1985 and it was agreed in 1986 that broadcasting be made permanent. The Commons, as in 1966, was more reticent. In 1985 the House voted by 275 to 263 against the idea. Three years later, however, it reached a different conclusion, approving in principle the holding of an experiment in television broadcasting. The vote was one of 318 to 264. After some delay, the cameras eventually started transmitting proceedings on 21 November 1989. The following year, the House agreed that broadcasting be made a permanent feature.

During the period of broadcasting solely from the Lords, coverage of the Upper House was more extensive – and popular – than was generally expected by broadcasters and parliamentarians. The same proved true of Commons' coverage from November 1989 onwards (Select Committee on the Televising of Proceedings of the House 1990: xxiv–xxx). Not only did proceedings, especially question time, in the chamber attract wide coverage, so too did committee meetings. In the first fifteen weeks of broadcasting, ninety-three select committee meetings and thirty-six standing committee meetings were televised. Committee meetings continued to prove popular. Thus, for example, some of the enquiries undertaken by the Trade and Industry Committee, listed in Chapter 6, such as the enquiry into the sale of the Rover Group to British Aerospace and the 'supergun' enquiry, attracted considerable television coverage.

Specialization

Parliament is thus a far more open institution than at any time in its history. It is also a far more specialized institution. The most significant change occurred, as we have seen already, in 1979 with the creation of the departmental select committees. Fourteen were established then. In the Parliament returned in 1992, sixteen were appointed (see Chapter 6). This new specialization has had two consequences. One has been to render government more open. The other has been to provide a more precise and extensive link between Parliament and outside groups.

By taking evidence from ministers and civil servants, the departmental select committees have elicited information that otherwise would not be on the public record. The committees (see Chapter 6), have proved prolific in taking evidence and producing reports. During the lifetime of a Parliament, the committees will usually interview at least two hundred ministers and more than one thousand civil servants (see Norton 1991a: 73). The committees have become more experienced at questioning witnesses and teasing details from them.

Obtaining such information benefits the committees. They are better informed than otherwise they would be. By virtue of each committee's concentration on a particular sector, and by each acquiring information and issuing reports, usually with recommendations for particular action, committee activity has also attracted the attention of a wide array of interested organizations. The creation of the committees has provided groups with a clear parliamentary target for lobbying activities (see Chapter 10). Groups lobby committees to investigate a particular topic. They submit evidence when enquiries are undertaken. Of more than 250 groups surveyed in 1986, two-thirds had presented written evidence to a Common's select committee or a joint committee of both Houses (Rush 1990: 283).

Select committees, then, have acted as magnets for such groups. However, groups are not simply providers of inputs to committees.

They are also consumers of the outputs. Representatives of organized interests are frequently present during committee hearings. They will be avid readers of committee reports in order to find out what impact their evidence has had. One survey of more than one hundred groups giving oral evidence to committees in the early 1980s found that virtually all of them obtained the committee findings (Marsh 1986: 171). Through their reports, committees thus reach an important audience. The televising of proceedings reaches both the general public and, to some extent, outside groups (just over two-thirds of groups questioned in 1986 used television as one means of keeping in touch with what goes on in Parliament), whereas select committee reports reach essentially the outside groups.

The House of Lords, as we have seen, has given a lead in terms of greater openness, but has not developed the degree of committee specialization of the Commons. Its committees on the European communities and on science and technology, both established in the 1970s, have nonetheless served to provide the House with the means to undertake detailed and informed enquiry and have acted as magnets for interested groups. The evidence flowing to both committees has been extensive.

On occasion, the evidence to a particular enquiry – such as that on civil research and development undertaken by the Science and Technology Committee in 1986–87 – has had to be published in more than one volume. The Science and Technology Committee, according to one informed observer, has always placed great emphasis on evidence taking:

> The quality of the reports has reflected the quality of the evidence, and it is a source of satisfaction to the committee that the scientific and technological communities have been so generous with their time and knowledge in contributing to evidence.
>
> (Hayter 1991: 151)

The various *ad hoc* committees appointed by the House have also served to mobilize the attention of interested bodies (Grantham and Moore Hodgson 1985: 115). The Committee on Laboratory Animal Protection, for example, received some 900 letters and memoranda from groups and individuals.

More independent behaviour

The change in members' behaviour in both Houses has already been identified in Chapter 2 and variously commented upon. Complete party cohesion results in constantly predictable outcomes and leaves little scope for fulfilling a teaching and mobilizing function outside the context of the party struggle. A greater willingness on the part of MPs and peers to act independently of party wishes serves to attract attention. It makes members of both Houses more attractive to those seeking to have some input into parliamentary deliberations (see Chapter 10). If members' actions are not predictable, those wishing them to act in a particular way have to pay attention to their views to know if they are supportive or likely to take a contrary line.

The willingness of members to co-operate on a bi-partisan basis also underpins the influence of select committees. Committees work hard to produce agreed reports. Divisions in select committees tend to be the exception rather than the rule (Drewry 1989). A committee report can be discounted by government, and by interested groups, if it is the product of a divided committee. It is less easy to dismiss a report that has the endorsement of every member of the committee.

Consequences

Since the time that Beer wrote, both Houses have thus moved to dismantle the obstacles he identified to achieving the capacity to mobilize support for measures of public policy. But have greater openness, specialization and independence resulted in parliamentarians serving as teachers and mobilizers of popular support?

The positive impact

The effect of a more open Parliament, particularly through the medium of television, would appear to be a more informed public. Televised proceedings, which means essentially televised extracts, reach a large audience, especially through news and regional programmes. Once televising got under way, dedicated programmes attracted audiences of between 200,000 and over 1 million (Select

Committee on the Televising of Proceedings of the House 1990: xxix).

The reaction to televised proceedings has generally been positive, both on the part of MPs (Hetherington, Weaver and Ryle 1990: Chapter 7; Select Committee 1990: xxxvi–xxxvii, 86–89) and on the part of the public (Select Committee 1990: 83–86). A two-wave survey of public opinion carried out by the BBC and IBA, the first wave shortly before broadcasting began and the other four months after the cameras had entered, found that support for televising proceedings increased from the first to the second wave (in the latter, eighty-three per cent thought it was a good idea and should be continued, compared with sixty-three per cent in the first wave) and that for over half of those questioned television was their principal source of information about what was going on in Parliament (Select Committee 1990: 83).

More importantly for our purposes, seven out of every ten respondents felt that 'people will begin to understand how Parliament works' and eight out of ten thought that 'people will feel more involved in what is going on in Parliament' (Select Committee 1990: 84; see also Barnett and Gaber 1992: 418). There was little or no change between the two waves in terms of perceptions of politicians and the capacity to identify the local Member of Parliament.

The effect of greater specialization also appears to have produced more attentive groups, learning from the process and the substance of committee work. The most extensive data on such effects were gathered by Ian Marsh from groups that gave oral evidence to committees in the 1981–82 session. Of the groups, just over half reported positive 'learning' of some kind or another and/ or forming new links to other groups (Marsh 1986: 169). Forty-one per cent received extra information about the issue or government or department attitudes. Virtually all, as we have already noted, got copies of the committees' findings; most then reported to their members on their participation in the enquiry (Marsh 1986: 171). In terms of the impact of the enquiry process on the attitudes and judgements of the groups, fifty-five per cent reported 'important' or 'very important' alterations of attitude (Marsh 1986: 173). Most were also stimulated to undertake fresh research.

These findings, concluded Marsh (1986: 178), 'point to the potential of committees to be catalysts in opinion formation within particular policy communities and to be agents for the restoration of political trust'. There is also some evidence that the potential effect may not be confined to policy communities in the UK. 'From our own experiences and contacts within the EEC', recorded the deputy Director-General of the CBI in the 1980s, 'we can affirm that select committee reports are highly regarded, read with considerable interest, and have been the object of highly favourable comment in Europe' (Edwards 1984: 49). We have seen that reports of the Lords' European Communities Committee are read within the Community (see Chapter 7); other committees also reach a community audience. The Lords EC Committee also fulfils an important role in informing UK groups of community proposals. One TUC official noted that the TUC found the committee reports useful 'because at the end of the day they do tell us quite a lot about the purposes of some European proposals, more clearly than the Commission itself' (Lea 1984: 53).

Nor, arguably, is the potential confined to select committees. The greater interest shown by groups in the legislative process has also increased the teaching capacity of standing committees. The impact is almost certainly limited but nonetheless there is some evidence of it occurring. Before sending briefing material to committee members, the representatives of organizations will often seek guidance on parliamentary practices and procedure. There was evidence, for example, of financial institutions seeking briefings from political consultants during the passage of the Financial Services Bill in 1986. There were also meetings between such institutions and members of the committee, one member attending 'perhaps twenty meetings and another twenty lunches or dinners organized by companies or organizations who wanted to discuss the provisions of the bill with me' (Norton 1990c: 197). More importantly, perhaps, is the experience of attending committee meetings. In Chapter 11, the potential for Parliament to allow groups to hear countervailing views was discussed. To quote the example of one committee:

> One member actively involved in the standing committee on the Animals (Scientific Procedures) Bill, and who had some contact with those in the public gallery, noted the effect on those attending: by being present and hearing the government's case they better understood both sides of the argument – and also better understood the role of the committee.
>
> (Norton 1990c: 199)

Through the educative role, Parliament may thus serve to reduce or resolve conflicts as well as increase support for certain provisions of public policy.

Televised proceedings allow citizens to see some of the activity of members of both Houses in their respective chambers, as well as in committees. This, as we have seen, is considered likely to increase knowledge of how Parliament works rather than the substance of policy. Committee activity increases knowledge of groups about both the parliamentary process as well as about the substance of policy under consideration. The more direct contact between MPs and constituents, and between members and groups, may also serve to further the learning process.

Contact between members and constituents is growing and growing rapidly (see Chapter 9). Members are in more frequent contact with constituents and they spent more time in their constituencies. They are more likely than before to exploit the local media, not least because there are more local media than before. Contact between individual backbenchers – in both houses – and organized groups is also more extensive than before (see Chapter 10). The contact is two way. Of the groups surveyed by the Study of Parliament Group in 1986, over half (fifty-six per cent) relied on direct contact with backbench MPs as one means of keeping in touch with what is going on in Parliament. Almost forty-five per cent used contact with backbench peers (Rush 1990: 292). Through such contact, members of both Houses have the capacity to inform, not only about processes but also about the substance of public policy.

Similarly, with unorganized publics, members are playing a greater – though not so extensive – role. (By virtue of the lack of organization, the opportunities for regular and structured contact are not so great.) By utilizing local media and being more proactive in locating such publics, MPs inform as well as learn. Members' newsletters reach not only constituents who may have contacted them but also those – the majority – who have not made contact and who, as the plurality of constituents, form a disorganized public. The more members – and, indeed, select committees (see Chapter 11) – go out to meet those not represented through established organizations, the more they serve to reach those who may previously have had little knowledge of and attachment to the parliamentary process and little knowledge of the reasoning behind the public policy that affects them.

In combination, then, this increase in contact between parliamentarians and those outside Westminster provides a greater capacity for teaching and for mobilizing the support of the public or attentive publics for particular measures of public policy. What evidence we have suggests that, to a small extent, that capacity is being realized.

Limitations

The capacity of parliamentarians to teach and mobilize is nonetheless limited. Television may have had some effect on viewers' attitudes towards Parliament, but the joint BBC–IBA survey in 1990 did not suggest a significant increase in knowledge, but rather the expectation of an increase. Furthermore, coverage of proceedings is in the form of extracts rather than a continuous feed. Coverage of an entire debate is very rare. Hence, the opportunities for increasing knowledge on the substance of issues is limited. Viewers may gain some understanding of Parliament, but increased knowledge of particular issues will tend to be confined to major issues that are already the focus of public discussion.

The capacity to educate and mobilize support among particular groups is also limited. The bi-partisanship of select committees is a strength but also a weakness. It discourages committees from addressing some central issues which are the subject of party conflict. Of the impact that committee reports have on group attitudes, most of those identified by Marsh took the form of clarifying attitudes. Less than one in five mentioned developing attitudes toward other issues as an important or very important outcome (Marsh 1986: 172). Marsh noted that his findings 'suggest substantive bases for mobilizing consent' (Marsh 1986: 178). However, he then immediately conceded that 'the process is clearly in an elemental stage. It can be observed in embryo, so to speak. . . . Further deliberate leadership from committees – further effort deliberately aimed at interest groups – is required for a forthright judgement about committee potential' (Marsh 1986: 178, 179).

Though contact between committees and groups, and between individual members and constituents, has increased and members have displayed a relatively greater willingness to act independently of their party leaders, party nonetheless continues to act as the principal barrier to mobilizing support behind a particular policy.

Where there is cross-party agreement, the potential is considerable. Where the parties take opposing stances, the opportunity to inform and mobilize support behind particular provisions is limited. As we have seen, in standing committee (see Chapter 5) the partisan conflict results in much of the detail being neglected in favour of argument over the principal contentious clauses. Individual members often find it difficult to avoid giving their communications with constituents – particularly speeches and press articles – a partisan slant. Once this practice is recognised, constituents tend to discount it accordingly.

The capacity for parliamentarians to educate and, more especially, mobilize support for particular provisions of public policy thus remains restricted. For members of either House to engage in a teaching role, they have first to be informed on the issue and be prepared to communicate with individuals, groups and less organized publics to inform them. Limited time and resources restricts the opportunity to obtain the information. Partisanship also acts as a barrier both to obtaining and to disseminating information and more especially to offering a united front to the public.

Conclusion

Since the 1970s, both Houses of Parliament have acquired a greater potential to educate both the public and particular groups and to mobilize support for specific provisions of public policy. Relative to past practice, both Houses are more open than before and, indeed, more open than some other legislatures. Relative to past practice, both Houses, especially the Commons, are more specialized than before. There is also a greater willingness to act independently of government and there is much greater contact between parliamentarians and those outside Westminster – individuals, organized groups and unorganized publics. This contact facilitates two-way communication.

However, that communication is restricted. Limited time and resources reduce the opportunity for committees and for members individually to inform themselves about the detail of policy. Party commitment severely limits members' ability to engage in mobilizing popular support.

Educating citizens is sometimes achieved by Parliament, and on occasion – primarily where there is cross-party agreement – members are able to assist in mobilizing popular support behind a particular policy. The evidence suggests that the occasions are more numerous than before. Parliament therefore has a greater impact than before. More importantly, though, Parliament has the potential to be a far more significant educator and mobilizer. As Marsh noted, it is at an elemental stage. If members grasp the resources, and develop their capacity to act independently of government, then the reality might start to match the potential.

Note

1. It is also possible for a committee to go into private session if it lacks a quorum. Without a quorum, it cannot continue to take evidence formally. By going into private session, it can continue on an unofficial basis. On 14 February 1990, the Procedure Committee adopted this approach when the departure of one of the members present deprived it of a quorum.

13

The Consequences of Parliament

This book addresses one central question. That question forms the title. Does Parliament matter? The answer, drawn from the preceding chapters, is 'Yes certainly. But . . .'. 'Yes' – and a resounding yes – because Parliament quite clearly has a number of consequences – significant consequences – for the political system. 'But' because those consequences vary in importance, with some not having the effect that they might have.

The environment in which Parliament exists is not a static one. The pressures on Parliament have changed over the centuries and Parliament has responded in different ways. Parliament has been shaped by, and itself helped shape, that environment. If Parliament has mattered and does matter, the question arises: to what extent will it continue to matter? Will pressures reduce its significance – limiting its consequences for government and for the citizen – or will it have greater significance in the future?

Parliament matters

Writing in 1977 on the question of whether Britain was worse governed than before, Peter Self ended with the words: 'This article hardly mentions Parliament. I suggest the reader asks himself why' (Self 1977). The reader was clearly expected to come up with one particular answer. However, there were two answers that the discerning reader might supply.

One – the expected one – is that Parliament is not a central actor in the determination of public policy. In this context, 'the significance of Parliament is its very insignificance' (Richardson and Jordan 1979: 121). The second answer is that Self rarely mentioned Parliament because he had adopted a narrow focus for his enquiry. Those concerned with the determination of public policy are not likely to find Parliament a central actor. That does not mean that Parliament does not matter. To establish that conclusion one would need to adopt a much wider focus.

That wider focus encompasses not just the relationship of Parliament to government in the making of public policy, but the relationship of Parliament to government in the formation and conduct of government and the relationship of Parliament to the citizen. This wider focus allows a more comprehensive picture of Parliament to emerge. In this wider systemic context, the significance of Parliament is not its insignificance but rather the reverse. Parliament is not just significant: it is indispensable.

What would the British polity be like without Parliament? How would the government be chosen? Who or what would 'represent' citizens and confer legitimacy on the actions of government and on measures that are intended to be binding on citizens? Who would check the actions of government? Who would champion the views and the demands of the individual citizen, and groups of citizens, in dealings with government? What forum would allow for the expression of conflicting sentiments in society?

In answer to most of these questions, it is possible to come up with an alternative, or complementary, body to that of Parliament. The press can act as a champion of the individual and of different publics. The National Audit Office and the media can scrutinize the actions of government departments. Ministerial actions can be challenged in the courts. Conflicting views can be expressed through opinion polls, television debates and referendums. What makes Parliament distinctive – and indispensable – is the fact that it alone enjoys the popular as well as the formal legitimacy to undertake all these tasks.

The functions of Parliament

Parliament has to be evaluated in this wider context. It is a multifunctional body. The consequences it has for the political system

Table 13.1 The functions of Parliament

Manifest legitimation
Recruiting, socializing and training ministers
Latent legitimation
Acting as a safety valve
Achieving a redress of grievance
Interest articulation
Administrative oversight
Law making
Mobilizing and educating citizens
Conflict resolution

are several and significant. A rank ordering of them, similar to that undertaken by Packenham for the Brazilian congress (see Chapter 1), is given in Table 13.1. The list encapsulates the principal consequences discussed in the preceding chapters. The ordering is a rough and necessarily subjective one, designed to give some sense of the relative position of the consequences that have so far been discussed in compartmentalized form.

The function of *manifest legitimation* – giving the formal seal of approval – is the one that constitutes the core defining function of legislatures. As we have seen, it is the oldest function of the House of Commons and since 1689 the assent of Parliament has been essential for a new law to be passed or dispensed with (see Chapter 2). The popular legitimacy of Parliament as the assent-giver to legislation makes it extremely powerful in terms of Luke's third face of power (see Chapter 8).

Similarly it is powerful in terms of *the recruitment of ministers* in that it enjoys virtual hegemony as the recruiting agency. Given that ministers remain within Parliament, the institution is also powerful in socializing ministers into parliamentary norms and expectations and creating an environment to which they have to adapt in order to survive. Indeed, as we noted in Chapter 3, there is a case for arguing that it may be too powerful, a capacity to handle Parliament enjoying undue influence as a criterion for ministerial selection.

By meeting regularly, by subjecting ministers to scrutiny, by allowing different views to be expressed and by retaining ministers as members, Parliament fulfils an important function of *latent legitimation* (see Chapter 8). That legitimation is of both Parliament and government. Parliament is seen to be active. By being derived from and subject to the attentions of Parliament, especially the elected House, government enjoys a degree of legitimacy over and above that conferred by Parliament's formal approval of its actions and measures.

The next three functions – those of *acting as a safety valve, achieving a redress of grievance* and *interest articulation* – are central to the relationship of Parliament, and especially parliamentarians, to the citizen. They encompass a more direct form of contact than that covered by the preceding functions. They are not exclusive to Parliament. There are alternative channels. Citizens can give vent to their feelings through writing to the press. They can pursue grievances through officials, councillors, citizens' advice bureaux, the media and the courts. Organized interests can, and do, express their needs and demands directly to government departments. However, as a safety valve and grievance chaser, none of these alternatives matches the popular expectations and legitimacy of Parliament.

Using Parliament is perceived as the route that should be employed and the route that is employed. As we have seen, citizens expect Members of Parliament to concentrate on local needs. Recent years have seen a dramatic growth in the use made by constituents of parliamentarians (see Chapter 9). The more parliamentarians respond to those demands and achieve outcomes satisfactory to those making them, then the greater the popular satisfaction with the institution of Parliament. Similarly, in terms of interest articulation, recent years have seen a remarkable increase in the use made of Parliament by organized interests (see Chapter 10) with similar effects. The principal vehicles of interest articulation – the political parties – retain their central role but they are now complemented by a host of organizations that use Parliament as a conduit for the authoritative expression of their particular interests.

It is these consequences, we would hypothesize, that explain the extent of popular satisfaction with Parliament. A MORI poll for the Rowntree Trust in 1991 found that almost sixty per cent of those questioned thought that Parliament was doing a good job (see Chapter 8). (Less than twenty per cent thought it as doing a bad job.) As we saw in Chapter 9, approval ratings increase following direct contact with MPs. Given that the local role of the MP is stressed by constituents, and that contact with MPs appears to produce a positive evaluation, then the activities of the MP discussed in Part Two would appear more central than those discussed in Part One to popular evaluations of Parliament.

The consequences of Parliament in terms of its relationship with government – those discussed in Part One – thus occupy the lower half of the list. Within what Packenham characterised as the decisional or influencing functions, that of *administrative oversight* – the focus of Chapter 6 – probably has greatest impact, both in terms of the effect on government and in the popular perceptions of Parliament's activity. Parliament helps keep government on its toes and is seen to do so.

In terms of *law making,* Parliament has some effect. The effect is important, but essentially at the margins: Parliament itself is rarely involved in the initiation and formulation of public policy (see Chapter 4) and achieves significant changes to the content of measures on an irregular rather than a regular basis (see Chapter 5). It is the emphasis on Parliament as law maker that leads to the evaluation of the institution as insignificant. The result is a skewed focus, leaving those adopting it unable to explain popular perceptions of Parliament as doing 'a good job'.

Parliament has some impact as an *educator* and *a mobilizer of popular support,* but it is essentially limited, important more for its potential than its realization (see Chapter 12). Parliamentarians have more effect in receiving and pursuing the needs expressed to them than they do in seeking to shape the views and mobilize the support of citizens and of different publics.

The capacity of Parliament to *resolve conflicts* has also proved limited. It is not non-existent. It is listed precisely because it is a consequence of Parliament but it does not have the impact that the other functions have. As argued in Chapter 11, it can and to some extent does serve as a arbiter, or broker, between competing interests, allowing the different sides to hear the arguments of the others engaged in the dispute. Again, though, as was suggested in Chapter 11, the potential is greater than the actuality. Serving to resolve conflict could be a more important consequence of Parliament than is the case at present.

Table 13.1 provides a relative evaluation of the functions of Parliament. Viewed as a whole, the functions demonstrate the centrality of Parliament to the political system. Parliament cannot be extricated from that system without destroying the system itself.

Government may seek to hide facts from Parliament, it may treat the institution with contempt, but every time it does so it diminishes its own position. The legitimacy of government derives from Parliament itself and whenever the institution is undermined in popular perception, the more government itself loses its popular legitimacy. Parliament may not make public policy, but to declare it insignificant is to misunderstand its role in the British polity. It serves as the central representative body of the nation (see Chapter 8). The consequences of Parliament for the political system are fundamental.

But . . .

To say that Parliament matters is important for understanding the British political system and the popular support that it enjoys. However, we have suggested that Parliament does not necessarily have the consequences that it could have. Hence the 'but . . .'. This brings us to the normative dimension. Our analysis so far has been neutral, focusing on what is rather than what should be. To establish that Parliament matters is not the same as establishing that it matters as much as it should do.

Should Parliament have more powerful consequences than it presently does? There is no definitive checklist against which Parliament can be evaluated. The essential basis for evaluation is subjective: that of popular and elite expectations. Does Parliament live up to what citizens expect of it?

To a large extent, we would argue that the answer is yes. The 1991 MORI poll already mentioned found that six out of every ten respondents felt that Parliament did a good job. As we saw in Chapter 8, a Gallup poll carried out at the same time found that almost half of all of those questioned had a 'great deal' or 'quite a lot' of confidence in Parliament, nine per cent more than had given the same responses two years earlier. In the 1991 poll, only nine per cent of respondents said they had no confidence at all in Parliament. In 1989, the figure had been eighteen per cent. On the face of it, these figures appear healthy and suggest a trend of increasing confidence in Parliament.

However, there is another side of the coin. In both the 1989 and 1991 Gallup polls, forty-three per cent of respondents expressed 'not very much' confidence in the institution. In comparative terms, popular confidence in the legislature is generally higher in other west European countries. The *Reader's Digest* Europe Survey at the beginning of 1991 found that the percentage expressing confidence in Parliament in the UK was eight per cent below the average in the countries of the European Community (EC) and the European Free Trade Area (EFTA). Particularly high levels of confidence were found in Germany, Switzerland, Portugal and Greece (Gallup Index, Report 366, February 1991; see also Saalfeld 1990: 83).

In terms of popular perceptions, Parliament would thus appear to occupy a position of 'satisfactory, but could do better'. How could it do better? In terms of the relationships of Parliament to government and to the citizen, we have seen the weight accorded the latter. The MP is expected to focus on local concerns. But what of members collectively? There are few data to inform our analysis. Our presumptions as to popular expectations were sketched in Chapter 8. Electors vote on a party basis yet expect Parliament to be more than a 'rubber stamp' for whatever the Government lays before it. Popular legitimacy is also questioned if particular sections of society – ethnic, regional or political – appear disadvantaged by the method by which Parliament is chosen.

We have suggested that popular expectations have been met in recent years to a greater extent than before as a result of the various changes we identified in Chapter 2 and developed in subsequent chapters. Both Houses have witnessed significant changes in resources, structures and behaviour. There have also been some changes that have moved closer to the expectations of particular publics as far as representation in the House of Commons is concerned. Nonetheless, problems remain.

These problems we have detailed in looking at the particular consequences of Parliament. The institution remains marginal in terms especially of the legislative process, both domestic and European. It is not a significant initiator of public policy and is an infrequent influencer of the content of public policy. In terms of administrative oversight, it has made great strides in providing for more regular scrutiny, and greater openness, of government, but remains limited in terms of the capacity to probe deeply and consistently across the range of sectors covered by government departments. It remains an essential forum for the expression of different views in society, but has a limited capacity to help resolve conflict and to mobilize the support of the public or particular publics for particular provisions of public policy. Members can act as grievance chasers but, collectively and individually, have limited resources and knowledge to challenge negative responses.

Hence, the 'but . . .'. Parliament matters. It has important consequences for the political system. But in terms of what is expected of it, it could do more.

The future

Parliament could do more. Will it do more? The evidence of recent years suggests it has the capacity to do so. The various changes we have sketched have resulted in a more active Parliament and, in so far as it is possible to infer a causal relationship between the two, a more supported Parliament. However, nothing about a trend ensures its continuation. Rather, we would suggest that Parliament faces two conflicting options in the years leading up to the twenty-first century.

From overload to collapse

The first option is that of collapsing under the strain. Parliamentarians – collectively and individually – are in danger of being overloaded with business (see Chapters 9 and 10). The growth of government has resulted not only in more ministers but in more public business being brought before both Houses. Bills are not more numerous but they are much longer than before. Membership of the European Community has added to the demands of public business. Expectations of Parliament are not static. The demands made by constituents, by organized interests and by wider publics have increased enormously the workload of members and of both Houses. The growth of career-oriented members has also increased the pressures on the time and resources of the House of Commons. Parliament's own increasing specialization, especially through the use of select committees, has added to the demands on members' time and efforts.

The result has been a volume of business that has exceeded the increase in the resources available to both Houses and to members individually (Norton 1992a). For the individual MP, 'a fourteen hour day is the norm from Monday to Thursday, in addition to whatever the Member does in his constituency' (Davis 1989: 49). Members are having to determine which of the demands made on their time have priority. Those at the bottom of the list get neglected. Pressure on the time of the Commons and of its members means that many bills get partial attention, the main burden of detailed scrutiny being left to the House of Lords to shoulder. The result is an increasingly overburdened Parliament. Members are under strain. That is a threat to their health. The institution is under strain. That is a threat to the health of the body politic.

There is, in effect, a danger of Parliament becoming a victim of its own success. The more members have taken up the demands made of them, the more demands have been made of them. The resources of both Houses and of members have so far proved sufficient – just – to meet these expectations, but there is little evidence of resources *continuing* to keep pace with the growing expectations. The resources themselves are better than ever before (see Chapter 2), but the improvement has been from a remarkably low base. In international comparison, the resources are poor. In terms of present demands, they are barely adequate. With increasing demands being made of the institution, they will cease to be adequate.

Building on strength

The second option is that of reforming procedures and improving resources in order to strengthen Parliament in its relationship with government and with the citizen. We have variously discussed ways in which this can be achieved. In terms of the legislative process, for example, there is the greater use of special standing committees and timetabling in the Commons and the use of public bill committees in the Lords (see Chapter 5). These are options that have found favour with a substantial proportion of the members in each House. More radical suggestions have also been floated, including reversing the order in which second reading and committee stage are taken (Norton 1992f). Evidence from other legislatures suggests that sending bills first to committee increases the influence of the legislature (Shaw 1979).

Improving the resources of each House, though, is necessary but not sufficient. They cannot be utilized effectively unless MPs and peers have the time and resources to make them work. Improving the resources of members is a prerequisite for an effective House. As we have seen, the burden on individual members as a result of constituency and group pressures is enormous. If members are to cope with the pressures detailed in previous chapters, they need the research and secretarial resources – and office infrastructure – that will allow them to cope with those demands. If they cannot keep pace with those demands, the quality of the service they can offer to constituents declines. Furthermore, the time and effort they can devote to legislation and more Westminster-oriented activities are also threatened. Hence the imperative of improving resources.

There are, though, two levels at which resources can be improved. One is the 'stand still' level. Given the increasing demands made of members, resources have to be improved just to remain at the present level of what members and both Houses can offer. In other words, both Houses have to run in order to stand still. The other is the 'value added' level. This entails not just doing that which is necessary to maintain the present level of operations but rather adding to it in order to provide a more effective institution, that is, one more capable of fulfilling popular expectations. What evidence we have suggests that Parliament could do more to meet the expectations held of it. If more citizens are to judge it to be doing a 'good job' – and in the MORI poll forty per cent of those questioned did not offer that evaluation – and if more than half are to express confidence in the institution, then it has to go beyond what it has presently achieved.

Whither Parliament?

Which of these options is likely to be pursued? The answer lies with the members of both Houses. Recent years have witnessed a growing body of members in both Houses favouring change. Demands for change, however, have found no authoritative outlet in the Commons. In the Lords, they have.

A MORI poll of MPs in 1990 found that fifty-eight per cent of those who responded considered the House to be a 'fairly poor' or 'very poor' place to work (House of Commons Commission 1990). A survey of select committee members by the BBC2 *Scrutiny* programme in the same year found that almost half of those questioned considered that the committees were not scrutinizing departments adequately and just over half favoured having more staff and resources. At the end of that year, Douglas Hurd made Commons' reform a central plank of his platform in contesting the Conservative Party leadership. The new Prime Minister, John Major, indicated he would not stand in the way of reform. (This distinguished him from his predecessor, a notable opponent of reform.) At the same time, an early day motion calling for a reform of hours and conditions attracted the signatures of more than ninety members (Norton 1991c).

A questionnaire sent to members in 1991 by the Select Committee on the Sittings of the House found widespread dissatisfaction with the timing of certain business, especially late-night sittings, and a majority of respondents favouring the timetabling of bills. By the end of the 1987–92 Parliament, there was an apparent groundswell in the Commons in favour of reform. In the 1992 general election, all three main parties committed themselves to parliamentary reform. In the new Parliament, one of the first notable acts of the House was to approve, by 324 votes to 197 and against government advice, a motion – in line with a recommendation of the top salaries review body – that the office cost allowance should be increased by approximately forty per cent, from £28,986 to £39,960 a year.

Nonetheless, pressure for substantial reform has not been overwhelming and it has found little expression in the reports of the Procedure Committee and in the speeches of the Leader of the House. From 1978 to 1986, the Procedure Committee was an important catalyst for reform, recommending the creation of the departmental select committees and later the use of special standing committees and the timetabling of bills, though, as we have noted (see Chapter 5), standing by its earlier recommendations, the Procedure Committee in recent years has adopted a 'steady as she goes approach', reflected most notably in its report on the first ten years of the departmental select committees (Select Committee on Procedure 1990; Norton 1990e). In the 1987–92 Parliament, it added no significant new thinking on how the House might meet the growing pressures to which it was subjected.

It was a stance that led to the creation of a new committee – the Select Committee on the Sittings of the House – to consider broader reform. However, in order to issue a report before the House was dissolved, the new committee moved quickly to take evidence and issue a report. The result was a fairly narrowly drawn report, favouring *inter alia* an earlier sitting of the House on a Wednesday and ten Fridays as non-sitting days. It did, though, reiterate the recommendation of the Procedure Committee for the timetabling of bills.

Following the 1979 general election, the Leader of the House, Norman St. John-Stevas, moved rapidly to get Cabinet approval for the Procedure Committee's 1978 recommendation for the creation of a series of departmental select committees. The Conservative manifesto in the election had supported reform and, on the basis of that, the Cabinet backed St. John-Stevas' proposals. In 1992, the conditions were set fair for a similar lead by the Leader of the House: a manifesto commitment and a parliamentary mood favouring change. However, on this occasion, no lead was forthcoming. The new Leader of the House, Tony Newton, adopted a cautious approach. Instead of leading, he ended up following, with the House going further than he recommended in increasing the office cost allowance.

The new Parliament returned in 1992 was thus one in which there was a mood of dissatisfaction with existing arrangements but one in which leadership that might allow the House to address fundamental questions of change was missing. Discussion was confined to the office cost allowance, the recommendations of the Sitting of the House Committee, and a fairly acrimonious debate on the selection of members to serve on the select committees. The 1990 report of the Procedure Committee was essentially a lost opportunity (Norton 1990e). The months between the 1992 general election and the summer recess – the time when the opportunity to mobilise parliamentary support in favour of change was greatest – similarly constituted a lost opportunity.

In the House of Lords, there is more evidence of leadership. A working group set up by the Leader of the House had concluded in

1987 that there was no fundamental problem with the procedures of the House. A more recent report, from the Select Committee on the Committee Work of the House in 1992 (see Chapter 5), adopted a more critical and constructive approach, recommending the employment of special standing committees and more regular use of *ad hoc* select committees. The report envisages no radical change, but did acknowledge the need for the existing procedures to be extended and kept under review. Underlying the report is a greater awareness than appears to exist within equivalent committees in the Commons of the need to run in order to stand still.

In the Lords, there thus appears to be some leadership that may allow the House to pursue the second option of change, albeit one favouring maintaining the present relationships rather than going beyond them. In the Commons, there is pressure for the second option – with some members favouring more extensive change that will allow the House to go beyond the present position – but with no leadership that will allow it to do so.

Conclusion

Parliament matters. It is a vital part of the body politic. In recent years it has shown a capacity to meet, more than before, the popular expectations held of it. By doing so, it appears to have encouraged even greater expectations. To meet them, it has to strengthen the resources at its disposal. That requires political will. Without that will-power, Parliament is in danger of being overloaded with work and unable to meet the demands made of it. Members alone can determine whether Parliament limps into the twenty-first century or enters it as a body more responsive than ever before to the demands of a changing society.

Further Reading

The following constitutes a selection of works recommended for those wishing to pursue research of Parliament. Those titles marked with an asterisk (*) are in print and available in paper editions.

Select committee reports and other parliamentary publications are available from Her Majesty's Stationery Office (HMSO).

Facts and figures

The most substantial work to appear recently providing extensive facts and figures on parliamentary activity is the 538-page volume by J. A. G. Griffith and Michael Ryle, *Parliament: Functions, Practice and Procedure* (1989; paper edn 1990)*. Valuable quantitative material for each parliamentary session is to be found in the *Sessional Information Digest* published each year by the public information office of the House of Commons. The *Digest* contains, *inter alia*, data on parliamentary questions, early day motions, debates, select committee reports, the amount of time spent by the House on particular items of business, and the bills introduced and the Acts passed.

Parliament and government

On party organization in Parliament, see Norton, 'The organization of parliamentary parties' in Walkland (1979) and – for the Conservative side only – Norton, 'The party in Parliament' in Seldon (1993). On backbench influence exerted through dissenting behaviour see Norton, 'The House of Commons:

behavioural changes' in Norton (ed), *Parliament in the 1980s* (1985). A recent analysis of backbench influence in both parties in the Commons is provided by Jack Brand, *British Parliamentary Parties* (1992).

On parliamentary scrutiny exerted through select committees, see especially the volume edited by Gavin Drewry, *The New Select Committees* (1989)*. The report of the Select Committee on Procedure – *The Working of the Select Committee System*, third report, session 1989–90, HC 19 – contains a mass of useful data and evidence, even if the conclusion disappoints. On scrutiny exerted through parliamentary questions, the classic work is that by Sir Norman Chester and Nona Bowring, *Questions in Parliament* (1962) which has now been superseded by Franklin and Norton (eds), *Parliamentary Questions* (1993).

On legislative scrutiny, see the classic work by Griffith, *Parliamentary Scrutiny of Government Bills* (1974), as well as Burton and Drewry, *Legislation and Public Policy* (1981). For more recent analyses, see Drewry, 'Legislation' in Ryle and Richards (eds), *The Commons Under Scrutiny* (1988)* and Norton, 'Public Legislation' in Rush, *Parliament and Pressure Politics* (1990). On private members' legislation, see Richards, *Parliament and Conscience* (1970) – analyzing the conscience issues of the 1960s – and Marsh and Read, *Private Members' Bills* (1988).

The most extensive and useful information on parliamentary scrutiny of European legislation is contained in the report of the Select Committee on Procedure, *The Scrutiny of European Legislation*, fourth report, session 1988–89, HC 622.

On the House of Lords, see especially Donald Shell, *The House of Lords*, second edition (1992)* and the volume edited by Shell and Beamish, *The House of Lords at Work* (1993). Valuable data also appear in the *Report from the Select Committee on The Committee Work of the House*, session 1991–92, HL paper 35, especially volume II containing the evidence submitted to the committee.

There are also some useful works analyzing the relationship between Parliament and government in particular sectors. Notable among recent works are David Judge, *Parliament and Industry* (1990) and Charles Carstairs and Richard Ware (eds), *Parliament and International Relations* (1991)*.

Parliament and citizen

On the backgrounds of Members of Parliament, see especially Mellors, *The British MP* (1978), Rush, 'The Members of Parliament' in Walkland (1979) and the chapter, also by Rush, with the same title in Ryle and Richards (eds), *The Commons Under Scrutiny* (1988)*. Valuable data on every Member of Parliament – and peer – are to be found in *Dod's Parliamentary Companion*, published at the beginning of each year.

On the relationship between Members of Parliament and constituents see especially Cain, Ferejohn and Fiorina, *The Personal Vote* (1987) and the forthcoming work by Norton and Wood, *Back to Westminster* (1993).

On the relationship of Parliament and pressure groups, see the volume edited by Rush, *Parliament and Pressure Politics* (1990). On the phenomenon of parliamentary lobbying, see the chapter by Cliff Grantham and Colin Seymour-Ure, 'Political consultants' in the Rush volume, Miller, *Lobbying*, 2nd ed. (1989) and Norton, 'The changing face of Parliament: lobbying and its consequences' in Norton (ed), *New Directions in British Politics?* (1991).

Parliament in perspective

For the purpose of analysing Parliament in terms of its consequences for the political system, see the various articles and chapters contained in the reader edited by Norton, *Legislatures* (1990)*. To consider parliament in comparative perspective, see Mezey, *Comparative Legislatures* (1979), Norton (ed), *Parliaments in Western Europe* (1990b) and Olson and Mezey, *Legislatures in the Policy Process* (1991). On the normative debate about Parliament's role in the political system, see the volume edited by Judge, *The Politics of Parliamentary Reform* (1983) and Norton, *Parliament in Perspective* (1987b)*.

References

Arkins, Audrey (1990), 'Legislative and executive relations in the Republic of Ireland', in Norton, P. (ed), *Parliaments in Western Europe*, London: Frank Cass.

Arter, David (1990), 'The Swedish Riksdag: The case of a strong policy-influencing legislature', in Norton, P. (ed), *Parliaments in Western Europe*, London: Frank Cass.

Bagehot, Walter (1867), *The English Constitution*, London: Chapman and Hall.

Baldwin, Nicholas D. J. (1985a), 'The House of Lords: behavioural changes', in Norton, P. (ed), *Parliament in the 1980s*, Oxford: Basil Blackwell.

Baldwin, Nicholas D. J. (1985b), 'The Contemporary House of Lords', Unpublished PhD Thesis, Exeter: University of Exeter.

Baldwin, Nicholas D. J. (1990), 'The House of Lords', in Rush, M. (ed), *Parliament and Pressure Politics*, Oxford: Oxford University Press.

Barker, Anthony and Rush, Michael (1970), *The Member of Parliament and his Information*, London: George Allen & Unwin.

Barnett, Steven and Gaber, Ivor (1992), 'Committees on Camera: MPs and lobby views on the effects of televising Commons select committees', *Parliamentary Affairs*, 45: 409–19.

Bates, T. St. John (1983), 'The drafting of European Community legislation', *Statute Law Review*, Spring: 24–34.

Batty, Ken and George, Bruce (1985), 'Finance and facilities for MPs', in Norton, P. (ed), *Parliament in the 1980s*, Oxford: Basil Blackwell.

Beer, Samuel H. (1966), 'The British legislature and the problem of mobilizing consent', in Frank, E. (ed), *Lawmakers in a Changing World*, Englewood Cliffs NJ: Prentice Hall.

Beer, Samuel H. (1969), *Modern British Politics*, revised edn, London: Faber.

Beer, Samuel H. (1982), *Britain Against Itself*, London: Faber.

Beith, Alan (1976), 'The MP as a grievance chaser', *Public Administration Bulletin*, 21: 6–10.

Berkeley, Humphry (1972), *Crossing the Floor*, London: George Allen & Unwin.

Blondel, Jean, Gillespie, P., Herman, V., Kaati, P. and Leonard, R. (1970), 'Legislative behaviour: some steps towards a cross-national measurement', *Government and Opposition*, 5: 67–85.

Blondel, Jean (1973), *Comparative Legislatures*, Englewood Cliffs NJ: Prentice Hall.

Bown, Francis A. (1990), 'The Shops Bill', in Rush, M. (ed), *Parliament and Pressure Politics*, Oxford: Oxford University Press.

Brand, Jack (1992), *British Parliamentary Parties*, Oxford: Clarendon Press.

Brandreth, Giles (1992), 'Post haste', *The House Magazine*, 18 (566): 5 October.

Bromhead, Peter (1958), *The House of Lords and Contemporary Politics 1911–1957*, London: Routledge & Kegan Paul.

Bruyneel, Gaston (1978), *Interpellations, Questions and Analogous Procedures for the Control of Government Actions and Challenging the Responsibility of the Government*, Association of Secretaries General of Parliaments.

Bryce, Lord (1921), *Modern Democracies*, London: Macmillan.

Buck, Philip W. (1963), *Amateurs and Professionals in British Politics 1918–59*, Chicago: University of Chicago Press.

Burch, Martin and Moran, Michael (1985), *A Reader in British Politics*, Manchester: Manchester University Press.

Burton, Ivor and Drewry, Gavin (1981), *Legislation and Public Policy*, London: Macmillan.

Butt, Ronald (1967), *The Power of Parliament*, London: Constable.

Cain, Bruce E., Ferejohn, J., and Fiorina, M. (1979), 'Popular evaluations of representatives in Great Britain and the United States', *California Institute of Technology Working Paper No. 288*, Pasadena: California Institute of Technology.

Cain, Bruce E., Ferejohn, J., and Fiorina, M. (1987), *The Personal Vote*, Cambridge, MA.: Harvard University Press.

Campion, Lord (1952), 'Parliament and democracy', in Campion, Lord (ed), *Parliament: A survey*, London: George Allen & Unwin.

Cannon, John and Griffiths, Ralph (1988), *The Oxford Illustrated History of the British Monarchy*, Oxford: Oxford University Press.

Carstairs, Charles and Ware, Richard (1991), *Parliament and International Relations*, Milton Keynes: Open University Press.

Cazalet-Keir, Thelma (1967), *From the Wings*, London: Bodley Head.

Chester, Norman and Bowring, Nona (1962), *Questions in Parliament*, Oxford: Oxford University Press.

Clarke, Sir Richard (1975), 'The machinery of government' in Thornhill, W. (ed), *The Modernization of British Government*, London: Pitman.

Clinton-Davis, Lord (1991), 'The Community and Britain: the changing relationship between London and Brussels', in P. Norton (ed), *New Directions in British Politics?*, Aldershot: Edward Elgar.

Cormack, Patrick (1992), 'Back to work, and bang goes September', *The House Magazine*, 18 (566): 5 October.

Cosgrove, Patrick (1985), *Carrington: A Life and a Policy*, London: J. M. Dent.

Couzens, K. (1956), 'A minister's correspondence', *Public Administration*, 34: 237–44.

Crewe, Ivor (1975), 'Electoral reform and the local MP', in Finer, S. E. (ed), *Adversary Politics and Electoral Reform*, London: Anthony Wigram.

Crick, Bernard (1964), *The Reform of Parliament*, London: Weidenfeld and Nicolson.

Crossman, Richard H. S. (1963), 'Introduction' to Bagehot, W., *The English Constitution*, London: Fontana edition.

Crowe, Edward (1986), 'The web of authority: party loyalty and social control in the British House of Commons', *Legislative Studies Quarterly*, 11: 161–85.

Currie, Edwina (1989), *Lifelines*, London: Sidgwick and Jackson.

Dalton, Russell J. (1988), *Citizen Politics in Western Democracies*, Chatham NJ: Chatham House.

Davis, David (1989), *The BBC Viewer's Guide to Parliament*, London: BBC Books.

Denver, David and Halfacree, Keith (1992), 'Inter-constituency migration and party support in Britain', *Political Studies*, 40: 571–80.

Dod's Parliamentary Companion, (annual), Etchingham, East Sussex: Dod's Parliamentary Companion Ltd.

Downs, Stephen (1985), 'The House of Commons: structural changes', in Norton, P. (ed), *Parliament in the 1980s*, Oxford: Basil Blackwell.

Dowse, Robert E. (1963), 'The MP and his surgery', *Political Studies*, 11: 333–41.

Drewry, Gavin (ed) (1989), *The New Select Committees*, revised edn, Oxford: Oxford University Press.

Dubs, Alf (1988), *Lobbying – An Insider's Guide to the Parliamentary Process*, London: Pluto Press.

Eddleston, Philip (1992), 'Parliament's continuing fall from grace: what should be done', Hull University Politics Department: Third-Year Undergraduate Dissertation.

Edwards, Kenneth (1984), 'An industrialist's view', in Englefield, D. (ed), *Commons Select Committees: Catalysts for Progress?* Harlow: Longman.

Elms, Tim and Terry, Tracy (1990), *Scrutiny of Ministerial Correspondence*, London: Cabinet Office Efficiency Unit.

Englefield, Dermot (1984) (ed), *Commons Select Committees: Catalysts for progress?* Harlow: Longman.

Field, Frank (1982), 'Backbenchers, the executive and theories of representation', in Royal Institute of Public Administration, *Parliament and the Executive*, London: RIPA.

Finer, Samuel E. (1958), *Anonymous Empire*, London: Pall Mall.

Finer, Samuel E. (ed) (1975), *Adversary Politics and Electoral Reform*, London: Anthony Wigram.

Fowler, Norman (1991), *Ministers Decide*, London: Chapmans.

Franklin, Mark (1985), *The Decline of Class Voting in Britain*, Oxford: Oxford University Press.

Franklin, Mark, Baxter, A. and Jordan, M. (1986), 'Who were the rebels? Dissent in the House of Commons 1970–1974', *Legislative Studies Quarterly*, 11: 143–59.

Franklin, Mark and Norton, Philip (eds) (1993), *Parliamentary Questions*, Oxford: Oxford University Press.

Freestone, David and Davidson, J. Scott (1988), *The Institutional Framework of the European Communities*, London: Croom Helm.

Gamble, Andrew (1988), *The Free Economy and the Strong State*, London: Macmillan.

Ganz, Gabriele (1989), 'The Transport Committee', in Drewry, G. (ed), *The New Select Committees*, 2nd ed., Oxford: Oxford University Press.

Gifford, Zerbanoo (1992), *Dadabhai Naoroji: Britain's first Asian MP*, London: Mantra.

Gordon, Strathearn (1948), *Our Parliament*, 3rd edn, London: Hansard Society.

Grantham, Cliff (1989), 'Parliament and political consultants', *Parliamentary Affairs*, 42: 503–18.

Grantham, Cliff (1993), 'Select committees', in Shell, D. R. and Beamish, D. R. (eds), *The House of Lords at Work*, Oxford: Oxford University Press.

Grantham, Cliff and Moore Hodgson, Caroline (1985), 'The House of Lords: structural changes', in Norton, P. (ed), *Parliament in the 1980s*, Oxford: Basil Blackwell.

Grantham, Cliff and Seymour-Ure, Colin (1990), 'Political consultants', in Rush, M. (ed), *Parliament and Pressure Politics*, Oxford: Oxford University Press.

Greer, Ian (1985), *Right to be Heard*, London: Ian Greer Associates.

Gregory, Roy and Alexander, Alan (1973), 'Our parliamentary ombudsman. Part 2: development and the problem of identity', *Public Administration*, 51: 41–59.

Griffith, John A. G. (1974), *Parliamentary Scrutiny of Government Bills*, London: George Allen & Unwin.

Griffith, John A. G. and Ryle, Michael (1989), *Parliament: Functions, Practice and Procedure*, London: Sweet & Maxwell.

Group on the Working of the House, House of Lords (1987), *Report by the Group on the Working of the House*, session 1987–88, HL 9, London: HMSO.

Hayter, P. D. G. (1991), 'The parliamentary monitoring of science and technology in Britain', *Government and Opposition*, 26: 147–66.

Headey, Bruce (1974), *British Cabinet Ministers*, London: George Allen & Unwin.

Hetherington, Alistair, Weaver, K. and Ryle, M. (1990), *Cameras in the Commons*, London: Hansard Society.

Hofferbert, R. I. and Budge, Ian (1992), 'The party mandate and the Westminster model: election programmes and government spending in Britain, 1945–85', *British Journal of Political Science*, 22: 151–82.

House of Commons Commission (1990), *House of Commons Services*, London: HMSO.

Ingelhart, Ronald (1977), *The Silent Revolution*, Princeton NJ: Princeton University Press.

Irwin, Helen, Kennon, A., Natzler, D. and Rogers, R. (1993), 'Evolving rules', in M. Franklin and P. Norton (eds), *Parliamentary Questions*, Oxford: Oxford University Press.

Jacobs, Francis and Corbett, Richard (1990), *The European Parliament*, London: Longman.

James, Simon (1992), *British Cabinet Government*, London: Routledge.

Jeger, Jenny (1978), 'The image of the MP', in Mackintosh, J. (ed), *People and Parliament*, Aldershot: Saxon House.

Jones, J. Barry (1990), 'Party committees and all-party groups', in Rush, M. (ed), *Parliament and Pressure Politics*, Oxford: Oxford University Press.

Jordan, A. Grant and Richardson, Jeremy (1982), 'The British policy style or the logic of negotiation?' in Richardson, J. (ed), *Policy Styles in Western Europe*, London: George Allen & Unwin.

Jowell, Roger and Witherspoon, Sharon (1985), *British Social Attitudes: The 1985 Report*, Aldershot: Gower.

Jowell, Roger, Witherspoon, Sharon, and Brook, Lindsay (1987), *British Social Attitudes: The 1987 Report*, Aldershot: Gower.

Judge, David (ed) (1983), *The Politics of Parliamentary Reform*, London: Heinemann.

Judge, David (1990), *Parliament and Industry*, Aldershot: Dartmouth.

King, Anthony (1974), *British Members of Parliament: A self-portrait*, London: Macmillan.

King, Anthony (1981), 'The rise of the career politician in Britain – and its consequences', *British Journal of Political Science*, 11: 249–85.

Kirchheimer, Otto (1966), 'The transformation of the western European party systems' in LaPalombara, J. and Weiner, M. (eds), *Political Parties and Political Development*, Princeton NJ: Princeton University Press.

Laugharne, Peter J. (1993), 'Specialist advisers and the British House of Commons: The Treasury and Civil Service Committee 1979–1990', Unpublished PhD Thesis, Hull: Hull University.

Lea, David (1984), 'A trade unionist's view', in Englefield, D. (ed), *Commons Select Committees: Catalysts for Progress?* Harlow: Longman.

Liaison Committee, House of Commons (1982), *First Report from the Liaison Committee*, 1982–83, HC 92, London: HMSO.

Locke, John (1689), *Second Treatise on Government*, London.

Lowell, A. Lawrence (1896), *Government and Parties in Continental Europe*, Cambridge, Mass.: Harvard University Press.

Lowell, A. Lawrence (1924), *The Government of England, vol. II*, New York: Macmillan.

Lukes, Steven (1974), *Power: A Radical View*, London: Macmillan.

McKenzie, Kenneth (1968), *The English Parliament*, London: Penguin.

Mackintosh, John P. (1977), *The British Cabinet*, 3rd edn, London: Methuen.

Marquand, David (1979), *Parliament for Europe*, London: Jonathan Cape.

Marsh, David and Read, Melvyn (1988), *Private Members' Bills*, Cambridge: Cambridge University Press.

Marsh, Ian (1986), *Policy-Making in a Three-Party System*, London: Methuen.

Marsh, James W. (1985), 'The House of Commons: representational changes', in Norton, P. (ed), *Parliament in the 1980s*, Oxford: Basil Blackwell.

Marshall, Geoffrey (ed) (1989), *Ministerial Responsibility*, Oxford: Oxford University Press.

Matthews, Donald R. (1985), 'Legislative recruitment and legislative careers', in Loewenberg, G., Patterson, S. C., and Jewell, M. E. (eds), *Handbook of Legislative Research*, Cambridge, MA: Harvard University Press.

Mellors, Colin (1978), *The British MP*, Aldershot: Saxon House.

Merkl, Peter H. (1988), 'Comparing legitimacy and values among advanced democratic countries', in Dogan, M. (ed), *Comparing Pluralist Democracies: Strains on legitimacy*, Boulder CO: Westview Press.

Mezey, Michael (1979), *Comparative Legislatures*, Durham NC: Duke University Press.

Miers, David R. and Page, Alan C. (1982), *Legislation*, London: Sweet & Maxwell.

Miliband, Ralph (1984), *Capitalist Democracy in Britain*, Oxford: Oxford University Press.

Miller, Charles (1989), *Lobbying*, 2nd edn, Oxford: Basil Blackwell.

Mitchell, Austin (1982), *Westminster Man*, London: Thames Methuen.

Mitchell, Austin (1986), 'A house buyer's bill: how not to pass a private member's bill', *Parliamentary Affairs*, 39: 1–18.

Montesquieu, Baron de (1748), *The Spirit of Laws* (*l'Esprit des Lois*).

Morrell, Frances (1977), *From the Electors of Bristol*, Nottingham: Spokesman.

Negrine, Ralph (1992), 'Reporting parliamentary committees: the investigation of the Rover Group sale to British Areospace', *Parliamentary Affairs*, 45: 399–408.

Nixon, Jaqi (1986), 'Evaluating select committees and proposals for an alternative perspective', *Policy and Politics*, 14: 415–38.

Norton, Philip (1975), *Dissension in the House of Commons 1945–74*, London: Macmillan.

Norton, Philip (1977), 'Private legislation and the influence of the backbench M.P', *Parliamentary Affairs*, 30: 356–62.

Norton, Philip (1978a), *Conservative Dissidents*, London: Temple Smith.

Norton, Philip (1978b), 'Government defeats in the House of Commons: myth and reality', *Public Law*, Winter: 360–78.

Norton, Philip (1979), 'The organization of parliamentary parties' in Walkland, S. A. (ed), *The House of Commons in the Twentieth Century*, Oxford: Oxford University Press.

Norton, Philip (1980), *Dissension in the House of Commons 1974–1979*, Oxford: Oxford University Press.

Norton, Philip (1981), *The Commons in Perspective*, Oxford: Martin Robertson.

Norton, Philip (1982a), *The Constitution in Flux*, Oxford: Martin Robertson/Basil Blackwell.

Norton, Philip (1982b), ' "Dear Minister" – the importance of MP-to-minister correspondence', *Parliamentary Affairs*, 35: 59–72.

Norton, Philip (1983), 'Party committees in the House of Commons', *Parliamentary Affairs*, 36: 7–27.

Norton, Philip (1985), 'The House of Commons: behavioural change', in Norton, P. (ed), *Parliament in the 1980s*, Oxford: Basil Blackwell.

Norton, Philip (1986), 'Independence, scrutiny and rationalisation: a decade of changes in the House of Commons', *Teaching Politics*, 15: 69–98.

Norton, Philip (1987a), 'Dissent in the House of Commons: rejoinder to Franklin, Baxter, Jordan', *Legislative Studies Quarterly*, 12: 143–52.

Norton, Philip (1987b), *Parliament in Perspective*, Hull: Hull University Press.

Norton, Philip (1989a), 'The constitutional position of parliamentary private secretaries', *Public Law*: 232–36.

Norton, Philip (1989b), 'Collective ministerial responsibility', *Social Studies Review*, 5: 33–36.

Norton, Philip (1990a), *The British Polity*, 2nd edn, New York: Longman.

Norton, Philip (ed) (1990b), *Parliaments in Western Europe*, London: Frank Cass.

Norton, Philip (1990c), 'Public legislation', in Rush, M. (ed), *Parliament and Pressure Politics*, Oxford: Oxford University Press.

Norton, Philip (1990d), 'Parliament in the United Kingdom: balancing effectiveness and consent?' in Norton, P. (ed), *Parliaments in Western Europe*, London: Frank Cass.

Norton, P. (1990e), 'Committee under scrutiny', *The House Magazine*, 15 (495): 12 November.

Norton, Philip (1991a), 'The changing face of Parliament: lobbying and its consequences', in Norton, P. (ed), *New Directions in British Politics?* Aldershot: Edward Elgar.

Norton, Philip (1991b), 'Parliament since 1945: a more open institution?' *Contemporary Record*, 5: 217–34.

Norton, Philip (1991c), 'Reforming the House of Commons', *Talking Politics*, 4: 16–20.

Norton, Philip (1991d), 'Crown and Parliament', in Jones, B. *et al.*, *Politics UK*, Hemel Hempstead: Philip Allan.

Norton, Philip (1992a), 'The House of Commons: from overlooked to overworked', in Jones, B. and Robins, L. (eds), *Two Decades in British Politics*, Manchester: Manchester University Press.

Norton, Philip (1992b), 'Building on Strength', in House of Lords, *Report from the Select Committee on the Committee Work of the House*, Vol. II: Evidence, HL Paper 35-II, London: HMSO.

Norton, Philip (1992c), 'The Conservative Party from Thatcher to Major', in King, A. (ed), *Britain at the Polls 1992*, Chatham NJ: Chatham House.

Norton, Philip (1992d), 'Does Britain need proportional representation?' in Blackburn, R. (ed), *Constitutional Studies*, London: Mansell.

Norton, Philip (1992e), 'Swings and roundabouts', *The House Magazine*, 18 (551), 27 April: 13.

Norton, Philip (1992f), 'A reform Parliament', *The House Magazine*, 18 (559), 22 June: 15.

Norton, Philip (1993a), 'Congress: comparative perspectives', in Bacon, D. C., Davidson, R. H., and Keller, M. (eds), *The Encyclopedia of the United States Congress*, New York: Simon & Schuster.

Norton, Philip (1993b), 'The party in Parliament', in Seldon, A. (ed), *The Conservative Party in the Twentieth Century*, Oxford: Oxford University Press.

Norton, Philip and Aughey, Arthur (1981), *Conservatives and Conservatism*, London: Temple Smith.

Norton, Philip and Grantham, Cliff (1986), 'The hyphen in British politics? Parliament and professional lobbying', *British Politics Group Newsletter (USA)*, 45: 4–8.

Norton, Philip and Wood, David (1990), 'Constituency service by Members of Parliament: does it contribute to a personal vote?' *Parliamentary Affairs*, 43: 196–208.

Norton, Philip and Wood, David (1993), *Back to Westminster: The Politics of Constituency Service in Britain*, Lexington KY: Kentucky University Press.

Olson, David and Mezey, Michael (1991), *Legislatures in the Policy Process*, Cambridge: Cambridge University Press.

Ostrogorski, Moisei (1902), *Democracy and the Organization of Political Parties, Vol. 1*, London: Macmillan.

Packenham, Robert (1970), 'Legislatures and political development' in Kornberg, A. and Musolf, L. D. (eds), *Legislatures in Developmental Perspective*, Durham NC: Duke University Press.

Patten, Christopher (1980), 'Policy-making in opposition', in Layton-Henry, Z. (ed), *Conservative Party Politics*, London: Macmillan.

Phillips, A. (1949), 'Post Office parliamentary questions', *Public Administration*, 27: 91–99.

Pitkin, Hanna (1967), *The Concept of Representation*, Berkeley: University of California Press.

Popper, Karl (1988), 'The open society and its enemies revisited', *The Economist*, 23 April.

Ramsden, John (1980), *The Making of Conservative Party Policy: The Conservative Research Department since 1929*, London: Longman.

Rawlings, Richard (1990), 'The MP's complaint service', *Modern Law Review*, 53: 22–42, 149–69.

Regan, Paul (1988), 'The 1986 Shops Bill', *Parliamentary Affairs*, 41: 218–35.

Rhodes James, Robert (1991), 'Thoughts before going', *The House Magazine*, 16, 7 October: 8–10.

Richards, Peter G. (1959), *Honourable Members*, London: Faber & Faber.

Richards, Peter G. (1970), *Parliament and Conscience*, London: George Allen & Unwin.

Richardson, J. Jeremy and Jordan, Grant (1979), *Governing Under Pressure*, Oxford: Martin Robertson.

Riddell, Peter (1992), 'Minister of Fun's antics failed to amuse the Tory back benches', *The Times:* 25 September.

Rose, Richard (1979), 'Ungovernability: is there fire behind the smoke?' *Political Studies*, 27: 351–70.

Rose, Richard (1980), *Do Parties Make a Difference?* London: Macmillan.

Rose, Richard (1983), 'Still the era of party government', *Parliamentary Affairs*, 36: 282–99.

Rush, Michael (1979), 'The Members of Parliament' , in Walkland, S. A. (ed), *The House of Commons in the Twentieth Century*, Oxford: Oxford University Press.

Rush, Michael (ed) (1983), *The House of Commons: Services and Facilities 1972–1982*, London: Policy Studies Institute.

Rush, Michael (1988), 'The Members of Parliament', in Ryle, M. and Richards, P. G. (eds), *The Commons Under Scrutiny*, London: Routledge.

Rush, Michael (ed) (1990), *Parliament and Pressure Politics*, Oxford: Oxford University Press.

Ryle, Michael and Richards, Peter G. (ed) (1988), *The Commons under Scrutiny*, London: Routledge.

Saalfeld, Thomas (1988), *Das britische Unterhaus 1965 bis 1986*, Frankfurt: Peter Lang.

Saalfeld, Thomas (1990), 'The West German Bundestag after 40 Years: the role of parliament in a "party democracy" ', in Norton, P. (ed), *Parliaments in Western Europe*, London: Frank Cass.

Schwarz, John E. (1980), 'Exploring a new role in policy making: the British House of Commons in the 1970s', *American Political Science Review*, 74: 23–37.

Sedgemore, Brian (1980), *The Secret Constitution*, London: Hodder & Stoughton.

Seldon, Anthony (ed) (1993), *The Conservative Party in the Twentieth Century*, Oxford: Oxford University Press.

Select Committee on the Committee Work of the House, House of Lords, (1992), *Report from the Select Committee on the Committee Work of the House*, session 1991–92, HL Paper 35-I, London: HMSO.

Select Committee on the European Communities, House of Lords (1990), *Twenty-Fourth Report: The Future of Rural Society*, session 1989–90, HL 80, London: HMSO.

Select Committee on Members' Interests, House of Commons (1991), *Third Report: Parliamentary Lobbying*, session 1990–91, HC 586, London: HMSO.

Select Committee on Members' Interests, House of Commons (1992), *First Report: Registration and Declaration of Members' Financial Interests*, session 1991–92, HC 326, London: HMSO.

Select Committee on Procedure, House of Commons (1978), *First Report from the Select Committee on Procedure*, session 1977–78, HC 588, London: HMSO.

Select Committee on Procedure, House of Commons (1984), *Public Bill Procedure: Minutes of Evidence*, 18 December, HC 49-iv, London: HMSO.

Select Committee on Procedure, House of Commons (1989), *Fourth Report from the Select Committee on Procedure: The Scrutiny of European Legislation*, session 1988–89, HC 622, London: HMSO.

Select Committee on Procedure, House of Commons (1990), *Second Report from the Select Committee on Procedure: The Working of the Select Committee System*, session 1989–90, HC 19-I, London: HMSO.

Select Committee on Sittings of the House, House of Commons (1992), *Report from the Select Committee on Sittings of the House*, session 1991–92, HC 20, London: HMSO.

Select Committee on the Televising of Proceedings of the House, House of Commons (1990), *First Report: Review of the Experiment in Televising the Proceedings of the House*, session 1989–90, HC 265-I, London: HMSO.

Select Committee on Trade and Industry, House of Commons (1988), *First Special Report: Monitoring the Department of Trade and Industry*, session 1987–88, HC 384, London: HMSO.

Select Committee on Trade and Industry, House of Commons (1992), *Second Special Report: Past Reports and Recommendations of the Trade and Industry Select Committee 1987–1992*, session 1991–92, HC 262, London: HMSO.

Self, Peter (1977), 'Are we worse governed?' *New Society*, 19 May.

Shaw, Malcolm (1979), 'Conclusions', in Lees, J. D. and Shaw, M. (eds), *Committees in Legislatures*, Oxford: Martin Robertson.

Shaw, Malcolm (1990), 'Members of Parliament', in Rush, M. (ed), *Parliament and Pressure Politics*, Oxford: Oxford University Press.

Shell, Donald R. (1988), *The House of Lords*, Deddington: Philip Allan.

Shell, Donald R. (1992), *The House of Lords*, 2nd edn, Hemel Hempstead: Harvester Wheatsheaf.

Shell, Donald R. and Beamish, David R. (eds) (1993), *The House of Lords At Work*, Oxford: Oxford University Press.

Shepherd, Robert (1991), *The Power Brokers*, London: Hutchinson.

Shipley, Peter (1979), *Directory of Pressure Groups and Representative Organizations*, 2nd edn, Sevenoaks: Bowker.

Silk, Paul (1987), *How Parliament Works*, London: Longman.

Sontheimer, Kurt (1984), 'Parliamentarianism in modern times – a political science perspective', *Universitas*, 26.

Stacey, Frank (1971), *The British Ombudsman*, Oxford: Oxford University Press.

Teeling, Sir William (1970), *Corridors of Frustration*, London: Johnson.

Theakston, Kevin (1987), *Junior Ministers in British Government*, Oxford: Basil Blackwell.

Topliss, Eda and Gould, Bryan (1981), *A Charter for the Disabled*, Oxford: Basil Blackwell.

Trevelyan, George M. (1938), *The English Revolution*, London: Thornton Butterworth.

Walkland, Stuart A. (1968), *The Legislative Process in Great Britain*, London: George Allen & Unwin.

Walkland, Stuart A. (ed) (1979), *The House of Commons in the Twentieth Century*, Oxford: Oxford University Press.

Westlake, Martin (1992), 'The formation of a "European political elite":
the British in the directly-elected European Parliament, 1979–1992',
Unpublished PhD Thesis, Florence, Italy: European University
Institute.

Wheeler-Booth, Michael (1989), 'The Lords', in Griffith, J. A. G. and
Ryle, M., *Parliament: Functions, practice and procedures*, London:
Sweet & Maxwell.

White, Albert B. (1908), *The Making of the English Constitution 449–1485*,
London: G. P. Putnam's Sons.

Wilson, H. H. (1961), *Pressure Group*, London: Secker and Warburg.

Wilson, Harold (1977), *The Governance of Britain*, London: Sphere
Books.

Wiseman, H. Victor (ed) (1966), *Parliament and the Executive*, London:
Routledge & Kegan Paul.

Wood, David M. and Norton, Philip (1993), 'Do candidates matter?
Constituency-specific vote changes for incumbent MPs, 1983–1987',
Political Studies, 40: 227–38.

Index

228